Sustainability Reporting Practices and the Circular Economy

Sarfraz Nazir · Alessandro Capocchi

Sustainability Reporting Practices and the Circular Economy

Analysis and Integrated Strategies

palgrave
macmillan

Sarfraz Nazir
Department of Business Economics and Law
University of Milano-Bicocca
Milan, Italy

Alessandro Capocchi
Department of Business Economics and Law
University of Milano-Bicocca
Milan, Italy

ISBN 978-3-031-51844-7 ISBN 978-3-031-51845-4 (eBook)
https://doi.org/10.1007/978-3-031-51845-4

This Palgrave Macmillan imprint is published by the registered company Springer Nature Switzerland AG
The registered company address is: Gewerbestrasse 11, 6330 Cham, Switzerland

Paper in this product is recyclable.

I would like to dedicate this book to my father, Qazi Nazir Ahmad; my mother, Shahnaz Sultana; my wife, Aman Sarfraz; and my mentor, Prof. Alessandro Capocchi. He is also the Coauthor of this Book. They play a magnificent role during my personal and professional adventures.

—Sarfraz Nazir

A special dedication to my wife Sara and my children Edoardo, Giorgio, and Vittoria Luisa.

—Alessandro Capocchi

Preface

Global warming, pollution, and declining soil fertility have increased environmental issues and demand for raw materials. The sustainability concept was first considered as the substitute/solution for social, ecological, and economic problems. The principles of sustainability and development have been increasing because in the 1980s, a milestone turned into the work of the World Commission on Environment and Development, known as the Brundtland Commission, which provided its report in 1987 entitled "Our Common Future." As the Brundtland Commission stated in 1987, "development that meets the needs of the present without compromising the ability of future generations to meet their very own demands." Although the discussion on Circular Economy (CE) was initiated in early 2000, in the last decades, the concept has attracted much attention from researchers, policymakers, and practitioners to enforce initiatives that allow the transition from a linear to a CE. Besides, the successful CE framework assumes to contribute to all three dimensions of sustainable development: environmental, social, and economic. Thus, reducing the environmental and social effects of intense industrialization and increasing consumption is possible. Balancing and intertwining environmental and social concerns is vital to sustainability issues and is hard to report in companies' reporting practices.

This book introduces CE and corporate reporting practices. This book provides a brief literature review on CE and reporting practices and suggestions on how companies deploy CE-related approaches in operations and discloses this information in reports. Researchers have considered social, economic, and environmental aspects, but a comprehensive framework with CE principles is still required to include the organization's social, environmental, economic, and governance factors. This book presented and used a content analysis approach for disclosure and key performance indicators (KPIs) to investigate how and to what extent companies disclosed this information in annual reporting practices and how and to what extent associated with social, economic, environmental, and governance and impact on companies' performance. In addition, the frameworks support supply chain management and highlight diverse stakeholders concerned. Stakeholders are concerned with the organization's economic, social, environmental, and governance for rational decision-making and economic development. Considering the above, the book proposes different frameworks to evaluate social, economic, and ecological aspects, promote CE in their organizations, and disclose practices in their reports. This book exploited sustainability subjects that can benefit managers and practitioners to provide systematized elements to the decision-making related to the circular economy, explicitly concerning social, environmental, governance, and economic issues.

Milan, Italy

Sarfraz Nazir
Alessandro Capocchi

Acknowledgments

Sarfraz Nazir

The Circular Economy is not an act of God. It is a philosophy that could save our land and promote sustainability. This book creates a mechanism for developing, evaluating, and promoting the circular economy and sustainable development for the present and future generations. The book provides different frameworks for evaluating organizations' contribution toward sustainability and integrated strategies for how organizations deploy the circular economy and participate in sustainable development.

Alessandro Capocchi

This book aims to be a bridge to the future. Sustainability and CE are always becoming more important, and the personal behavior of humans is changing very fast. In front of these changes also, companies must start to be more responsible. In this direction, it is very important to define proper corporate behaviors in terms of communication and accounting representation of the economic and social dynamics. Working better today is creating a better future for the next generations. In this view, I hope that this book may contribute to increasing awareness of how we must all together build a better future for all.

Contents

About the Authors

Dr. Sarfraz Nazir is a Research Fellow at the University of Milano-Bicocca. He holds a Ph.D. in Business Administration and Management, a joint doctoral program, Universities Pisa, Florence and Siena, Italy, on the topic of circular economy and sustainable development. I am teaching Ph.D. Students in financial and non-financial accounting, sustainability accounting, operation management, sustainability risk management, sustainable supply chain management, governance, corporate social responsibility, Economics for sustainable development, System Dynamics, and social innovation. My areas of expertise are in the circular economy (including financial, non-financial accounting, and management control), sustainable development, corporate governance, operational management, system dynamics, and board games. I am an expert in quantitative, qualitative, and Simulation research methods. I have published Circular Economy and Integrated Reporting, Systems Thinking, System Dynamics, Board Games, Simulations, Environment management, Economic and Stakeholder pressures papers in international academic journals and made over 20 presentations at international conferences. I managed two EU projects with SYDIC, such as the project of Project Management Board Game (PMBGs) and the SYSTEMA project. And also, a member of the Scientific Committee and Coordinator of the 4th Edition of SDCR Summer School, which the European Union funds. The program aims to deepen participants' knowledge and understanding and build their competencies on the role and value of sustainability reporting.

https://it.linkedin.com/in/sarfraz-nazir-448779137.

Prof. Alessandro Capocchi is a Full Professor of Business Economics (SSN 13/B1) at the University of Milano-Bicocca, where he has taught since 1 October 2005. He holds the Business Economics course (9 CFU in the first year of the three-year degree in economics and business) and the Risk Management (8 CFU in English in the second year of the master's degree in Economic and Business Sciences).

Appointed by the Presidency of the Council of Ministers Department of Public Function (resolution no. 39/2023) member of the examining commission for a public competition of the National Anti-Corruption Authority (ANAC).

Appointed in January 2023 by the Ministry of Business and Made in Italy MIMIT expert to support the permanent Technical Secretariat of the inter-ministerial committee for attracting foreign investments (CAIE).

Appointed by the company Eutalia srl (formerly Studiare Sviluppo srl), within the Framework Agreement with Sogei—Societàgenerale Informatica SpA for the performance of support activities for the structures of the General Accounting Office of the State and Local Authorities in terms of definition, management, control, monitoring, and reporting of public interventions included in the PNRR, signed on 11/23/2021 as an expert in economic-financial accounting.

January 2023, appointed by Ca Foscari University of Venice as independent reviewer within the G@V COFUND call for proposals.

Appointed by LAZIOcrea S.P.A. "Expert in planning" for the training courses to be carried out as part of the "Regional training plan for the qualification and empowerment of institutions, operators, and stakeholders." Assignment in progress.

Appointed by the Autonomous Province of Trento as a member of the technical evaluation team for the project proposals presented within the European Social Fund Operational Program 2014–2020, the European Social Fund Plus Program 2021–2027, and the provincial implementation plan for youth employment (Youth Guarantee). Assignment in progress.

Appointed by the company Studiare Sviluppo SRL (an in-house company of the MEF) as a senior specialist expert on corporate and public administration organization on a project for the Public Function, Presidency of the Council of Ministers. Position completed at the end of February 2022.

Appointed by the MISE as an expert to be assigned to the functioning of the group of industrial policy experts, referred to in art. 3 law 11 May 1999, n. 140. The appointment concluded on 30 November 2022.

List of Figures

Chapter 4

Chapter 5

Chapter 6

List of Tables

Chapter 2

Chapter 3

Chapter 4

Chapter 5

Chapter 6

1

Introduction

1 Introduction

Background of Sustainability Reporting

Over the last three decades, the sustainable development [SD] debate on corporate sustainability has increased. Subsequently, many remarkable pieces of literature have been published on sustainable development; the concept of "sustainable development" began from the Brundtland report (WECD, 1987); the Brundtland report highlights the environment and social pictures while the economic idea was ignored. Furthermore, UN (2015), Agenda 2030 for Sustainable Development (UN, 2015) emphasizes economic, social, and environmental development concepts. Subsequently, organizations' intensifying demand to act toward SD development and policymakers have settled rules, standards, and norms to improve organization reporting and accounting standards. In 1995, Europe announced its primary sustainability report program, the "Eco-Management and Audit Scheme" (EMAS), and then, in 2000, the Global Reporting Initiative produced the first sustainability reporting guidelines. Later, in June 2000, the European Commission (2000a) distributed the "EU Financial Reporting Strategy: 'The Way Forward',"

S. Nazir and A. Capocchi, *Sustainability Reporting Practices and the Circular Economy*,
https://doi.org/10.1007/978-3-031-51845-4_1

which recommended that the yearly report should not be constrained distinctly to the financial-related feature of a business, adding that "appropriate investigation of environmental and social aspects important for a comprehension organization's development, performance and position" (European Commission, 2000b) should be disclosed.

In April 2014, the European Parliament passed a directive concerning non-financial disclosure for more than 500 public organizations to increase transparency and contribute toward SD. The European Union Directive 2014/95/EU necessitates that more than 6,000 big organizations release non-financial information in their annual or semi-annual business report that would be useful to the stakeholders to discover organizational risks, opportunities, future outlooks, governance, and strategies. Directive 2014/95/EU aims to create and enhance consistency and similarity of non-financial information within the EU organization while providing good news to the stakeholders. Organizations may utilize global, European, and public rules, policies, trends, and regulations to disclose their business position or condition (i.e., UN Global Compact, GRI, A4S Integrated Reporting).

Moreover, these rules broadly fluctuate and cover laws and regulations about sustainable development. For instance, A4S and GRI provide various guidelines to enhance sustainability and cover economic, social, and environmental aspects. However, the international IIRC (International Integrated Reporting Council) provides a framework that mentions the organization's financial and non-financial information. In this book, the term "reporting approaches" includes reporting standards, guidelines, frameworks, models, and other tools designed to present the sustainability disclosure that not only fulfill typical non-financial stakeholders' demands (e.g., from consumers, local communities, and non-governmental organizations [NGOs] but also those from the investment communities (e.g., shareholders and banks) who are increasingly asking transparency of business practices. Thus, the quantity and quality of information disclosed in sustainability reports can be used by stakeholders to measure an organization's legitimacy (Maroun & Prinsloo, 2020). However, with a growing landscape of competing reporting options available to companies that intend to reduce bias in self-assessment, the decision of which one to implement could be more complex, as highlighted by Stewart and Niero (2018). Moreover, scholars and practitioners are engaged in the debate on improving the quality of sustainability reports and transparency of non-financial disclosures (de Villiers & Sharma, 2020; Gacser & Szoka, 2021; Stewart & Niero, 2018). Transparency demonstrates how internal changes (e.g., CE implementation) impact on company's sustainability performance that often formally communicated through "corporate sustainability reporting" (EC, 2021; EC, 2020). Gacser and Szoka (2021) stated that sustainability reporting can contribute to a company's formation and conceptualization of sustainability, as well as the strategic integration of sustainability principles. Reporting frameworks and approaches were constructed to facilitate the reporting writing process to ensure comparable, measured, and reliable disclosures from companies across sectors (EC, 2021).

Background of Circular Economy

The circular economy [CE] approach has been developed with various characteristics considering social, economic, environmental, and political frameworks. In the mid-1990s, Germany carried the CE approach as a framework (Cameron, 1997; Jacobs, 1996) to address environmental issues related to raw materials and resource use for maintaining economic development. In 1990, China developed an eco-industrial framework, which was later implemented with attention to waste prevention, reusing post-consumer, and improving waste-based closed-loop circles inside and outside organizations. At the same time, the CE approach is used in the organization for product development, innovation, sustainable development, and keeping and updating of products and parts. Stahel (1982) presented specific points of the CE that emphasize modern economic matters and conceptualize contemporary waste reduction, job creation, resource reduction, reuse, and recycling techniques in the current economy.

Policymakers and trendsetters have argued for optimal strategies toward SD, and the CE model is gaining momentum as a promising pathway (Geissdoerfer et al., 2017). With this trend comes a proliferation of CE definitions, terminology, and performance assessment approaches adopted by various stakeholders (Kirchherr et al., 2017; Kraaijenhagen et al., 2016; Kühl et al., 2022; Lacy & Rutqvist, 2015; Lamba et al., 2023). The main principles of the CE model are becoming increasingly adopted and promoted by companies and policymakers (Lacy et al., 2020).

CE is described as a policy approach that first prevailed as a national-level policy with the "Circular Economy Promotion Law of the People's Republic of China" in 2008 (The Standing Committee of the National People's Congress, 2008; Wen & Meng, 2015). Within this document, CE is described as "a generic term for reduce, reuse and recycle activities in the process of production, flow, and consumption" (The Standing Committee of the National People's Congress, 2008, p. 1). European Commission (EC) developed publications promoting the implementation of CE, including the Circular Economy Action Plan (EC, 2015b). CE is defined as "A circular economy intention to maintain the value of products, materials, and resources for as long as possible by returning them into the product cycle at the end of their use while minimising the generation of waste" (EC, 2015a, p. 2).

CE has also become influential across business circles, where work done by organizations, such as the Ellen MacArthur Foundation (EMF), promote CE as an "economic model which seeks to decouple global economic development from finite resource consumption ultimately" often illustrated with the butterfly diagram distinguishing between technical and biological cycles (EMF, 2015b, p. 2). Meanwhile, the European Commission's action plan for the CE can make 600 billion euros yearly in economic increases in the EU manufactured sector alone (EMAF, 2013; EU, 2014). Finland's Independence Celebration Fund (FICF, SITRA) and McKinsey (2014) together measure 2.5 billion euros yearly gains for the national economy of Finland through the circular economy. The global economy would profit from 1000 billion US dollars annually (EMF, 2013; FICF and McKinsey, 2014).

Besides, the CE has been picking up footing as a practice for achieving regional, national, and global sustainability. It has become a prolonged consideration for international organizations (Lacy et al., 2020) and policymakers in industrialized nations (EC, 2015b). The EU has passed several regulations and directives regarding plastic, food, packaging, and waste sectors. The Directive 2008/98/EC of waste is the most important directive of the EU Commission of the waste Directive Framework (WDF), described as the essential features of the waste management framework like recycling, repair, reuse, remanufacture, and recovery. These goals describe that 50% of the waste should be recovered for recycling and reuse of household waste, as well as 70% of the destructed waste, which needs to be equipped for reuse, recycling, and recovery.

The regional and national governments are free to implement their strategies for waste reduction and manage business models to achieve SD goals. At the same time, the most significant regulation of the EU commission is the REACH [Registration, Evolution, Authorization, and Restriction of Chemicals] Regulation (EC1907/2006), which pertains to adopting a closed-loop strategy for recycling and reuse of material. This regulation aims to protect human and environmental issues and deals with chemical substances and their impact on humans and ecosystems (EU Commission, 2015a).

The reason behind these directives is that previously, the countries and companies effectively presumed a linear model of manufacturing and consumption. This model pertains to the "take, make, use, waste" stream, where natural resources are highly consumed in manufacturing and waste without considering resource preservation and environmental issues (Murray et al., 2017).

The researchers, scholars, and practitioners are involved in exploring new business frameworks for decreasing the impact of the linear model and want to enhance sustainable development globally. The circular economy approach in business pertains to reuse, remanufacturing, refurbishing, repurposing, repairs, redesigning, recovering products, and improving product life-cycle approaches (EMF, 2013). CE is an economic framework where closed-loop cycles apply for trading products and services (EMF, 2015a) and regenerative, redesigning, and remanufacturing products, parts, and material life as much as possible (EMF, 2020).

Bocken et al. (2016) describe CE as a "closed-loop business model framework that enhances resource productivity", this characteristic refers to a regenerative framework that enhances resource inputs and, through continuing strategies, reduce, redesign, recycling, repair, remanufacturing, refurbishing, reusing, and recover of products and parts by using the strategy of the closed-loop circle and supply chains (Govindan et al., 2015), product structure in circular form (Burke & Clark, 2016), and business models and framework circularity (Bocken et al., 2016). However the CE incorporates with 3Rs (Reduce, reuse, recycle), 6Rs (Reduce, reuse, recycle, reproduce, redesign, recover) (Jawahir & Bradley, 2016) and 10Rs (refuse, reduce, reuse/resale, repair reproduce, remanufacturing, redesign, recover, recycling, recover remain) (Reike et al., 2018).

Despite the increasing promotion of CE by international institutions and private organizations, academic research has identified potential sustainability trade-offs and recovery outcomes from implementing CE principles (Geissdoerfer et al., 2017; Kirchherr et al., 2017). These "recovery outcomes" can be defined as the reduction of material practice in expected benefits from new and more efficient technologies because of changes in consumer behavior or the extent to which producers have responsibilities for developing new products. To monitor and reduce the environmental externalities effects of implementing CE strategies and subsequent companies must be transparent regarding the assessment and reporting of progress on circularity by use of quantitative metrics as well as qualitative evaluation approaches. When using these options, organizations can consider the impacts of their CE practices on their organizational sustainability goals.

Concerning sustainability narratives, such as CE, the guidance included within reporting approaches will influence the terminology, definitions of concepts promoted, and the assessment approaches companies use to produce sustainability reports moving forward (Stewart & Niero, 2018). How these reporting approaches suggest companies communicate CE within a sustainability report and the challenges surrounding CE reporting remains to be seen and largely unexplored. This book reviews corporate sustainability reporting approaches and how and to what extent reports integrate with CE aspects. Therefore, the main research aim is to explore how sustainability reporting approaches and literature guide companies to include CE issues. This book outlines how and to what extent CE incorporates organizational and sustainable development. The book explored how and to what extent the companies disclosed CE activities in their reporting and helped provide shape information to all stakeholders and policymakers for better decision-making and setting trends.

2 Book Aims and Questions

This section provides the key pillars of the book structure, questions, and research aims. The book is divided into different chapters. Every chapter entails a paper that explores other prospects of CE and Sustainable development.

- Chapter 2 consists of a paper that reflects systematic literature. The research question is based on

  (A) What are the similarities, differences, and relationships between circular economy and sustainable development, as reported in the business economics literature?

This literature review contributes to the CE and SD concepts at a micro-level and sheds light on several aspects particularly relevant to the CE and SD research community. The CE refers to the regenerative framework in which resource reduction, waste, outflow, and energy spillage techniques reduce material consumption by closed-loop circles. This can be accomplished through continuing frameworks like maintenance, reuse, remanufacturing, restoring, and reduction. Literature found that SD for the stable incorporation of economic performance, social comprehensiveness, and environmental strength benefits present and future outcomes. This literature review highlights the similarities, differences, and relationships and investigates the research gaps, agendas, practices, and trends of CE and SD.

- The third chapter reflects paper two and addresses two research questions:

  (A) If integrated reporting provides the principles and elements to support the representation of CE-related activities?

(B) How and to what extent do current integrated reports practices disclose CE activities and information?

To address these aims, the research searched for textual elements (number and frequency of concepts) and images (number and typologies of figures and graphical representations, e.g., closed-loops). The study explores the primary nexus of IR with CE issues and activities. In this context, through content analysis, the study provided data valid to investigate how and to what extent integrated reports disclose circular economy-related information.

- In chapter 4, paper three explores circular economy (CE) principles concerning companies' reporting and whether CE supports environmental disclosure. The research searched CE-related principles, reducing (R1), reusing (R2), recycling (R3), remanufacturing/reproducing (R4), redesigning/repurposing (R5), and recovering (R6) in the top 100 corporate sustainable companies and research integrated with the GRI-300 environmental disclosure standards.

The study addresses two questions:

(A) How and to what extent are CE-related R1-R6 principles disclosed in companies' reports?
(B) How and to what extent do CE-related R1-R6 principles engage with environmental performance? The study proposed a unison glossary of CE-6Rs principles, intending to explore the CE-6Rs-related activities and could motivate the academia and policymakers to reorganize the organization strategies for creating new CE-related activities and reporting perspectives.

- While Chapter 5 consists of paper four, which explores CE-6Rs principles in integrated reporting, the paper addresses two research questions:

(A) How and to what extent does integrated reporting support circular economy 6Rs-related activities?

(B) How and to what extent do institutional pressures (coercive, normative, and mimetic) impact integrated reporting in the context of circular economy 6Rs activities?

The research highlights CE-6Rs (reduce, reuse, recycle, reproduce, redesign, recover) practices in six regions (Europe, Africa, Asia, Australasia, South America, and North America) and 13 industries. The 6R principles draw upon a basic practical framework of CE (Reike et al., 2018), and research used institutional theories approach for developing hypotheses mechanism yearly, industry and region-wise, for exploring the concept. The study also contributes to CE practices in IR and supports organizations to make better decisions for contributions to SD.

- In Chapter 6, the primary purpose of this fifth paper was to endorse a framework for assessing social, environmental, economic, and governance impact evaluation by indicators, which became possible through the CE-BSC approach. The research investigates the framework's validation using services and the manufacturing industry.

  The primary research questions are:

(A) To what extent do companies disclose financial/economic perspectives and support CE principles by the balanced scorecard framework?
(B) To what extent do companies disclose customer/environment perspectives and support CE principles by the balanced scorecard framework?
(C) To what extent do companies disclose Internal business processes/social perspectives and support CE principles by the balanced scorecard framework?
(D) To what extent do companies disclose Learning and Growth Perspectives/Governance perspectives and support CE principles by the balanced scorecard framework?

The study goal was to provide a framework inside the overall performance dimension of CE more rapidly for sustainability and waste management.

Chapter 7 contains the conclusion that identifies the research philosophy and explores the corporate sustainability agenda.

3 Methodology

The book research entails qualitative and quantitative methods to explore circular economy activities in corporate reporting practices. The research mainly adopts the content analysis and KPIs in this book study, which primarily focuses on the triple bottom line of the corporate sustainability agenda. The book directly appeals to these methodologies due to measuring and integrating corporate sustainability and reporting strategies.

- Chapter 2 consists of a systematic literature review followed by a methodical technique that considers the available published literature in terms of titles, references, and keywords (Bellis, 2009). According to White and Schmidt (2005, p. 13), "Before the reviews become systematic, the writer is free to pick and choose the papers that support his or her viewpoint [...] a biased approach." First, the data were collected through a search of the databases Web of Science (www.webofknowledge.com) and Scopus using the key terms circular economy and sustainable development. This allowed for identifying all the relevant literature in a specific period.
- In Chapter 3, the research design searched for CE-related concepts and visual representations in integrated reporting documents. The former items (concepts) were searched through content analysis (Krippendorff, 2004) based on the use of the NVivo software; the latter were searched manually by the researchers analyzing the reports in the sample. In both cases, *codebooks* of words and images (Neuendorf, 2002) were defined as *ex-ante* (Schilling, 2006).

- Chapters 4–6 study a mixed methodology approach of qualitative and quantitative analysis. Qualitative content analysis is "a research technique for the objective, systematic, and quantitative description of the manifest content of communication" (Krippendorff, 1989, p. 403). This technique can be used with either qualitative or quantitative data and allows for organizing "the text of writing into various groups or categories based on selected criteria" (Guthrie et al., 2004, p. 287) using NVivo software. Additionally, for the test of the hypothesis, the research used SPSS software to analyze the hypothesis, whether the variable has significant or non-significant effects, and whether the hypothesis rejects or fails to reject the hypothesis by using the *P*. Value and *T*-test.

References

Bellis, N. D. (2009). *Bibliometrics and citation analysis*. Scarecrow Press.

Bocken, N. M., De Pauw, I., Bakker, C., & Van Der Grinten, B. (2016). Product design and business model strategies for a circular economy. *Journal of Industrial and Production Engineering, 33*(5), 308–320.

Burke, J. J., & Clark, C. E. (2016). The business case for integrated reporting: Insights from leading practitioners, regulators, and academics. *Business Horizons, 59*(3), 273–283.

Cameron, E. J. (1997). *A formal AIN service creation, feature interactions analysis and management environment: An industrial application*. In Proceeding of Fourth Workshop on Feature Interactions in Telecommunications Systems, July 1997.

De Villiers, C., & Sharma, U. (2020). A critical reflection on the future of financial, intellectual capital, sustainability and integrated reporting. *Critical Perspectives on Accounting, 70*, 101999.

Ellen MacArthur Foundation. (2013). *Opportunities for the consumer goods sector, towards a circular economy*. https://www.ellenmacarthurfoundation.org/publications

Ellen MacArthur Foundation. (2015a). *Delivering the circular economy—A toolkit for policymakers*. https://www.ellenmacarthurfoundation.org/publications

Ellen MacArthur Foundation. (2015b). *Potential for Denmark as a circular economy*. https://www.ellenmacarthurfoundation.org/publications

Ellen MacArthur Foundation. (2015c). *Towards a circular economy: Business rationale for an accelerated transition*. https://www.ellenmacarthurfoundation.org/publications

EMF—Ellen-Macarthur Foundation. (2020). *Global-Commitment-2020-Progress-Report*. https://emf.thirdlight.com/link/il0mcm1dqjtn-knjubr/@/preview/1?o

European Commission. (2000a). *EU financial reporting strategy: The way forward*. https://eur-lex.europa.eu/legal-content/en/ALL/?uri=CELEX:52000DC0359

European Commission. (2000b). *Company reporting*. https://ec.europa.eu/info/business-economy-euro/company-reporting-and-auditing/company-reporting_en

European Commission. (2015a). *EU resource efficiency scoreboard*. https://ec.europa.eu/environment/resource_efficiency/targets_indicators/scoreboard/index_en.htm

EC—European Commission. (2015b). *First circular economy action plan*. https://ec.europa.eu/environment/topics/circular-economy/first-circular-economy-action-plan_en

EC—European Commission. (2020). *Circular economy action plan*. https://ec.europa.eu/environment/strategy/circular-economy-action-plan_en

EC—European Commission. (2021). *Proposal for a Corporate Sustainability Reporting Directive (CSRD)*. https://ec.europa.eu/info/business-economy-euro/company-reporting-and-auditing/company-reporting/corporate-sustainability-reporting_en

EU—European Union. (2014). *Scoping study to identify potential circular economy actions, priority sectors, material flows and value chains*. Publications Office of the European Union. https://op.europa.eu/en/publication-detail/-/publication/0619e465-581c-41dc-9807-2bb394f6bd07

Finland's Independence Celebration Fund (FICF, Sitra) and Mckinsey Kiertotalouden Mahdollisuudet Suomelle. (2014). The possibilities of circular economy for Finland.

Gacser, N. G., & Szoka, K. (2021). Sustainability accounting-historical development and future perspectives of the discipline. *PressAcademia Procedia, 14*(1), 1–4.

Geissdoerfer, M., Sayaget, P., Bocken, N. M. P., & Hultin, E. J. (2017). The circular economy—A new sustainability paradigm? *Journal of Cleaner Production, 143*, 757–768.

Govindan, K., Soleimani, H., & Kannan, D. (2015). Reverse logistics and closed-loop supply chain: A comprehensive review to explore the future. *European journal of operational research, 240*(3), 603–626.

Guthrie, J., Petty, R., Yongvanich, K., & Ricceri, F. (2004). Using content analysis as a research method to inquire into intellectual capital reporting. *Journal of Intellectual Capital, 5*(2), 282–293.

Jacobs, L. F. (1996). The economy of winter: Phenotypic plasticity in behavior and brain structure. *The Biological Bulletin, 191*(1), 92–100.

Jawahir, I. S., & Bradley, R. (2016). Technological elements of circular economy and the principles of 6R-based closed-loop material flow in sustainable manufacturing. *Procedia CIRP, 40*, 103–108.

Kirchherr, J., Reike, D., & Hekkert, M. (2017). Conceptualizing the circular economy: An analysis of 114 definitions. *Resources, Conservation and Recycling, 127*, 221–232.

Kraaijenhagen, C., Van Oppen, C., & Bocken, N. (2016). Circular business: Collaborate and circulate. Circular collaboration.

Krippendorff. K. (1989). Content analysis. In E. Barnouw, G. Gerbner, W. Schramm, T. L. Worth, & L. Gross (Eds.), *International Encyclopaedia of communication* (Vol. 1, pp. 403–407). Oxford University Press.

Krippendorff, K. (2004). *Content analysis: An introduction to its methodology*. SAGE Publications.

Kühl, C., Bourlakis, M., Aktas, E., & Skipworth, H. (2022). Product-service systems and circular supply chain practices in UK SMEs: The moderating effect of internal environmental orientation. *Journal of Business Research, 146*, 155–165.

Lacy, P., & Rutqvist, J. (2015). *Waste to wealth: The circular economy advantage*. Macmillan.

Lacy, P., Long, J., Spindler, W., Lacy, P., Long, J., & Spindler, W. (2020). Introduction: The path to transformation is circular. *The Circular Economy Handbook: Realizing the Circular Advantage*, 1–14.

Lamba, H. K., Kumar, N. S., & Dhir, S. (2023). Circular economy and sustainable development: A review and research agenda. *International Journal of Productivity and Performance Management* (ahead-of-print).

Maroun, W., & Prinsloo, A. (2020). Drivers of combined assurance in a sustainable development context: Evidence from integrated reports. *Business Strategy and the Environment, 29*(8), 3702–3719.

McKinsey. (2014). Sustainability's strategic worth McKinsey global survey results. https://www.mckinsey.com/capabilities/sustainability/our-insights/sustainabilitys-strategic-worth-mckinsey-globalsurvey-results

Murray, A., Skene, K., & Haynes, K. (2017). The circular economy: An interdisciplinary exploration of the concept and application in a global context. *Journal of Business Ethics, 140*(3), 369–380.

Neuendorf, K. (2002). The content analysis guidebook Sage Publications, Inc. In *Library of congress. CA: United States.*

Reike, D., Vermeulen, W. J. V., & Witjes, S. (2018). The circular economy; New or refurbished as CE 3.0? Exploring controversies in the conceptualization of the circular economy through a focus on history and resource value retention options. *Journal of Cleaner Production, 135*, 246–264.

Schilling, J. (2006). On the pragmatics of qualitative assessment. *European Journal of Psychological Assessment, 22*(1), 28–37.

Stahel, W. (1982). *Product-life factor.* http://product-life.org/en/major-publications/the-product-life-factor.

Standing Committee of the National People's Congress. (2008). Circular Economy Promotion Law of the People's Republic of China. https://www.gov.cn/flfg/2008-08/29/content_1084355.htm

Stewart, R., & Niero, M. (2018). Circular economy incorporates sustainability strategies: A review of corporate sustainability reports in the fast-moving consumer goods sector. *Business Strategy and the Environment, 27*(7), 1005–1022.

UN—United Nations. (2015). *Transforming our world: The 2030 agenda for sustainable development.* https://sustainabledevelopment.un.org/

WCED SWS. (1987). World commission on environment and development. *Our Common Future, 17*(1), 1–91.

Wen, Z., & Meng, X. (2015). Quantitative assessment of industrial symbiosis for the promotion of circular economy: A case study of the printed circuit boards industry in China's Suzhou New District. *Journal of Cleaner Production, 90*, 211–219.

White, A., & Schmidt, K. (2005). Systematic literature reviews. *Complementary Therapies in Medicine, 13*, 54–60.

2

Systematic Literature Review of Circular Economy and Sustainable Development

1 Introduction

The current economic model exhibits conflicting values due to the different agendas emerging from business, manufacturing, utilization, and recovery. However, there is a consensus that given the rate of population growth, our current utilization of resources could be more sustainable. The global population is predicted to achieve 9 "G" by 2050, which raises the alarm about natural resources as the demand for them and energy intensifies (Riding et al., 2014). In 1985, the first directive EEC (85/339) was issued on the containers of liquids for human consumption, which lays down rules for producing, recycling, reusing, remanufacturing, and reducing packaging for products intended for human consumption (European Commission, 2015a). The European Union (EU) set an agenda that, by 2025, 65% of plastic packaging will be reused, this figure being 22.5% in 2008. The EU set targets for maximizing waste recovery, expecting chemical components to be removed in redesigning and recycling. Furthermore, the EU adopted the first circular economy (CE) action plan (EC, 2015) for the smooth transition toward

S. Nazir and A. Capocchi, *Sustainability Reporting Practices and the Circular Economy*,
https://doi.org/10.1007/978-3-031-51845-4_2

the circular economy for sustainable development, to boost the global economy, foster sustainable economic growth, and generate new jobs. For this, the EU passed several action plans and directives, i.e., the EU Green Deal (2019), the new action plan of CE (2020), new regulations on sustainable batterie (2020), global alliance on circular economy and resources efficiency (European Union, 2020), organic pollutant waste directive (EU, 2021), and sustainable product design and packages (EU, 2022).

Under CE, the emphasis is on less consumption of natural resources, reuse of products, parts, and materials, remanufacturing, renovation, repairs, cascading, updating, renewable energy, human well-being, social equity, and low-carbon emissions. Similarly, SD is associated with human prosperity through food and water security, sanitation, medical services, training, sustainable energy, sex equality, social values, voice (e.g., political support, liberty of speech), and employment (UN, 2030). A mutually agreed framework for manufacturing, distribution, utilization, and recovery is required to fulfill the SD agenda. The research contribution not only discloses CE practices and SD but also identifies which CE practices and SD are similar and which are different, as well as ascertaining the extent to which a relationship exists between the two. The research explores the corporate reporting practice's role in implementing CE activities by firms, which is informative for the internal and external stakeholders in the decision-making process. The review also contributes to international research (based on CE and SD practices internationally), thus providing the opportunity to compare present and future goals and see the big picture of CE-related trends and SD practices. The structure of the paper is as follows: Sect. 2, Defining Circular Economy; Sect. 3, Defining Sustainable Development; Sect. 4, Research Design; Sect. 5, Results; Sect. 6, Discussions and Conclusion; and Sect. 7, Practical Implications, Limitations, and Further Research.

2 Defining Circular Economy

The CE approach usually considers various social, economic, and environmental frameworks. In Germany, in the mid-1990s, the CE concept was considered through an ecological approach (Cameron, 1997) addressing fundamental material issues and resource use for maintaining economic development, also called social-ecological economics. Later, this was implemented with consideration of reusing, recycling, and developing a closed circle framework for organizations or among various businesses and customers.

A CE is an economic framework where products and services are traded in closed-loop cycles (EMF, 2012): "*The CE is characterized as an economy which is regenerative by design, with the aim to retain value as much as possible of products, parts, and resources.*" The primary aim of this framework is to create a system that could permit the preservation of natural resources, redesign products and parts, and enhance product and parts life cycle (EMF, 2016, p. 17; Kirchherr et al., 2018). Today, technological leaps forward have empowered the implementation of a third step, where the life cycle of products can be increased without affecting the quality (EMF, 2015b, p. 13). Under the linear product model, any waste after the product's sale is discarded.

In contrast, with CE, this waste is reused as an input in the following product run, thereby delivering product price-saving advantages and opening doors to obtaining new benefits associated with this framework (EMF, 2015a, p. 8). CE positively impacts the economy, environment, and society (EU, 2019; Lang and Marsden, 2018) by working on cyclical energy frameworks and closed-loop frameworks for materials (Reike et al., 2018). It is "*beneficial or regenerative by purpose and plan*" (EMF, 2012, p. 25) while also allowing for circular supply chain management (Jain et al., 2018) for reducing greenhouse emissions, waste (including packaging and product-based), and increasing the reuse and recycle ability regarding the product and packaging (DeLorenzo et al., 2019).

In the last few years, the CE has emerged as a key principle for the industrial and environmental policies in China (Winans et al., 2017; Zhu et al., 2019), Africa (World Economic Forum [WEF], 2020) and the European Union (EU, 2020), as well as for a growing list of corporations and local governments (see, e.g., the strategic partners of the EMF, 2012).

CE promoted "a regenerative system in which resource input and waste, emission, and energy leakage are minimized by slowing, closing, and reduction material usage and energy loops to long-lasting design, maintenance, repair, reuse, remanufacturing, refurbishing, and recycling" (Geissdoerfer et al., 2017, p. 759). Correspondingly, circular business models reduce costs, increase revenues, and manage risks, as well as provide possibilities for the finance sector to contribute to a transition of sustainability (EMF, 2020).

Moreover, the European concept of the CE and circular business models is also widely questioned on their premises, practicality, and consequences. In particular, these analyses suggest that policy advocacies of the CE appear to be "approbatory, uncritical, descriptive and deeply normative" (Gregson et al., 2015, p. 219), to support a deliberately vague, but principally uncontroversial CE (Lazarevic & Valve, 2017), and to feature a consensual win–win policy that is particularly difficult to criticize (Kovacic et al., 2020) despite the lack of any actual consensus on the magnitude of eventual economic, social, and environmental "win–win–win" benefits (Aguilar-Hernandez et al., 2021). While this vagueness might be perceived as a strength by policymaking actors, the win–win policies restrict the focus to conflict-free solutions and strategies. Thereby, initiatives outside the–win paradigm that address the conflicts, trade-offs, and problems of leaving the linear economy are overlooked (Völker et al., 2020), and this might result in circularity becoming naturalized with little space for critical and hesitative reflection (Lazarevic & Valve, 2017).

Although often presented as a revolutionary innovation, the CE is a familiar idea. It is another rehearsal of how to imagine a reconciliation and compatibility of economic and environmental concerns that have already been expressed by the terms "sustainable growth," "green growth," and "sustainable development"; the 1990s and 2000s imaginaries of dematerialization of the economy; and already with the Brundtland Commission's concept of (simultaneous) environmental, social, and economic sustainability (…) (Völker et al., 2020 p. 116).

Circularity is viewed "as a refurbished rather than [...] virgin concept" (Reike et al., 2018, p. 247). The various strategies to prolong resource use gathered together under the CE banner are new. If the concept offers some newness, it offers a new framing of these strategies and an ability to connect them (Blomsma & Brennan, 2017).

The CE builds on a heterogeneous collection of scientific and semi-scientific concepts, for example, "ecological economics, industrial ecology, cradle-cradle design, [...] performance economy, biomimicry, eco-efficiency, resilience science, natural capitalism, and cleaner production" (Korhonen et al., 2018, p. 549). Over a hundred definitions of circularity have been inventoried with the consequences (Kirchherr et al., 2017). This could be because the concept and its application have almost exclusively been developed and driven by practitioners, policymakers, business consultants, business associations, and business foundations (Korhonen et al., 2018). Chairman of the International Solid Waste Association (ISWA) stated that "[t]here is no single commonly accepted definition of the term 'Circular Economy', but different definitions share the basic concept of decoupling of natural resource extraction and use from the economic output, having increased resource efficiency as a major outcome" (Mavropoulos & Nilsen, 2020).

Moreover, there are distinct differences, separations, and exclusions between research communities engaged in CE research, for example, between scholars in engineering and business (Korhonen et al., 2018). Hence, different definitions of CE are typically adopted for different theoretical uses (Kirchherr et al., 2017). As a result, the CE becomes characterized by its conceptual fragmentation (Blomsma & Brennan, 2017; Korhonen et al., 2018) and a perceived lack of paradigmatic strength (Inigo & Blok, 2019).

The outcome is the perception that the CE needs to address ontological and epistemological questions, such as what is considered of ethical value, that underlie the complex and interrelated environmental, social, and economic issues that are facing nowadays (Temesgen et al., 2021). It is indeed easier to say what the CE is not than to say what it is (Kovacic et al., 2020). The CE "is not a theory but an emerging approach to industrial production and consumption" (Korhonen et al., 2018, p. 551).

CE circularity concept creates excitement and enthusiasm as it seemingly provides a new framing to resolve many problems.

3 Defining Sustainable Development

The Brundtland Commission's report (1987) briefly defines the concept of SD as the "*ability to make development sustainable to ensure that it meets the needs of the present without compromising the capacity of future generations to meet their own needs.*" SD can be explained in terms of natural challenges associated with the over-consumption of resources worldwide. According to global measurements, the portion of materials extracted has increased substantially since 1980, reaching 72 gigatons (Gt) in 2010 and is expected to be 100 Gt by 2030 (OECD, 2015a). Different strategies have been adopted for waste and the environment aimed at cleaner production, pollution reduction, and energy efficiency in the industry (EC COM, 2015). SD agendas have opened doors for businesses that embrace the issues of the well-being of humans and sanitation in developing nations (Schroeder et al., 2018). Resourceful, sustainable practices can help address hygiene challenges in developing countries; for instance, human waste can be utilized to develop bacteria to be used as feed for fish farms and other animal generation frameworks (Schroeder et al., 2018), thereby adding to horticultural efficiency and sustainable nutrition creation systems (UN, 2015), closed-loop frameworks for wastewater recycling and reuse (Flores et al., 2018) will have vital role in the accomplishment of UN agenda 2030 (UN, 2015).

In line with the sustainable development goals (SDGs), governments have enforced clean energy plans (nuclear renewable) to combat the above environmental threats. Countries have prioritized using renewable and nuclear energy sources in line with the target of decarbonizing the energy sector (Pata & Samour, 2022). As an essential clean energy source, renewable energy refers to naturally regenerative sources (Yang et al., 2016). Renewable sources can regenerate themselves quickly (Nathaniel et al., 2020), while their utilization provides energy security (Hao et al., 2021). Renewable energy sources are highly reliable and sustainable and improve environmental quality without harming the economic growth process (Rahman et al., 2022). In this sense, renewable energy sources replace fossil fuels, reduce the demand for polluted resources, and contribute to the enrichment of the Earth's biocapacity (Pata, 2021).

Despite this rising trend, the consumption of renewable energy is still limited in many countries due to high installation costs and technological barriers (Nguyen & Kakinaka, 2019). Looking at global trends in renewable energy sources, member countries of the UN Agenda 2030, in particular, have directed their investments in renewable energy to achieve the SDGs. Sustainable development goals 7, 11, 12, 13, 14, and 15 can likely be achieved through the widespread use of renewable energy. As a result of the great interest in realizing these six SDGs, renewable energy accounted for 28.5% and 28.3% of global electricity generation in 2020 and 2021, respectively.

Human consumption has exceeded nature's regenerative capacity and humanity currently requires 1.6 Earths to meet its ecological service needs (Nathaniel, 2021). Therefore, many countries are facing the problem of environmental sustainability and the need for sufficient energy supply to meet their growing energy demands. Various global conferences and measures such as the Paris Agreement—COP-21—have been taken to minimize environmental degradation. At the forefront of global efforts was the need to balance environmental and economic activities (Abbasi & Choukolaei, 2023). As such, green growth has been accepted as an essential global strategy to mitigate environmental pollution in all areas of economic activities (Abbasi et al., 2023) and to promote economic expansion (Abbasi et al., 2022).

4 Research Design

This research systematic technique considers the available published literature regarding titles, references, years, and keywords (Bellis, 2009). According to White and Schmidt (2005, p. 13), "before the reviews become systematic, the writer is free to pick and choose the paper that supports his or her viewpoint [...] a biased approach." To start with, the data were collected through a search of the databases Web of Science (WOS) (www.webofknowledge.com) and Scopus (www.scopus.com) using the key terms/words circular economy, sustainability, and sustainable development, reporting. This allowed for identifying all the relevant literature at a specific time. It also began the process of eliciting the differences, similarities, and relationships between CE, sustainability, and sustainable development, which would inform the subsequent construction of a combined framework for these concepts (Fetscherin & Heinrich, 2015), WOS published 1522 and Scopus published 2026, In total in both databases 3548 articles published up until 2 July 2022 on CE, sustainability and SD were found, and 20 international organizations reported (see Fig. 1).

Top Ranked journal list, the Journal of Cleaner Production has published more than 250 articles in Scopus, followed by Sustainability Journal with 185. In comparison, the top rank in WOS is 350 articles in sustainability journal, followed by the Journal of Cleaner Production with 161. Google Scholar and the ResearchGate network were utilized to

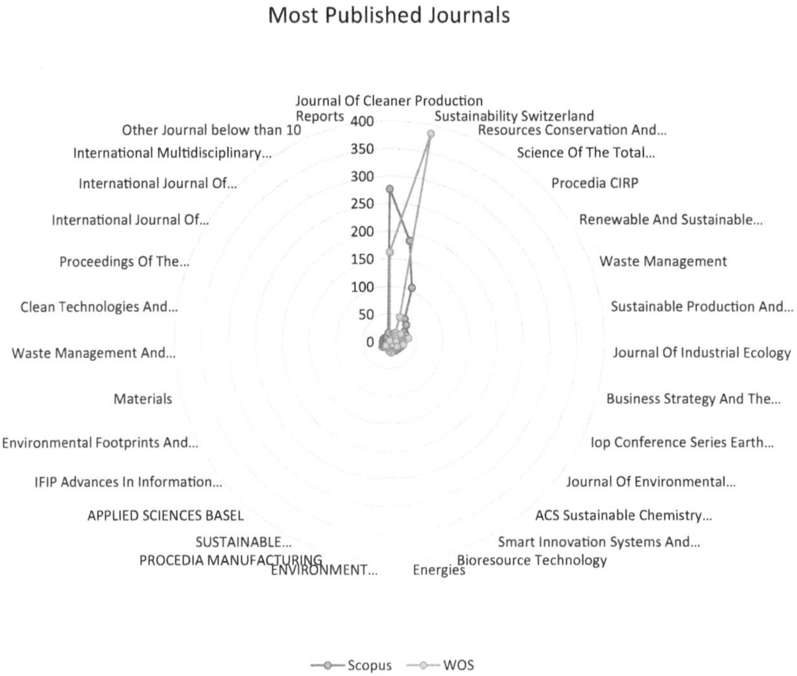

Fig. 1 Most published journals

retrieve academic papers reports from the leading CE organization (e.g., EMF), official research bodies (e.g., European Environmental Agency, UN, EU), legislative bodies (e.g., EC, OECD), and web pages through Google search. This research is focused on the business economic domain, where the dominant linear economic framework shifting to a CE one has been getting significant attention from vital global companies, e.g., Google, Unilever, and Renault, as well as governments, NGOs, and policymakers. Companies disclose this information in financial and non-financial reporting, informing their stakeholders about sustainable practices. The retrieved articles emphasize the significance of the business models as well as the environment, social and economic perspectives, e.g., supply chain management, marketing, circular business model, rethinking approach, technology transfer, low carbon, sustainable technology, economic performance, remanufacturing plastic, sustainability, and corporate reporting practices. For a more in-depth investigation, the following research question is posed.

RQ: What are the similarities, differences, and relationships between circular economy and sustainable development, as reported in the business economics literature?

5 Results

The data collection process for the systematic literature review is provided in Fig. 2.

As mentioned above, the Web of Science, Scopus, and Google Research databases identified 3548 articles and 20 reports from world-leading organizations that have published articles, book chapters, and conference papers on the circular economy, sustainability, reporting, and sustainable development in previous years. After the screening, it was found that 548 articles were replicated. Subsequent in-depth screening found that 297 articles had no text. After that, the authors excluded the sample because they did not belong to business management, accounting, business finance, economics, and operational research

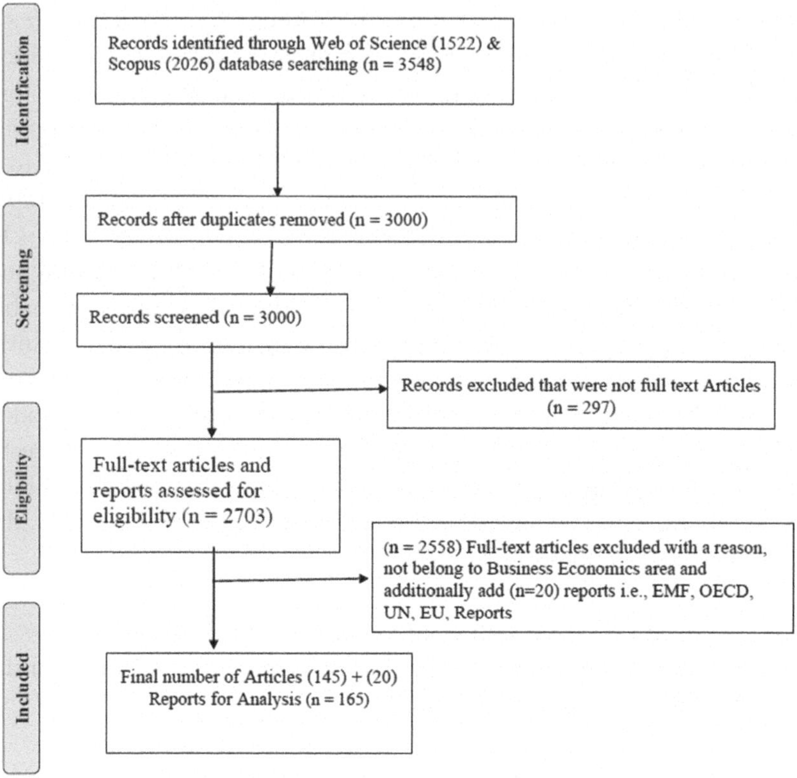

Fig. 2 Data collection for the related literature review

management. We found 145 publications and 20 reports (see Appendix) from different organizations being identified for the qualitative analysis. Appendix provides the keywords and the focus and publication of those articles/book chapters/conference papers/reports that refer to CE and/or Sustainability and/or SD in the business economics area. Appendix 1 displays the titles of the relevant articles, book chapters, conferences and reports, author/years, keywords, findings, and sources. This is an inductive study aimed at identifying similarities and differences and the relationship between the CE and SD concepts. Figure 3 illustrates the number of articles, book chapters, and conferences published per year in Scopus and WOS (see Fig. 3), i.e., from 2009 to 2021, WOS has

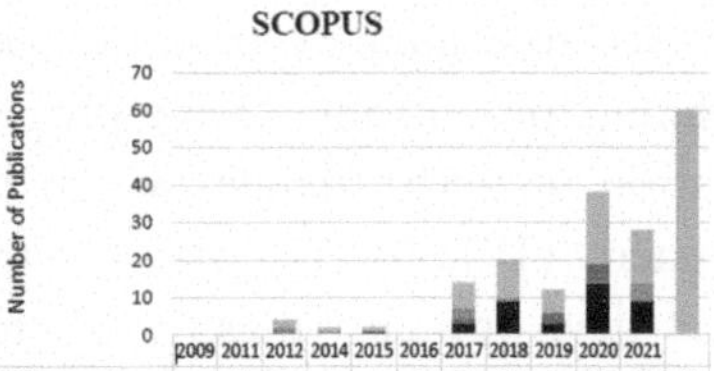

	2009	2011	2012	2014	2015	2016	2017	2018	2019	2020	2021	
Scopus Total	0	0	2	1	1	0	7	10	6	19	14	60
Scopus Book Chapters	0	0	1	1	0	0	3	1	0	0	5	
Scopus Conference Papers	0	0	1	0	0	0	1	0	3	5	0	
Scopus Articles	0	0	0	0	1	0	3	9	3	14	9	

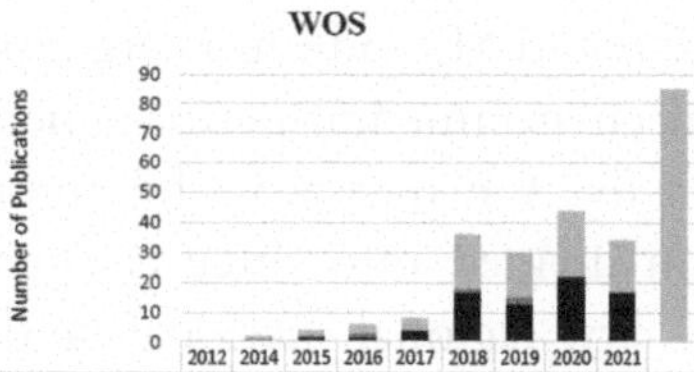

	2012	2014	2015	2016	2017	2018	2019	2020	2021	
WOS Total	0	1	2	3	4	18	15	22	17	85
WOS Book Chapters	0	0	0	0	0	0	0	0	0	
WOS Conference Papers	0	1	0	1	0	1	2	0	0	
WOS Articles	0	0	2	2	4	17	13	22	17	

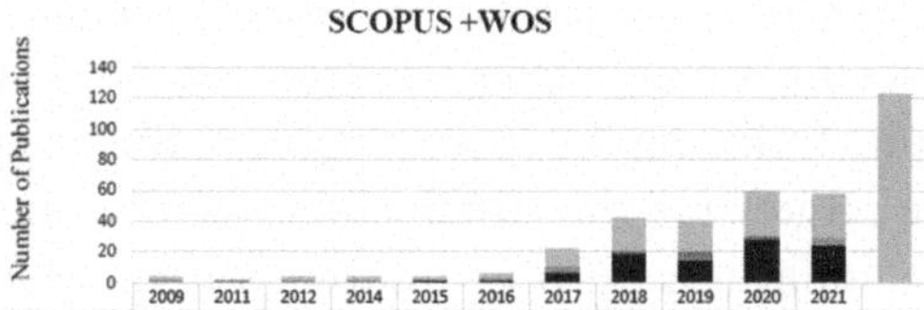

	2009	2011	2012	2014	2015	2016	2017	2018	2019	2020	2021	
Total	2	1	2	2	2	3	11	21	20	30	29	123
Book Chapters		0	1	1			3	1			5	
Conference Papers	2	0	1	1		1	1	1	5	2		
Articles		1			2	2	7	19	15	28	24	

Fig. 3 Yearly book chapter, conference papers, and articles published

published more than Scopus. There are 145 publications in these two databases on CE, SD, and sustainability in Business economics. While some publications were both in Scopus and WOS, after careful screening, the author removed published articles and book papers that were twice in both databases. Thus, this subject matter has increasingly grabbed the attention of researchers and, no doubt, practitioners as well.

Similarities Between CE and SD

For both the CE and SD concepts, the literature emphasizes social and economic commitments to address environmental threats and the importance of sustainable connections and strategic frameworks toward economic, environmental, and social perspectives (Jain et al., 2018). Stakeholders view CE and SD share as similar, emphasizing global-scale problems that require shared responsibilities and appropriate coordination.

CE and SD indicators are typically used to evaluate economic, social, and environmental performance. Different practitioners have proposed fifty-five CE indicators for the evaluation of performance, which have been divided into three categories: macro (19), for the assessment of the city, regional, national, and global development; meso (16), for a circular index of business, eco-industrial parks, and industrial associations; and micro (20), for material, components, products, and parts (Kristensen, & Remmen, 2019). The European Economic Area (EEA) (Eaton et al., 2003) characterized sustainability-related indicators into five types: (i) descriptive indicators (government, NGO roles); (ii) performance indicators (utilizing the same variable as the descriptive indicators and fixing the targets for the sustainability of the present and future); (iii) efficiency indicators (giving information on the effectiveness of products and procedures); (iv) plan practicality indicators (about the difference between the environmental factors to planned endeavors); and (v) social well-being indicators. Moreover, the OECD (2015b) and Reike et al. (2018) argue that comparing CE with sustainability regarding the economic parameters, cost and price, redesign, and recycling are commonly used. Regarding the environmental indicators, CO_2, eco-efficiency, energy, and ecosystem are referred to for both CE and SD. Some companies adopt these indicators to disclose their financial and non-financial information to their stakeholders. These are used as evidence of robust economic performance through flexible strategies, such as remanufacturing and value creation for an organization, to obtain increased investment).

CE stimulates stakeholder collaboration, e.g., food manufacturers, packaging companies, plastic producers, waste supervisors, etc. Also, it changes stakeholders' decision-making behavior in that they tend to act in alignment with SD (EMF, 2016, 2017). Climate change and environmental degradation are existential hazards to Europe and the world (EU, 2019). To address these challenges, the European Green Deal (EU, 2019) will rework the EU into cutting-edge assistance on the competitive economic framework and ensure zero-emission greenhouse gases by 2050, while the economic development framework is linked with the preservation of resources, gender diversity, and circularity. The European Green Deal (EU, 2019) is the EU lifeline for recovery from the COVID-19 pandemic. While SD needs technological innovation abilities and industry symbiosis in material production, innovation has continuously increased (Murray et al., 2017). There is evidence that circular business model innovation allows for the development of sustainable technologies (EU, 2019; Martins, 2016). This refers to the sustainable framework facilitating flow and control over the production process by the circular business model (Reike et al., 2018). CE and SD consider value creation a closed-loop system (Barnabè & Nazir, 2021, 2022). Specifically, CE explicitly builds on the shift from a circular to a "circular" (i.e., closed-loop) design of the economic system and corporate integrated thinking (Barnabè & Nazir, 2021, 2022). Different practitioners and academic disciplines specifically stress the need for short-term closed-loops, assessing stakeholder impact, and forming strategies for sustainability. They also strive to embed CE practices with SD goals and influence national, regional, and global business agendas (EC, 2015b; EU, 2019, 2022).

Differences Between CE and SD

The CE and SD literature reveals a few differences between the concepts, including objectives, targets, framework strategies, and stakeholders' responsibilities. Moreover, the idea behind CE is more recent than SD, and the former has been referred to through concepts such as candle to candle, industrial associations, and ecosystems (EMF, 2013; UN, 2015). After the publication of the Brundtland report in 1987, environmental initiatives and supranational bodies were established for the SD of society. Moreover, different literature has varying objectives related to CE and SD. Most authors emphasize CE as a short closed-loop framework where all-natural resources are preserved, waste is utilized, and there is control over the release of GHGs.

In contrast, the objectives of SD are more of an open-ended question, with some authors stressing stakeholders' (government, NGOs) interest in the concept and long-term closed-loop framework for society and the environment. However, the study identified four elements concerning CE closed-loop circle assessment and reported it on companies' annual and semi-annual reports. The first aim is to measure the economic, environmental, and social effects through a short-term closed-loop framework and, second, to compare various kinds of closed-loop circles and to identify the most appropriate one. The third aim is to promote the usage of the chosen framework. The final objective is to evaluate the framework outcomes and then modify the closed-loop circles by sustainable development. While it has been acknowledged that the economic and environmental aspects of closed-loop geared toward SD can be assessed, the social one is hard to measure (EC, 2015b, Resource efficiency scoreboard, EU, 2022).

CE practice in SD relies on an alternative framework emphasizing economic and environmental benefits. Geissdoerfer et al. (2018) point out that most CE indicators relate to economic and ecological sustainability, while social indicators still need improvement. There is a general agreement about estimating the economic indicators through expenditure and income, ecological through CO_2 emissions, and social ones through job creation, gender diversity, and the level of safety in the workplace. However, despite several indicators being proposed regarding social measurement, there has yet to be a consensus on how these should be measured. Companies measure sustainability through agreed standards, e.g., GRI and G4, but these indicators cannot assess the social impact of those firms exercising CE practices. A difference between the recipients of sustainability and CE is noted by Geissdoerfer et al. (2018), "*Sustainability goals for making the environment, the economy, and society everywhere, while the principal recipients of the Circular Economy appear to be the economy on-screen characters that execute the framework.*"

The primary motive of CE is to provide financial advantages to companies through remanufacturing, waste utilization, less resource consumption, and control over the ecological effects. The Ellen Macarthur Foundation has identified clear examples where companies refer to the *"circular economy," "circular model," "circular business," "circular development," "circularity"* or *"circular thinking."* However, many companies do not disclose in their financial and non-financial reporting what practices they implement to support SD by circularity frameworks. Negative associations between CE and SD have been presented by Cristina et al. (2018), who argue that the expenditure on closed-loop cycle frameworks must be adjusted to ensure that there is no creation of negative value on the social side. These are appropriate in various contexts: global economy, national economy, value chains of interlinked organizations, "material flow," "waste flow," and the end of product life (EU, 2019).

Relationship Between CE and SD

Jain et al. (2018) contend that circularity in business frameworks for the sustainable production of goods is essential for improving industries' financial and environmental performance in developed and developing nations. The United Nations Agenda 2030 defines 17 sustainable development goals, including 169 targets, as measured by impact and value (UN, 2015). For instance, direct link relations and cooperative dynamics between CE practices and SDG targets exist for SDG 6 (Clean Water and Sanitation), SDG 7 (Affordable and Clean Energy), SDG 8 (Decent Work and Economic Growth), SDG 12 (Sustainable Consumption and Production), and SDG 15 (Life on Land), registering high scores both for direct and circular commitments. CE activities make indirect contributions to, such as SDG 1 (No Poverty), SDG 2 (Zero Hunger), and SDG 14 (Life Below Water). The UN Agenda 2030 regarding CE refers to SDG 4 (Quality Education), SDG 9 (Industry, Advancement, and Infrastructure), SDG 10 (Reduced Inequalities), SDG 13 (Climate Action), SDG 16 (Peace, Justice, and Solid Institutions), and SDG 17 (Partnerships for the Goals) among others, being attained its worldwide adoption (UN, 2015). At the same time, some targets have demonstrated only weak connections with CE practices, e.g., SDG 3 (Good Health and Well-being), SDG 5 (Gender Equality), SDG 10 (Decreased Inequities), SDG 11 (Sustainable Cities and Communities), and SDG 16 (Peace, Justice and Strong Institutions). For instance, SDG 5 (Gender Equality) demonstrates the gender diversity and female proportions in top-level directors' positions while ignoring how female activists promote the CE and SD in their organization by making decisions and rethinking operations. Aside from SDG 9 (Industry, Innovation, and Infrastructure) and SDG 16, particularly SDG 17 (Partnerships for the Goals/ Means of Implementation), all goals have targets involving collaboration regarding CE practices. Table 1 demonstrates that SD dramatically benefits the economy, environment, and society. It overviews the similarities, differences, and relationships between CE and SD.

CE activity offers the benefits of transferring waste into resources, reducing the consumption of resources, and reducing carbon emissions (EU, 2019; Liu et al., 2017). Today, the concept of CE is widely embraced by companies, associations, and regulators worldwide. *"A circular economy pursues regenerating capital, whether financial, manufactured, human, social or natural. It ensures enhanced flows of goods and services"* (EMF, 2013; EU, 2019, 2022), which extends beyond a single company or the economic dimension. It emerges that most companies produce a sustainability report and make disclosures on CO_2 emissions and the recycling capacity. Still, many do not embrace the gender diversity role in reducing carbon emissions. All African governments have declared their support for the companies to disclose their information (financial and non-financial) by following the International Integrated Reporting Council framework (IIRC, 2013). If all over the world, companies, stakeholders, and practitioners followed suit and implemented CE where appropriate, this would enhance the environmental, economic, and social dimensions (Barnabè & Nazir, 2021, 2022). Drawing on the identified literature from the systematic review, a framework is required for combining CE and SD to achieve comprehensive sustainability, which integrates the environmental, economic, and social aspects. The concept of "circular economy" *is specifically connected with the terms "closed-loop" and "close the loop"* (Murray et al., 2017). A comparable representation was provided by the United Nations Environment Program), which demonstrates how CE can be a strategy for delivering economic development (Kirchherr et al., 2018). Subsequently, the global alliance on circular economy and resource efficiency (European Union, 2020) provided by the EU related to CE transition initiatives, resource efficiency, sustainable production, and consumption on efforts being deployed internationally.

Table 1 Overview of the similarities, differences, and relationships regarding CE and SD found in the literature

Concept	Similarities	Differences	Relationships	Sources
History of concept		✓		Brundtland Report (1987)
Objectives		✓		UN (2015) SDGs Agenda 2030, Green Deal (EU, 2019)
UNO agenda 2030		✓		UN (2015) SDGs Agenda 2030
Targets (Rules and regulations)	✓	✓	✓	UN (2015) SDGs Agenda 2030
Stakeholders	✓	✓	✓	Kirchherr et al. (2018) and EMF (2015b)
Circular supply chain management for sustainable development practices	✓		✓	Linder & Williander (2017), Geissdoerfer et al. (2018)
Circular sustainable business models enhance sustainable practices	✓		✓	EMF (2015c)
Ecology economics sustainability practices	✓		✓	Martins (2016), EMF (2020) and Mathews & Tan (2011)
Technology transfer and low-carbon energy technology for sustainability	✓		✓	Kirchherr et al. (2018) and Liu et al. (2017)
Product Service Model	✓		✓	Linder et al. (2017) and Tukker (2015)
3Rs, 6Rs, 10Rs, principles, and sustainable design strategies	✓		✓	Stahel (1982), EMF (2012), Reike et al. (2018) and Barnabè & Nazir (2021, 2022)
Sustainable technology and circular business model innovation	✓		✓	Linder & Williander (2017) and Cristina et al. (2018)

(continued)

Table 1 (continued)

Concept	Similarities	Differences	Relationships	Sources
Waste Management Framework (Zero waste)	✓		✓	Kirchherr et al. (2018), EMF (2012), EC (2015), Casiano Flores et al. (2018), and EU (2019)
Plastic Recycling Strategy for Sustainability	✓		✓	EMF (2016, 2017)
Eco-Innovation, Ecosystem, Industry Ecology, Eco design	✓		✓	Martins (2016) and Kirchherr et al. (2018)
Design Thinking, and Education for Sustainability	✓		✓	Andrews (2015)
Industry Symbiosis and GHG	✓		✓	Liu et al. (2017) and Mathews & Tan (2011)

6 Discussion and Conclusion

A systematic technique has been used to analyze the articles/reports on CE and SD to address the research question. The focus has been on the similarities, differences, and relationships between the two, as found in the business literature. Researchers and practitioners are stressing the importance of CE practices for a progressive economy and protection of the environment, but fewer have referred to social prosperity. The social aspects include job creation, gender diversity, corporate board diversity, social culture, and organizational culture, which could promote a country's prosperity. It has been elicited that most companies do not disclose a social perspective, i.e., gender diversity, females on board, audit committee role, the independent auditor in their reporting practices, only highlighting the economic advantages through CE, i.e., reducing resource consumption, efficiency, gains, and waste reduction, with moderately quick outcomes associated with sustainability (Linder & Williander, 2017; Martins, 2016).

Linder and Williander (2017) highlight critical issues of CE that carry with SD, e.g., the technical difficulties of a closed-loop cycle equilibrium between the demand and supply of the product and the energy required for recycling waste materials. While companies usually report both the economic and environmental dimensions of CE and sustainable development, they rarely do so regarding the social one, which can be attributed to the lack of robust indicators for the companies that cannot be avoided. Also, even if there were suitable measurements, there are no enforceable directives that require firms to report their contribution to social (gender diversity participation) development that enhances CE practice. Some researchers and practitioners, e.g., Martins (2016), have endeavored to identify connections with the different components of ethical and social areas of CE by seeking an organic endogenous (EU, 2022) relationship of these with the real economy and environmental issues. Other researchers have sought to develop sustainable frameworks that guide those utilizing CE into more comprehensive sustainable practices, which include the social dimension (Kirchherr et al. 2017). The product-service system (PSS) has been considered an applicable circular business model that can incorporate SD (Tukker, 2015; Linder & Williander, 2017) in service industries primarily.

The implication and the concept of CE are applied to developing many businesses and even countries that preserve natural resources and the environment for prompt and achieving SD (Kirchherr et al., 2017; Linder & Williander, 2017; Tukker, 2015). The circular design concept also covers the manufacturing and services sectors as one of the most important economic sectors. CE aims to use raw materials of natural origin and design the products and parts as they can be recoverable and quickly reproduce, combat obsolescence while preserving products and materials to produce maximum value, and so forth.

The relationship between CE, sustainability (CSR), and accounting information disclosure started to be studied together with the effects of corporate ownership governance and institutional pressure on environmental protection (Barnabè & Nazir, 2021; Kirchherr et al., 2018). Many researchers and practitioners are developing and merging the concept of CE and CSR and defining corporate social responsibility as "management policy that sets the practice and fireworks for sustainable product operations in present and meets future needs."

Linear to CE transformation (where material flows regenerate and consequently reduce the demand for virgin raw materials, leaving room for models of reuse and recycling of products) represents a valid opportunity to respond to the challenges of the future both nationally and internationally (Barnabè & Nazir, 2021). The corporate management philosophy of companies also started to be stated into mandatory and non-mandatory reports that better frame CE identifying and communicating specific objectives and disseminating best practices to achieve SDGs.

The implementation of the CE framework still encounters many limitations and barriers that prevent its diffusion (Barnabè & Nazir, 2021; McDonough & Braungart, 2002). Some authors observe that CE-relevant research has evolved primarily as research on waste management, reducing raw material consumption, and eliminating environmental externalities (Lieder & Rashid, 2016). Other authors criticize the lack of strategic and managerial perspective in CE research able to support changes to business models and operations that managers need to cope with and communicate throughout the entire organization when going circular and may also imply changes in the company's organizational culture (Barnabè & Nazir, 2021, 2022).

Another gap to CE diffusion has been identified in performance indicators or assessment methodologies, lacking in most CS reports that involved only CE. Stewart and Niero (2018) observe that only a minority of companies present a dedicated set of key performance indicators (KPIs) for their CE approach. The circular design minimizes the use of raw materials by minimizing loss of value, extending the life cycle, and improving resources.

The importance of the design and role of designers in creating increasingly sustainable models have been discussed for developing green and eco-friendly products. Particular attention has been devoted to environmental well-being obtained by creating and optimizing new business models to transition to a CE (Barnabè & Nazir, 2022). Environmental sustainability scenarios are linked to some fundamental principles such as the use of production processes capable of significantly reducing energy consumption, more outstanding durability of the product, ease of disassembly of materials, and the possibility of reusing a product or service at the end of its life. These principles translated into environmental, social, and economic terms and disclosed in non-financial reports become a tangible benefit for the society.

Terms such as "circularity," "environmental stewardship," "eco-design," and "suppliers environmental assessment" are increasingly used and testify to a change in the companies' managerial approach. It refers to new strategies that address relevant issues of environmental protection, water pollution, air quality, and waste management, with an approach that is recognized also from the use of different terms (Nathaniel, 2021). In the industry, the transition to circular models can be used to change the product "design" to increase durability. This is a pivotal element in instilling confidence in the consumer.

Design more "durable products" with "green formulation," design for standardization and compatibility for certain parts of the product, design for disassembly and reassembly where the products and their parts can be easily separated and reassembled and "reused" (Bocken et al., 2016) are specific themes regarding new processes of production oriented to circularity. Environmental disclosure literature also discusses problems regarding the limited use of indicators and quantitative assessments of circularity objectives. Market logic underpins climate policy without an actively constructed ideological project requiring the mobilization of significant economic interests and resources. The environmental decline has provided scope for new forms of policymaking, yet these emergent policies and policymaking bodies still need to be better understood in many cases. Many authors undertake empirical analysis mainly through content analysis and case studies in several sectors, including consumer goods, ICT and services, automotive, and manufacturing. The systematic literature review also identified gaps in the ability of companies to adapt to frameworks and standards provided by emergent policies and policymaking bodies, using effective indicators to assess circularity and cover the sustainability perspective.

Concerning the above, CE aligns with a range of R imperatives, e.g., 3Rs, 4Rs, 5Rs, 6Rs, 7Rs, 8Rs, 9Rs, and 10Rs (Reike et al., 2018), but most practitioners, academic researchers, and organizations are using 3Rs (reduce, reuse, recycle) because of quickly implement in services and manufacturing industries efficiently. The CE-4R's framework is the official EU policy framework aimed at a zero-waste program (EC 2015a) (waste), wastewater reuse and sanitation, industrial symbiosis, and remanufacturing (product-by-product). Some modern manufacturing companies have been trying to implement CE practices in their production framework, like Marks and Spencer and H&M, which means including remanufacturing and redesigning. However, the services industries, i.e., tourism, asset management, and insurance companies, still ignore CE practices for sustainable development. This has been pursued by exploiting artificial intelligence, achieving greater sustainability in their organization (EMF, 2017).

According to their reports, most companies do not offer employees CE transformation training, social awareness programs, gender equality frameworks, or work harmony models. They do not disclose them in their social responsibility reports and integrated reports. Waste management, involving reducing its flow, reuse, and recycling, led to job creation and stimulation of the local economy, thereby positively impacting the societal dimension. Are non-male executive directors more effective in participating in waste management? A question remains open. Stewart and Niero (2018) and Barnabè and Nazir (2021, 2022) included Integrated (besides other sustainability, environmental reports integrated reports) in their review of corporate reports in the fast-moving consumer goods sector to explore how far companies have incorporated CE-related concepts in their sustainability agendas and embedded these practices into one account while not considered the gender diversity aspects, as well only focused on manufacturing industries not focusing on services industries. They found that many modern organizations have yet to recognize the potential opportunities available from CE. The evidence from these reviews suggests that reporting may help them think and rethink the relationships among resources across the various sectors of the organization and deliver new accounting information for better strategic decision-making on green investment and revenue. The CE and SD article abstracts were processed for review using NVivo 12 Pro software to create a word cloud. This "is a special visualization of text in which the most frequent words are effectively highlighted by occupying more prominence in the representation. (…) Word clouds can be useful for preliminary analysis and validation of previous findings" (McNaught & Lam, 2010, p. 630) (see Fig. 4).

As shown in the figure, the articles' more frequently used words on the business economic area, like circular economy, social, economic development, sustainable, sustainability, business models, and framework words, are highly cited. This reflects that all the retrieved articles and reports for the review closely relate to the CE and SD concepts.

The research question is: What are the similarities, differences, and relationships between circular economy and sustainable development, as reported in the business economics literature? CE is a regenerative framework for resource reduction, reuse, recovery, energy spillage remediation techniques, and materials consumption reduction in a closed-loop circle. UN (2030) contends that SD benefits present and future outcomes for firms regarding economic performance, the social dimension, and environmental protection. However, the review revealed little concern for social aspects, specifically corporate gender diversity and role in reporting, and there are several reasons behind this, including a lack of stakeholder interest and knowledge and poor consumer awareness/

Fig. 4 Words cloud of article abstracts

education. Most companies do not offer CE and SD skill development training programs for their employees' social awareness programs.

Moreover, generally, SME companies do not disclose social gender proportion information in their reporting practices. EU (2019) and the UN (2015) SD agenda both hold that the SD social aspect should be incorporated into CE activities and reporting around such issues as, e.g., job creation, job satisfaction, safe working environment, employee involvement, non-male and male on board, non-male executive score, and employees' participation in the decision-making process. Hence, policymakers should consider requiring organizations to report these socially related elements in their non-financial information. The term CE is associated with the closed-loop for achieving long-term and short-term goals, while SD only relates to the long-term prosperity of society. If short-medium and medium-long-term closed-loop circular frameworks are developed and followed, regional, national, and international prosperity could be enhanced by delivering the benefits of such processes on an ongoing basis. If reporting practices are embedded within CE activities, then this would stimulate companies to focus directly on social aspects (as well as governance aspects), thereby aligning CE with SD.

7 Practical Implications

While the literature has revealed a relationship between CE practices and SD, much remains to be done to comprehensively align the two concepts. Hence, organizations must encourage or even require actions to foster such alignment. CE-related practices are already used in industry on a large scale following the 3Rs 4Rs and 6Rs principle of reduce, recycle, and reuse in manufacturing industries. However, the 6R's arrangement in the services industry could be more beneficial regarding sustainable development. While firms engaging in CE practices have to report economic and environmental information with recognized indicators, widely accepted indicators are unavailable. Hence, there is a pressing need for their development in the sustainability context of financial and non-financial reporting.

8 Limitations

Moreover, if such a move occurred, wider industries not engaged in CE would have to consider adopting a more sustainable product production method. The literature review has certain limitations. First, there is a small size of sample of articles, and second, only the business economics research area has been covered.

9 Future Research

For further research, content analysis and a qualitative exploratory case study are proposed to shed different light on the relationship between CE activities and SD. Moreover, such inquiry should be extended to industrial sectors other than business economics. On the other hand, the research only covers the business economics research area; however, in the future, other areas like material engineering, construction, etc., can be used for comparative analysis.

Appendix: Explicit Reference to the Main Theme of CE and SD

Number	Authors	Year	Keywords	Document type	Journal name
(1)	Skvarciany, V; Lapinskaite, I; Volskyte, G	2021	Performance, business	Article	Oeconomia Copernicana
(2)	Zhang, DW; Huang, XL; Wen, YF; Trivedi, P; Joghee, S	2021	Circular economy; supply chain management; circular business models; sustainable development	Article	Journal of Theoretical and Applied Electronic Commerce Research
(3)	Gonzalez, VV	2021	Strategies; public policies; circular economy; sustainable development; Colombia	Article	Cuadernos De Administracion-Universidad Del Valle
(4)	De Angelis, R	2021	Circular economy; circular competitiveness; economy-ecology reintegration; environmental paradigms; sustain centrism	Article	Management Decision

(continued)

(continued)

Number	Authors	Year	Keywords	Document type	Journal name
(5)	Ly, B	2021	Apparel multinationals; circular economy; competitive advantage; covid; fast fashion; OLI paradigms; sustainable solutions; value creation	Article	Cogent Business & Management
(6)	Mansilla-Obando, K; Jeldes-Delgado, F; Guinez-Cabrera, N; Ortiz-Henriquez, R	2021	Altruism; circular economy; nongovernmental organization; sustainability; charity shop	Article	Cuadernos De Administracion-Universidad Del Valle
(7)	Rok, B; Kulik, M	2021	Sustainability; start-ups; sustainable innovation; circular economy; positive impact	Article	Corporate Governance-The International Journal of Business in Society
(8)	Smitha, JS; Thomas, A	2021	Circular economy; recycling; integrated model; index; built environment	Article	Construction Economics and Building

(continued)

(continued)

Number	Authors	Year	Keywords	Document type	Journal name
(9)	Svensson, G; Padin, C	2021	Sustainable development; business-driven; Spinoffs; trade-offs; sustainability; triple bottom line; sustainable development goals; UN 2030 agenda	Article	Journal of Business & Industrial Marketing
(10)	Mikelsone, E; Atstaja, D; Koval, V; Uvarova, I; Mavlutova, I; Kuzmina, J	2021	Urban; sustainable urban transformation; economic development; Covid-19; critical literature review	Article	Estudios De Economia Aplicada
(11)	Rainville, A	2021		Article	Research Policy
(12)	Islam, MM; Perry, P; Gill, S	2021	Environmental sustainability; fashion supply chain; sustainable practices; sustainable supply chain management; systematic literature review	Article	Journal of Fashion Marketing and Management

(continued)

(continued)

Number	Authors	Year	Keywords	Document type	Journal name
(13)	D'Inverno, G; Carosi, L; Romano, G	2021	Performance evaluation; composite indicator; water utilities; undesirable indicator; environmental impact; sustainable development	Article	Socio-Economic Planning Sciences
(14)	Christmann, P	2021	Minerals; metals; sustainable development; policies; regulations; International Minerals and Metals Agency; European Union; World	Article	Mineral Economics
(15)	Brones, F; Zancul, E; Carvalho, MM	2021	Ecodesign; product development; change management; transition; sustainability; innovation management	Article	International Journal of Managing Projects in Business
(16)	Ouhimmou, M; Ronnqvist, M; Lapointe, LA	2021	Forest value chain; new product assessment; sustainability; decision support tool; biorefinery; network design	Article	Omega-International Journal of Management Science

(continued)

(continued)

Number	Authors	Year	Keywords	Document type	Journal name
(17)	Zebek, E; Zilinskiene, L	2021	Food waste legal regulation; waste management; food waste; bio-waste; waste hierarchy	Article	Entrepreneurship and Sustainability Issues
(18)	Morganti P., Vannozzi A., Memic A., Coltelli M.-B	2021	Advanced medications; beauty masks; Chitin nanofibrils; circular economy; cosmetics; food waste; lignin; plastic waste; pollution packaging	Book Chapter	An Introduction to the Circular Economy
(19)	Morganti P., Morganti G	2021	Circular economy; environment; food systems; Green cities; Green economy; innovation; pollution; recycling; sustainability; waste	Book Chapter	An Introduction to the Circular Economy
(20)	Piu M., Rossetti M	2021	Chemical substances; circular economy; environmental impact; fashion; recycling; textile fibers; textile waste; traceability	Book Chapter	An Introduction to the Circular Economy

(continued)

(continued)

Number	Authors	Year	Keywords	Document type	Journal name
(21)	Leyva-Díaz J.C., Molina-Moreno V., Sánchez-Molina J., Belmonte-Ureña L.J	2021	Bibliometric analysis; circular economy; indicator; sustainability; technological nutrient; water management	Book Chapter	An Introduction to the Circular Economy
(22)	Alcalde-Calonge A., Ruiz-Palomino P., Sáez-Martínez F.J	2021	Bioeconomy; circular economy; competitive advantage; dynamic capabilities; forest industry; Social capital	Book Chapter	Social Capital: Issues, Challenges and Perspectives
(23)	Cantù C.L., Schepis D., Minunno R., Morrison G	2021	Circular economy; innovation platform; inter-organizational relationships; living lab; relational governance; sustainability	Article	Journal of Business and Industrial Marketing
(24)	Bag S., Rahman M.S	2021	Capabilities; circular economy; dynamic capabilities; environmental uncertainty; supply chain management; sustainable supply chain flexibility	Article	Supply Chain Management

(continued)

(continued)

Number	Authors	Year	Keywords	Document type	Journal name
(25)	Lichtenthaler U	2021	Competitive advantage; firm performance; natural resource-based view; sustainability; sustainability innovation; sustainable development goals	Article	Journal of Strategy and Management
(26)	Jesus G.M.K., Jugend D	2021	Circular economy; circular oriented innovation; open innovation; Sustainability	Article	European Journal of Innovation Management
(27)	Hasheminasab H., Hashemkhani Zolfani S., Kazimieras Zavadskas E., Kharrazi M., Skare M	2021	Circular economy; cradle-to-cradle; extended stepwise weight assessment ratio analysis extended SWARA (E-SWARA); fossil fuel; MCDM; Measurement of Alternatives and Ranking according to Compromise Solution (MARCOS); sustainability	Article	Economic Research-Ekonomska Istrazivanja

(continued)

(continued)

Number	Authors	Year	Keywords	Document type	Journal name
(28)	Saroha M., Garg D., Luthra S	2021	Circular economy; circular supply chain management (CSCM); Developing countries; F-DEMATEL; practices; sustainable development	Article	International Journal of Productivity and Performance Management
(29)	Sehnem S., Lopes de Sousa Jabbour A.B., Conceição D.A., Weber D., Julkovski D.J	2021	Circular economy; developing economy; green supply chain; sustainability	Article	Benchmarking
(30)	Karpova, SV; Cherenkov, VI; Cherenkova, NI	2020	Arctic environment; circular economy; consumer behavior; consumers' consumption; sustainability construct; sustainability literacy; sustainable consumption and production; sustainable development	Article	International Scientific Conference Digital Transformation on Manufacturing, Infrastructure and Service

(continued)

(continued)

Number	Authors	Year	Keywords	Document type	Journal name
(31)	Zwiers, J; Jaeger-Erben, M; Hofmann, F	2020	Circular economy; circular literacy; sustainable development; transformation knowledge	Article	Culture and Organization
(32)	Kristoffersen, E; Blomsma, F; Mikalef, P; Li, JY	2020	Digital circular economy; digitalization; circular economy; Sustainability; Industry 4.0; Big data analytics	Article	Journal of Business Research
(33)	Sebestova, J; Sroka, W	2020	Circular economy; recycling; sustainable business; waste management	Article	Journal of Eastern European and Central Asian Research
(34)	Volker, T; Kovacic, Z; Strand, R	2020	Circular economy; indicator politics; sociotechnical imaginaries; centers of calculation; epistemic communities; environmental governance	Article	Culture and Organization

(continued)

(continued)

Number	Authors	Year	Keywords	Document type	Journal name
(35)	Bui, TD; Ali, MH; Tsai, FM; Iranmanesh, M; Tseng, ML; Lim, MK	2020	Sustainable corporate finance; bibliometric analysis; network analysis; co-wording analysis; circular economy; triple bottom line	Article	Journal of Risk and Financial Management
(36)	Krysovatyy, A; Zvarych, R; Zvarych, I; Krysovatyy, T; Krysovata, K	2020	Inclusiveness; circularity; circular economy; inclusive growth; eco-security; methodology; ecology; value chain; self-organization	Article	Economic Annals-XXI
(37)	Ramakrishna, S; Ngowi, A; De Jager, H; Awuzie, BO	2020	Industry 4; 0 technologies; circular economy; innovation; higher education	Article	Science Technology and Society
(38)	Rodriguez-Anton, JM	2020	Africa; circular economy; SDG; Tourism Competitiveness	Article	Estudios De Economia Aplicada
(39)	Koszewska, M; Bielecki, M	2020	Circular economy; sustainability; circular product design; consumer; furniture; closed-loop supply chain	Article	Entrepreneurship and Sustainability Issues

(continued)

(continued)

Number	Authors	Year	Keywords	Document type	Journal name
(40)	Al Hosni, IS; Amoudi, O; Callaghan, N	2020	Recycling & reuse of materials; sustainability; waste management & disposal	Article	Proceedings of The Institution of Civil Engineers-Management Procurement and Law
(41)	Khudyakova, T; Shmidt, A; Shmidt, S	2020	Smart city; sustainable city; circular economy; waste management; economic effect; resource-saving technologies; tire recycling	Article	Entrepreneurship and Sustainability Issues
(42)	Zralek, J; Burgiel, A	2020	Consumer behavior; perceived consumer effectiveness; perceived difficulty; perception matrix; sustainable consumption	Article	Review of Business
(43)	Marrone, M; Linnenluecke, MK; Richardson, G; Smith, T	2020	Environmental accounting; Review; Topic burst; Carbon; Circular economy; Ecosystem services; Literature review	Article	Accounting Auditing & Accountability Journal

(continued)

(continued)

Number	Authors	Year	Keywords	Document type	Journal name
(44)	Piwowar, A	2020	Low-carbon economy; development challenges; rural areas; environmental protection; farmers' behaviors; Poland	Article	Economics & Sociology
(45)	Drabik, P; Rehak, R; Vernerova, D; Kukura, M	2020	Environment; eco-product; marketing; sustainability; sustainable consumption	Article	Ekonomicky Casopis
(46)	Naqvi, MHA; Jiang, YS; Miao, M; Naqvi, MH	2020	Sustainable user-generated content; social influence process; uses and gratification theory; online technologies; trust; Instagram; attitude; sustainable intention to use SNS; social media communication and interaction	Article	Cogent Business & Management

(continued)

(continued)

Number	Authors	Year	Keywords	Document type	Journal name
(47)	Monciardini, D; Mahonen, JT; Tsagas, G	2020	Non-financial reporting; European regulation; sustainability; corporate social accountability; integrated reporting; non-financial reporting directive; accounting	Article	Accounting Economics and Law Convivium
(48)	Martens, R; Fan, SK; Dwyer, RJ	2020	Additive manufacturing; 3D printing; innovation adoption; disruptive innovation; supply chain management	Article	World journal of Entrepreneurship Management and Sustainable Development
(49)	Drábik P., Rehák R., Vernerová D., Kukura M	2020	Eco-product; environment; marketing; sustainability; sustainable consumption	Article	Ekonomicky Casopis
(50)	Mitra A., Gaur S.S	2020	Asian markets; emerging markets; environmental performance; Governance in Asia; social equity	Article	Journal of Asia Business Studies

(continued)

(continued)

Number	Authors	Year	Keywords	Document type	Journal name
(51)	Pagan N.M., Pagan K.M., Teixeira A.A., de Moura Engracia Giraldi J., Stefanelli N.O., de Oliveira J.H.C	2020	Circular economy; environmental performance; marketing; neuromarketing; sustainable consumption; sustainable development goals	Article	Global Journal of Flexible Systems Management
(52)	Lin B.C.-A	2020	Circular economy; circular GDP; economic growth; sustainability issues; sustainable growth	Article	Journal of Economic Issues
(53)	Šebestová J., Sroka W	2020	Circular economy; recycling; sustainable business; waste management	Article	Journal of Eastern European and Central Asian Research
(54)	Thatta S., Polisetty A	2020	Circular economy; linear; MUD jeans; recycling; sustainable circular model; sustainable development	Article	FIIB Business Review

(continued)

(continued)

Number	Authors	Year	Keywords	Document type	Journal name
(55)	Urmínová M., Kusá A	2020	Circular fashion; education; social media; sustainability communications; sustainability fashion	Conference Paper	Proceedings of the European Conference on Innovation and Entrepreneurship, ECIE
(56)	Khan T., Badjie F	2020	Blended Islamic finance; circular economy; Islamic social finance; Sadaqa; sustainable development goals; sustainable human development; Waqf; Zakah	Article	Singapore Economic Review
(57)	Rodríguez-Antón, Miguel J	2020	Africa; circular economy; SDG; tourism competitiveness	Article	Estudios De Economia Aplicada
(58)	Piispanen V.-V., Henttonen K., Aromaa E	2020	BMC; business model; business model canvas; business opportunity; case study; circular economy; innovation; sustainability; value creation	Conference Paper	International Journal of Entrepreneurship and Innovation Management
(59)	Nasution A.H., Aula M., Ardiantono D.S	2020	CBMC; circular business model canvas; circular economy; Dairy industry	Article	International Journal of Integrated Supply Management

(continued)

(continued)

Number	Authors	Year	Keywords	Document type	Journal name
(60)	Holtström J., Bjellerup C., Eriksson J	2019	Apparel industry; business model; business model innovation; circular economy; sharing economy; sustainability	Article	Journal of Strategy and Management
(61)	Barrett J., Makale K	2019		Article	Journal of Australian Taxation
(62)	Tamasila M., Ivascu L., Turi A., Artene A	2019	Circular economy; competitiveness; corporate sustainability efficiency; evaluation; ISO; sustainable development	Conference Paper	Proceedings of the 33RD International Business Information Management Association Conference, IBIMA 2019: Education Excellence and Innovation Management Through Vision 2020
(63)	Ivascu L., Ardelean B.-O., Turi A., Gaureanu A., Balan M	2019	Life-cycle assessment; model for sustainable development; models; risk management; stakeholder; sustainability	Conference Paper	Proceedings of the 33RD international Business Information Management Association Conference, IBIMA 2019: Education Excellence and Innovation Management Through Vision 2020

(continued)

(continued)

Number	Authors	Year	Keywords	Document type	Journal name
(64)	Brendzel-Skowera K	2019	Circular economy; medium enterprises; small; sustainable development	Conference Paper	Proceedings of the 33RD International Business Information Management Association Conference, IBIMA 2019: Education Excellence And Innovation Management Through Vision 2020
(65)	Gureva, MA; Butko, VV	2019	Circular economy; linear economy; sustainable development; social and economic development; The Ellen MacArthur Foundation (EMF)	Conference Paper	Vision 2025: Education Excellence and Management of Innovations Through Sustainable Economic Competitive Advantage
(66)	Nilsen, HR	2019	Sustainability; ecology; resources; social justice; waste hierarchy; circular economy	Article	International Journal of Social Economics
(67)	Sharma, YK; Mangla, SK; Patil, PP; Liu, SF	2019	Sustainable development; stakeholders; supply chain management; emerging markets; environment; organizational performance	Article	Management Decision

(continued)

(continued)

Number	Authors	Year	Keywords	Document type	Journal name
(68)	Razminiene, K	2019	Clusters; circular economy; resource efficiency; performance evaluation; knowledge transfer; sustainability; sustainable growth; sustainable use of resources	Article	Equilibrium-Quarterly Journal of Economics and Economic Policy
(69)	Trigkas, M; Mpyrou, K; Karagouni, G; Papadopoulos, I	2019	Circular economy; product life cycle; innovation; resource efficiency; economic model; Greek industries; sustainable development	Article	Business Management Theories and Practices in a Dynamic Competitive Environment
(70)	de Assuncao, GM	2019	Environmental management; circular economy; solid waste; sustainability	Article	Sistemas & Gestao
(71)	Zaidi, SAH; Mirza, FM; Hou, FJ; Ashraf, RU	2019	Sustainable procurement; sustainable development; interpretive structural modeling; Pakistan	Article	Socio-Economic Planning Sciences

(continued)

(continued)

Number	Authors	Year	Keywords	Document type	Journal name
(72)	Holtstrom, J; Bjellerup, C; Eriksson, J	2019	Business model; sustainability; business model innovation; Sharing economy; apparel industry; circular economy	Article	Journal of Strategy and Management
(73)	Pinheiro, MAP; Seles, BMRP; Fiorini, PD; Jugend, D; Jabbour, ABLD; da Silva, HMR; Latan, H	2019	Stakeholders; new product development; barriers; drivers; sustainable design; circular design	Article	Management Decision
(74)	Farooque, M; Zhang, A; Liu, YP	2019	China; sustainability; sustainable supply chain; circular supply chain; food industry; circular economy; Barrier; Fuzzy DEMATEL	Article	Supply Chain Management: An International Journal
(75)	Fulconis, F; Pache, G; Reynaud, E	2019	Sustainability; Stakeholders; Supply chains; Frugality; Circular economy; Degrowth	Article	Society and Business Review

(continued)

(continued)

Number	Authors	Year	Keywords	Document type	Journal name
(76)	Andronie, M; Simion, VE; Gurgu, E; Dijmarescu, A; Dijmarescu, I	2019	Social responsibility; bioeconomy; natural resources; sustainability; intelligent use of resources	Article	Amfiteatru Economic
(77)	Horvath, B; Khazami, N; Ymeri, P; Fogarassy, C	2019	Business model innovation; circular economy; biotechnology; SME; circular value proposition	Article	Journal of Business Economics and Management
(78)	Mircea, AT; Ciplea, SA	2019	Sustainability; environmental impact; waste management; environmentally compatible structures and materials	Conference paper	Vision 2025: Education Excellence and Management of Innovations Through Sustainable Economic Competitive Advantage
(79)	Banwo, AO; Du, JG	2019	China; Comprehensive action determination model; context; employees; Jiangsu Province; small and medium-sized enterprises; workplace pro-environmental behavior	Article	Journal of Global Entrepreneurship Research

(continued)

(continued)

Number	Authors	Year	Keywords	Document type	Journal name
(80)	Di Tullio P., Valentinetti D., Rea M.A	2018	Business model; competitiveness; sustainability; sustainable business model	Article	Industria
(81)	Casiano Flores C., Bressers H., Gutierrez C., de Boer C	2018	Business ethics and sustainability; circular economy; Mexico water management; Presa Guadalupe Mexico; wastewater treatment policy; water basin management; water governance	Article	Management Research Review
(82)	Moon C.J	2018	Education; entrepreneurship; innovation; mindset; sustainability; UN HESI; UN SDGs	Book Chapter	Contemporary Issues in Entrepreneurship Research
(83)	Raphaëlle Stewart, Monia Niero	2018	CSR report, food and beverage, household, packaging, sustainable development, textile	Article	Business Strategy and the Environment

(continued)

(continued)

Number	Authors	Year	Keywords	Document type	Journal name
(84)	Fonseca L.M., Portela A.R., Duarte B., Queirós J., Paiva L	2018	Circular economy; education; higher education institutions; Portugal; social responsibility; sustainability; sustainable development	Article	Management and Marketing
(85)	Menegaki A.N	2018	Circular economy; hotel business; resources; smart sustainable technologies	Article	International Journal of Tourism Policy
(86)	Pamfilie, R; Firoiu, D; Croitoru, AG; Ionescu, GHI	2018	Sustainable development; circular economy; circular tourism; integrated management system; economic performance	Article	Amfiteatru Economic
(87)	Ievdokymov, V; Oliinyk, O; Ksendzuk, V; Sergiienko, L	2018	Circular economy; sustainable development; environment and economic security; state administration; state policy; Ukraine	Article	Ekonomista

(continued)

(continued)

Number	Authors	Year	Keywords	Document type	Journal name
(88)	Fonseca, LM; Domingues, JP	2018	Circular economy; sustainability; closed-loop economy; sustainable consumption; change; engineering students	Conference Paper	Proceedings of the International Conference on Business Excellence
(89)	Julian Kirchherr, Laura Piscicelli, Ruben Bour, Erica Kostense-Smit, Jennifer Muller, Anne Huibrechtse-Truijens, Marko Hekkerta	2018	Circular economy, sustainability transitions, sustainable development, barriers, European Union	Article	Ecological Economics
(90)	Julian Kirchherr, Frauke Urban	2018	Technology transfer, solar PV, wind hydropower, dams, low-carbon development, sustainability transitions	Article	Energy Policy
(91)	Jonathan Sze Choong Low, Yen Ting Ng	2018	Sustainable development, circular economy, reverse logistics, life-cycle cost, the total cost of ownership, flexibility in design	Article	Business Strategy and the Environment

(continued)

(continued)

Number	Authors	Year	Keywords	Document type	Journal name
(92)	Denise Reike, Walter J.V. Vermeulen, Sjors Witjes	2018	Circular economy, circularity, closed-loop economy, value preservation, literature review	Article	Resources, Conservation, and Recycling
(93)	Jouni Korhonen, Antero Honkasalo, Jyri Seppälä	2018	Circular economy, business strategy, scientific research, global net sustainability, thermodynamics, system boundaries, six limitations	Article	Ecological Economics
(94)	Goyal, S; Esposito, M; Kapoor, A	2018	Business models; circular economy; cradle-to-cradle; cradle-to-grave; developing economies; linear economy; reduce-reuse recycle	Article	Thunderbird International Business Review
(95)	Mishenin, Y; Koblianska, I; Medvid, V; Maistrenko, Y	2018	Management of flows; flow thinking; industrial ecology; logistics; region's sustainable development; circular economy; regional policy	Article	Entrepreneurship and Sustainability Issues

(continued)

(continued)

Number	Authors	Year	Keywords	Document type	Journal name
(96)	Immacolata, V	2018	Tourism system; circular economy; sustainable tourism; sustainability indicators; sustainability paradigm; circular paradigm	Article	Quality-Access to Success
(97)	Lang, M; Marsden, T	2018	Circular economy; growth; place; sustainability; well-being	Article	Local Economy
(98)	Jain, S; Jain, NK; Metri, B	2018	Performance management; environment management; supply chain management; circular economy	Article	Benchmarking-an International Journal
(99)	Vegera, S; Malei, A; Sapeha, I; Sushko, V	2018	Industrial waste; technological cycle; costs; waste of ferrous and non-ferrous metals; construction waste and waste arising from reservoirs cleaned	Article	Entrepreneurship and Sustainability Issues

(continued)

(continued)

Number	Authors	Year	Keywords	Document type	Journal name
(100)	Borrelli, IP	2018	Agriculture; circular economy; circular paradigm; case study; winery; Tuscany region	Article	Quality-Access to Success
(101)	Skene K., Murray A	2017		Book	Sustainable Economics: Context, Challenges and Opportunities for the 21st-Century Practitioner
(102)	Roorda N., Corcoran P.B., Weakland J.P	2017		Book	Fundamentals of Sustainable Development: Second ED
(103)	e Jesus and Sandro Mendonça	2017	Circular economy; eco-innovation; barriers; drivers; survey	Article	Ecological Economics
(104)	Liu, Zhe & Adams, Michelle & Cote, Raymond P. & Geng, Yong & Chen, Qinghua & Liu, Weili & Sun, Lu & Yu, Xiaoman	2017	GHG emissions in mitigation, industrial symbiosis, comprehensive development, opportunities, challenges, China	Article	Energy Policy
(105)	Alan Murray, Keith Skene & Kathryn Haynes	2017	Circular economy, closed-loop cycle, sustainability, sustainable development	Article	Journal of Business Ethics

(continued)

(continued)

Number	Authors	Year	Keywords	Document type	Journal name
(106)	Marcus Linder and Mats Williander	2017	Circular business model, business model innovation, customer development, product-service-system, circular economy, remanufacturing	Article	Business Strategy and the Environment
(107)	Pajula T., Behm K., Vatanen S., Saarivuori E	2017	Carbon footprint; carbon handprint; life-cycle assessment; sustainability; water footprint	Book Chapter	Dynamics of Long-Life Assets: From Technology Adaptation to Upgrading the Business Model
(108)	Moon C	2017	Education; entrepreneurship; innovation; sustainability; UN SDGs	Conference Paper	Proceedings of the European Conference on Innovation and Entrepreneurship, ECIE
(109)	Kralj D., Tramšek M., Homšak M	2017	Business; Circular economy; Environment; Excellence; Management; Organization model	Article	WSEAS Transactions on Business and Economics
(110)	García B., Ferat M	2017		Article	International Journal of Economic Research

(continued)

(continued)

Number	Authors	Year	Keywords	Document type	Journal name
(111)	Saritas O., Proskuryakova L.N	2017	Horizon scanning; Russia; sustainable water systems; water goods and services; water resources; water use	Article	Foresight
(112)	Antikainen, M; Valkokari, K	2016	Circular economy; sustainability; business model; business canvas; innovation; case study	Article	Technology Innovation Management Review
(113)	Cabrita, MD; Cruz-Machado, V; Matos, F; Safari, H	2016	Proceedings of the 17th European Conference on Knowledge Management	Conference	Circular Economy; Eco-Innovation; Green Knowledge; Greening Innovation; Knowledge Management; Sustainability
(114)	Nuno Ornelas Martins	2016	Ecosystem, classical political economy, value, scarcity, strong sustainability	Article	Ecological Economics
(115)	Andrews D	2015	Circular economy; education for sustainability; sustainable design and manufacture	Article	Local Economy

(continued)

(continued)

Number	Authors	Year	Keywords	Document type	Journal name
(116)	Golinska-Dawson, P; Nowak, A	2015	Remanufacturing process; suppliers; cores	Article	Log Forum
(117)	Bran, F; Ioan, I; Radulescu, CV	2014	Proceedings of the 8th international Management Conference: Management Challenges for Sustainable Development	Conference Paper	Waste; Entropy; Value; Circular Economy; Product Service Systems
(118)	Bermejo R	2014	Biomimicry; environmental economics; sustainable economy; sustainable future; sustainable production and consumption	Book	Handbook for a Sustainable Economy
(119)	Webster K., Vare P	2012		Book Chapter	Learning for Sustainability in Times of Accelerating Change
(120)	Bi X., Shan S., Xue Y	2012	Circular economy; DEA; ecological efficiency; sustainability; weight set	Conference Paper	2012 International Symposium on Management of Technology, ISMOT 2012

(continued)

(continued)

Number	Authors	Year	Keywords	Document type	Journal name
(121)	Mathews (2011)	2011	China, circular economy, eco-industrial park, eco-industrial development, industrial ecology, latecomer strategy	Article	Asian Business & Management
(122)	Li, H; Deng, J	2009	Bauxite; circular economy; mineral resources; financial crisis; sustainable development	Conference Paper	Proceedings of 2009 International Conference on Management Science and Engineering
(123)	Wang, HD; Li, CX	2009	Circular economy; small and medium-sized enterprises; industrial cluster; development strategy	Conference Paper	Enterprise Grows in Sustaining Efficiency and Effectiveness, Conference Proceedings

(continued)

(continued)

Number	Authors	Year	Keywords	Document type	Journal name
(124)	Ellen MacArthur Foundation	2012, 2014, 2013, 2015, 2016, 2017, 2018, 2019	Towards the Circular Economy Vol. 1, 2, 3, A new Dynamic: effective business in the Circular Economy, Growth within, a circular economy vision for a competitive Europe, Business Rationale for an acceleration transition, Delivering the circular economy, a tool kit for the policymaker, the new plastic economy, the new plastic Economy, Rethinking the future of plastic, A wealth of Flow-2nd Edition, Circular economy in cities	Reports	Ellen MacArthur Foundation Org

(continued)

(continued)

Number	Authors	Year	Keywords	Document type	Journal name
(125)	European Commission Reports and Directives	2012, 2014, 2015, 2016, 2019, 2020, 2021, 2022	Towards a Circular Economy: A Zero Waste Programme for Europe, COM (2015) 614/2, Directive 2014/24/EU, EC commission (2015b) Resource Efficiency scoreboard, EU green Deal (2019), new action plan of CE (2020), new regulations on sustainable batterie (2020), global alliance on circular economy and resources efficiency (GACERE, 2021), organic pollutant waste directive (2021), and sustainable product design and packages (2022)	Reports	European Union
(126)	OECD Reports	2015a, 2015b	Enabling the next productivity revolution, productivity indicators	Reports	https://www.oecd.org/

(continued)

(continued)

Number	Authors	Year	Keywords	Document type	Journal name
(127)	2030 Agenda of Sustainable Development	2015	17 sustainable goals, 169 Targets		United Nations Organization

References

Abbasi, K. R., Hussain, K., Haddad, A. M., Salman, A., & Ozturk, I. (2022). The role of financial development and technological innovation towards sustainable development in Pakistan: Fresh insights from consumption and territory-based emissions. *Technological Forecasting and Social Change, 176*, 121444.

Abbasi, S., & Choukolaei, H. A. (2023). A systematic review of green supply chain network design literature focusing on carbon policy. *Decision Analytics Journal*, 100189.

Abbasi, S., Zahmatkesh, S., Bokhari, A., & Hajiaghaei-Keshteli, M. (2023). Designing a vaccine supply chain network considering environmental aspects. *Journal of Cleaner Production, 417*, 137935.

Aguilar-Hernandez, G. A., Rodrigues, J. F. D., & Tukker, A. (2021). Macroeconomic, social and environmental impacts of a circular economy up to 2050: A meta-analysis of prospective studies. *Journal of Cleaner Production, 278*, 123421.

Andrews, D. (2015). The circular economy, design thinking and education for sustainability. *Local Economy, 30*(3), 305–315.

Barnabè, F., & Nazir, S. (2021). Investigating the interplays between integrated reporting practices and circular economy disclosure. *International Journal of Productivity and Performance Management, 70*(8), 2001–2031.

Barnabè, F., & Nazir, S. (2022). Conceptualizing and enabling circular economy through integrated thinking. *Corporate Social Responsibility and Environmental Management, 29*(2), 448–468.

Bellis, D. N. (2009). *Bibliometrics and citation analysis*. Scarecrow Press.

Blomsma, F., & Brennan, G. (2017). The emergence of circular economy: A new framing around prolonging resource productivity. *Journal of Industrial Ecology, 21*(3), 603–614.

Bocken, N. M., De Pauw, I., Bakker, C., & Van Der Grinten, B. (2016). Product design and business model strategies for a circular economy. *Journal of Industrial and Production Engineering, 33*(5), 308–320.

Cameron, E. J. (1997). A formal AIN service creation, feature interactions analysis and management environment: An industrial application. In Proceedings of Fourth Workshop on Feature Interactions in Telecommunications Systems, July 1997.

Casiano Flores, C., Bressers, H., Gutierrez, C., & de Boer, C. (2018). Towards circular economy—A wastewater treatment perspective, the Presa Guadalupe case. *Management Research Review, 41*(5), 554–571.

Corvellec, H., Böhm, S., Stowell, A., & Valenzuela, F. (2020). Introduction to the special issue on the contested realities of the circular economy. *Culture and Organization, 26*(2), 97–102.

Cristina, D. M, Popescu, M.F., Jean, A., & Mieila, M. (2018). Developments of the circular economy in Romania under the new sustainability paradigm. *Economic Computation and Economic Cybernetics Studies and Research, 52*(2), 125–183.

DeLorenzo, A., Parizeau, K., & Von Massow, M. (2019). Regulating Ontario's circular economy through food waste legislation. *Society and Business Review, 14*(2), 200–216.

Eaton, K. A., Newman, H. N., & Widström, E. (2003). A survey of dental hygienist numbers in Canada, the European Economic area, Japan and the United States of America in 1998. *British Dental Journal, 195*(10), 595–598.

Ellen MacArthur Foundation. (2012). *Economic and business rationale for an accelerated transition. Towards a circular economy*. https://www.ellenmacarthurfoundation.org/publications

Ellen MacArthur Foundation. (2013). *Opportunities for the consumer goods sector. Towards a circular economy*. https://www.ellenmacarthurfoundation.org/publications

Ellen MacArthur Foundation. (2014). *Accelerating the scale-up across global supply chains. Towards the circular economy*. https://www.ellenmacarthurfoundation.org/publications

Ellen MacArthur Foundation. (2015a). *Delivering the circular economy—A toolkit for policymakers*. https://www.ellenmacarthurfoundation.org/publications

Ellen MacArthur Foundation. (2015b). *Potential for Denmark as a circular economy*. https://www.ellenmacarthurfoundation.org/publications

Ellen MacArthur Foundation. (2015c). *Towards a circular economy: Business Rationale for an accelerated transition*. https://www.ellenmacarthurfoundation.org/publications

Ellen MacArthur Foundation. (2016). *The new plastic economy: Rethinking the future of plastics*. https://www.ellenmacarthurfoundation.org/publications

Ellen MacArthur Foundation. (2017). *The new plastic economy: Rethinking the future of plastics & catalysing action*. https://www.ellenmacarthurfoundation.org/publications

EMF—Ellen-Macarthur Foundation. (2020). *Global-Commitment-2020-Progress-Report*. https://emf.thirdlight.com/link/il0mcm1dqjtn-knjubr/@/preview/1?o

European Commission. (2012). *Manifesto for a resource-efficient Europe, MEMO 12/989/*. http://europa.eu/rapid/press-release_MEMO-12-989_en.htm.

European Commission. (2014a). *Scoping study to identify potential circular economy actions, priority sectors, material flows, and value chains*. https://op.europa.eu/en/publication-detail/-/publication/0619e465-581c-41dc-9807-2bb394f6bd07

European Commission. (2014b). *Towards a circular economy: A zero waste programme for Europe, COM (2014)398*. https://www.eumonitor.eu/9353000/1/j9vvik7m1c3gyxp/vjl4tamjogxb

European Commission. (2015a). *Communication from the commission to the European Parliament, the council, the European Economic and Social Committee and the committee of the regions. COM (2015) 614/2*. https://ec.europa.eu/transparency/documents-register/detail?ref=COM(2015)614&lang=en

European Commission. (2015b). *Resource efficiency scoreboard*. https://ec.europa.eu/environment/resource_efficiency/targets_indicators/scoreboard/index_e

European Union. (2014). Directive 2014/24/EU of the European Parliament and of the Council of 26 February 2014 on public procurement and repealing Directive 2004/18/EC. Office Journal European Union, 65–242. https://eur-lex.europa.eu/legal-content/EN/TXT/PDF/?uri=CELEX:32014L0024

European Union. (2019). *The European Green Deal*. https://ec.europa.eu/info/strategy/priorities-2019-2024/european-green-deal_it

European Union. (2020). *Global alliance on circular economy and resource efficiency*. https://ec.europa.eu/environment/international_issues/gacere.html

European Union. (2022). *Communication from the commission to the European parliament, the council, the European Economic and Social Committee and the committee of the regions on making sustainable products the norm, com/2022/140 final*. https://eur-lex.europa.eu/legal-content/EN/TXT/?uri=CELEX%3A52022DC0140&qid=1649112555090

Fetscherin, M., & Heinrich, D. (2015). Consumer brand relationships research: A bibliometric citation meta-analysis. *Journal of Business Research, 68*(2), 380–390.

Fonseca, L. M., Portela, A. R., Duarte, B., Queiros, J., & Paiva, L. (2018). Mapping higher education for sustainable development in Portugal. *Management & Marketing: Challenges for the Knowledge Society, 13*(3), 1064–1075.

Geissdoerfer, M., Morioka, S. N., de Carvalho, M. M., & Evans, S. (2018). Business models and supply chain for the circular economy. *Journal of Cleaner Production, 190*(20), 712–721.

Geissdoerfer, M., Savaget, P., Bocken, N. M., & Hultink, E. J. (2017). The Circular Economy–A New Sustainability Paradigm? *Journal of Cleaner Production, 143*, 757–768.

Gregson, N., Crang, M., Fuller, S., & Holmes, H. (2015). Interrogating the circular economy: The moral economy of resource recovery in the EU. *Economy and Society, 44*(2), 218–243.

Hao, L. N., Umar, M., Khan, Z., & Ali, W. (2021). Green growth and low carbon emission in G7 countries: How critical the network of environmental taxes, renewable energy and human capital is? *Science of the Total Environment, 752*, 141853.

Hermann, R. R., Jensen, A., & Gianiodis, P. (2021). Opportunity domains for new entrants in the circular economy: A keyword-in-context analysis of Norwegian RD tax incentive projects. In *Research handbook of innovation for a circular economy* (pp. 316–325). Edward Elgar Publishing.

IIRC. (2013). *The international IR framework*. International Integrated Reporting Council. https://integratedreporting.org/resource/international-ir-framework/

Inigo, E. A., & Blok, V. (2019). Strengthening the socio-ethical foundations of the circular economy: Lessons from responsible research and innovation. *Journal of Cleaner Production, 233*, 280–291.

Jain, S., Jain, N. K., & Metri, B. (2018). Strategic framework towards measuring a circular supply chain management. *Benchmarking: An International Journal, 25*(8), 3238–3252.

Kirchherr, J., & Urban, F. (2018). Technology transfer and cooperation for low carbon energy technology: Analysing 30 years of scholarship and proposing a research agenda. *Energy Policy, 119*, 600–609.

Kirchherr, J., Piscicelli, L., Bour, R., Kostense-Smit, E., Muller, J., Huibrechtse-Truijens, A., & Hekkert, M. (2018). Barriers to the circular economy: Evidence from the European Union (EU). *Ecological Economics, 150*, 264–272.

Kirchherr, J., Reike, D., & Hekkert, M. (2017). Conceptualizing the circular economy: An analysis of 114 definitions. *Resources, Conservation and Recycling, 127*, 221–232.

Korhonen, J., Honkasalo, A., & Seppala, J. (2018). Circular economy: The concept and its limitations. *Ecological Economics, 143*, 37–46.

Kovacic, Z., Strand, R., & Völker, T. (2020). *The circular economy in Europe: Critical perspectives on policies and imaginaries* (p. 208). Taylor & Francis.

Kristensen, H., & Remmen, A. (2019). A framework for sustainable value propositions in product-service-system. *Journal of Cleaner Production, 223*, 25–35.

Lang, M., & Marsden, T. (2018). Rethinking growth: Towards the well-being economy. *Local Economy, 33*(5), 496–514.

Lazarevic, D., & Valve, H. (2017). Narrating expectations for the circular economy: Towards a common and contested European transition. *Energy Research & Social Science, 31*, 60–69.

Levi Jaksic, M., Rakicevic, J., & Jovanovic, M. (2018). Sustainable Technology and business innovation framework comprehensive approach. *Amfiteatru Economic, 20*(48), 418–436.

Linder, M., & Williander, M. (2017). Circular business model innovation: Inherent uncertainties. *Business Strategy and the Environment, 26*(2), 182–196.

Liu, Z., Adams, M., Cote, R. P., Geng, Y., Chen, Q., Liu, W., Sun, L., & Yu, X. (2017). Comprehensive development of industrial symbiosis for the response of greenhouse gas emission mitigation: Challenges and opportunities in China. *Energy Policy, 102*(C), 88–95.

Low, J. S. C., & Ng, Y. T. (2018). Improving the economic performance of remanufacturing systems through flexible design strategies: A case study based on remanufacturing laptop computers for the Cambodian market. *Business Strategy and the Environment, 27*, 503–527.

Martins, N. O. (2016). Ecosystems, strong sustainability, and the classical circular economy. *Ecological Economics., 129*, 32–39.

Mathews, J. A., Tang, Y., & Tan, H. (2011). China's move to a circular economy as a development strategy. *Asian Business & Management, 10*(4), 463–484.

Mathews, J. A., & Tan, H. (2011). Progress toward a circular economy in China: The drivers (and inhibitors) of ecoindustrial initiative. *Journal of industrial ecology, 15*(3), 435–457.

Mavropoulos, A., & Nilsen, A. W. (2020). *Industry 4.0 and circular economy: Towards a wasteless future or a wasteful planet?* Wiley.

McDonough, W., & M. Braungart. 2002. Cradle to Cradle. Remaking the Way We Make Things. New York: North Point Press.
McNaught, C., & Lam, P. (2010). Using Wordle as a supplementary research tool. *The Qualitative Reports, 15*(3), 630–643.
Murray, A., Skene, K., & Haynes, K. (2017). The circular economy: An interdisciplinary exploration of the concept and application in a global context. *Journal of Business Ethics, 140*, 369–380.
Nathaniel, S. P. (2021). Environmental degradation in ASEAN: Assessing the criticality of natural resources abundance, economic growth and human capital. *Environmental Science and Pollution Research, 28*(17), 21766–21778.
Nathaniel, S., Anyanwu, O., & Shah, M. (2020). Renewable energy, urbanization, and ecological footprint in the Middle East and North Africa region. *Environmental science and pollution research, 27*, 14601–14613.
Nguyen, K. H., & Kakinaka, M. (2019). Renewable energy consumption, carbon emissions, and development stages: Some evidence from panel cointegration analysis. *Renewable Energy, 132*, 1049–1057.
Niskanen, J., Anshelm, J., & McLaren, D. (2020). Local conflicts and national consensus: The strange case of circular economy in Sweden. *Journal of Cleaner Production, 261*, 121117.
OECD. (2015a). *Enable the productive revolution.* OECD Publishing. https://www.oecd.org/sti/OECD-Innovation-Strategy-2015
OECD. (2015b). *OECD compendium of productivity indicators.* OECD Publishing. https://www.oecd.org/sti/OECD-Innovation-Strategy-2015
Pata, U. K. (2021). Renewable and non-renewable energy consumption, economic complexity, CO_2 emissions, and ecological footprint in the USA: Testing the EKC hypothesis with a structural break. *Environmental Science and Pollution Research, 28*, 846–861.
Pata, U. K., & Samour, A. (2022). Do renewable and nuclear energy enhance environmental quality in France? A new EKC approach with the load capacity factor. *Progress in Nuclear Energy, 149*, 104249.
Rahman, M. M., Alam, K., & Velayutham, E. (2022). Reduction of CO_2 emissions: The role of renewable energy, technological innovation and export quality. *Energy Reports, 8*, 2793–2805.
Reike, D., Vermeulen Walter, J. V., & Witjes, S. (2018). The circular economy: New or refurbished as CE 3.0?—Exploring controversies in the conceptualization of the circular economy through a focus on history and resource value retention options. *Resource Conservation & Recycling, 135*, 246–264.
Riding, J. M., Herbert, B. M. J., Ricketts, L., Dodd, I., Ostle, N., & Semple, T. K. (2014). Harmonising conflicts between science, regulation, perception

and environmental impact: The case of soil conditioners from bioenergy. *Environmental International, 74*, 52–67.

Schroeder, P., Angraeni, K., & Uwe, Weber. (2018). The relevance of circular economy practices to the sustainable development goals. *Journal of Industrial Ecology, 23*(1), 77–95.

Stahel, W. (1982). *Product-life factor*. http://product-life.org/en/major-publications/the-product-life-factor.

Stewart, R., & Niero, M. (2018). Circular economy in corporate sustainability strategies: A review of corporate sustainability reports in the fast-moving consumer goods sector. *Business Strategy and the Environment, 27*, 1005–1022.

Stewart, R., Niero, M., Murdock, K., & Olsen, S. I. (2018). Exploring the implementation of a circular economy strategy. In Procedia CIRP 25th Life Cycle Engineering Conference, 30 April–2 May, Copenhagen, Denmark.

Temesgen, A., Storsletten, V., & Jakobsen, O. (2021). Circular economy–reducing symptoms or radical change? *Philosophy of Management, 20*(1), 37–56.

Tukker, A. (2015). Product services for a resource-efficient and circular economy—A review. *Journal of Cleaner Production, 97*, 76–91.

United Nation. (2015). *Sustainable Development Agenda 2030*. https://www.un.org/sustainabledevelopment/development-agenda/

Valenzuela, F., & Böhm, S. (2017). Against wasted politics: A critique of the circular economy. *Ephemera: Theory & Politics in Organization, 17*(1), 23–60.

Velis, C. (2018). No circular economy if current systemic failures are not addressed. *Waste Management & Research, 36*(9), 757–759.

Völker, T., Kovacic, Z., & Strand, R. (2020). Indicator development as a site of collective imagination? The case of European Commission policies on the circular economy. *Culture and Organization, 26*(2), 103–120.

World Economic Forum (WEF) (2020). Nature Risk Rising: Why the Crisis Engulfing Nature Matters for Business and the Economy. New Nature Economy Series. https://www.weforum.org/publications/nature-riskrising-why-the-crisis-engulfing-nature-matters-for-business-and-the-economy/

Winans, K., Kendall, A., & Deng, H. (2017). The history and current applications of the circular economy concept. *Renewable and Sustainable Energy Reviews, 68*, 825–833.

White, A., & Schmidt, K. (2005). Systematic literature reviews. *Complementary Therapies in Medicine, 13*, 54–60.

Yang, X. J., Hu, H., Tan, T., & Li, J. (2016). China's renewable energy goals by 2050. *Environmental Development, 20*, 83–90.
Zhu, J., Fan, C., Shi, H., & Shi, L. (2019). Efforts for a circular economy in China: A comprehensive review of policies. *Journal of industrial ecology, 23*(1), 110–118.

3

Circular Economy Key Concepts and Reporting Practices: An Exploratory Study

1 Introduction

This article builds on the current debate on how to include (or even integrate) sustainability-related data and information into accounting corporate reporting practices. In detail, the article focuses on *Circular Economy* and *Integrated Reporting* as the two building blocks for the research. On the one hand, circular economy (CE) is gaining interest and is said to rapidly raise political as well as business agendas (European Commission, 2014a, 2014b); on the other hand, integrated reporting (IR) represents corporate sustainability reporting in a new pattern and trends (e.g., Adams, 2015; Atkins et al., 2015a; Eccles & Krzus, 2010), being able to provide a holistic representation of organizations, its resources, and the value creation process put in place (Adams & Simnett, 2011; Atkins et al., 2015b).

Specifically, the study first focuses on the CE and provides a brief literature review of the concept and its management-related implications. In contrast to today's essentially linear-oriented systems, "a circular economy represents a development strategy that enables economic growth while aiming to optimize the chain of consumption of biological and technical materials" (European Commission, 2014a, 2014b, p. iv).

S. Nazir and A. Capocchi, *Sustainability Reporting Practices and the Circular Economy*, https://doi.org/10.1007/978-3-031-51845-4_3

This entails a profound transformation of production and consumption processes, the redesign of the industrial system, and the ability to exploit the so-called 3Rs of CE (reduce, reuse, and recycle). Notably, this also requires *accounting and reporting frameworks* to facilitate the integration of information on systemic and long-term activities and intangible and non-financial assets. In this light, the Integrated Reporting Framework (IIRC, 2013a), which strictly follows a circular approach of strategies, resource allocation, outlook, and performance, may represent the ideal fit not only to assist organizations in representing and disclosing CE-related activities information but also to stimulate them to fully integrate such issues in their value creation processes and with a holistic approach (i.e., considering simultaneously economic, social, and environmental issues).

In this specific regard, although previous research demonstrated that IR is spreading and is increasingly used to communicate environmental, social, and financial information (e.g., Adams, 2015; Atkins et al., 2015b; Beattie & Smith, 2013; Burke & Clark, 2016; Busco et al., 2013; de Villiers & Sharma, 2020; Eccles & Krzus, 2010), its actual use to disclose effectively data about CE activities is still under-researched, this calling for more investigation and evidence (e.g., Stewart & Niero, 2018).

Starting from the considerations above, this article aims to discuss:

a) if integrated reporting provides the principles and elements to support the representation of CE-related activities.
b) How and to what extent do current integrated reports practices disclose CE data and information?

The research design searched for textual elements (number and frequency of concepts) and images (number and typologies of figures and graphical representations, e.g., closed-loops) to address these aims. The former items were searched through content analysis (Krippendorff, 2004) based on the use of the NVivo software; the latter were searched manually by the researchers throughout the reports included in the sample. In both cases, *codebooks* of words and images were defined *ex-ante* (Schilling, 2006). To guide the analyses.

The rationale behind the two analyses is justified by previous research: content analysis is a well-known research methodology to analyze the main object of the information. On the other hand, images, business charts, graphs, matrixes, etc., are considered by a recent stream of literature in management accounting (e.g., Bell & Davison, 2013; Davison, 2014, 2015; Quattrone, 2017) as very relevant when investigating how *visual representations* may be used to disclose data and conceive information about the relationships between an organization (and/or various organizational actors) and its stakeholders, mainly external ones (e.g., Davison, 2014 and Quattrone, 2017).

At the same time, previous research also advocated more research on these topics, specifically regarding CE and IR (e.g., Kamp-Roelands, 2013; Stewart & Niero, 2018).

The structure of the paper is the following: Sect. 2 provides the literature review on CE and CE-related reporting tools and options, highlighting the role that in this context might be played by IR; Sect. 3 describes the research design; Sect. 4 presents the results; Sect. 5 provides our discussion of results; Sect. 6 concludes the research, also underlying some limitations to this study and future research agenda.

2 Circular Economy and Reporting Literature Review

Circular Economy and CE-related Reporting Options

Although the literature provides several definitions for the concept we analyze in this study (e.g., Kirchherr et al., 2017 analyzed 114 definitions of this concept), a circular economy is where products and services are treated in circularity to minimize the negative externalities. A circular economy is characterized as an economy that is regenerative by design to retain as much value as possible of products, parts, and materials. This means that the aims of the circular economy permit the redesign and remanufacturing of products and services as possible (Ellen MacArthur Foundation, 2016; Kraaijenhagen et al., 2016).

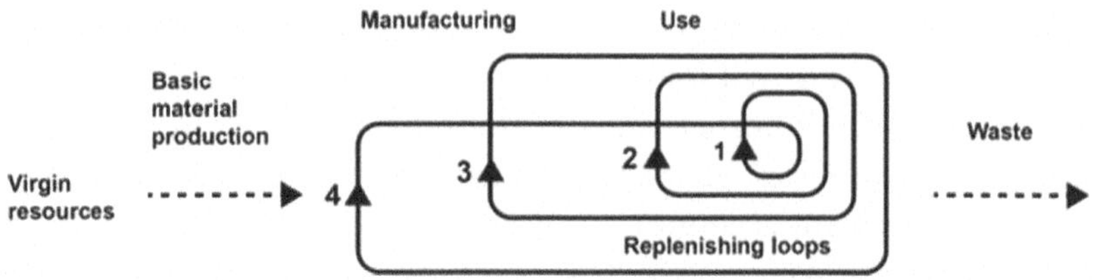

Fig. 1 Circular economy system diagram (*Source* Economic alternative: Closed-loop system with minimized material in and outflow, Stahel [1982])

Therefore, the economy can be viewed as a circle framework which is dependent on four exercises (see Fig. 1):

1. Reuse (circle 1) indicates the reuse of the product many times, as a whole or about its parts after its first life cycle is completed, to reduce the usage of raw materials and favor the manufacturing of newer products or components.
2. Repair (circle 2) includes updating the product by repair for the subsequent use of products utilizing components, materials, and resources from the previous generation of products.
3. Remanufacturing (circle 3) entails reprocessing products that have already been used, bringing them back to their original state using as many components as possible without losing functionality.
4. Recycling (circle 4) is converting materials that would be considered waste into new materials or products.

The objective of this framework is to create a renewable economy with the aim of less use of virgin material and reducing environmental impacts or social and technological development (Stahel, 1982). As shown in the reasoning of CE, unused does not exist. Parts of an item can be intended to fit inside a material life cycle, reasonable for dismantling and restoration, remanufacturing or repurposing, and, subsequently, "waste" is to be treated to generate value. Figure 1 represents enhanced products and parts life-cycle framework with a closed-loop.

As the Ellen MacArthur Foundation (2015) advocates, a circular economy is beneficial through having a structure that intends to keep products, parts, and materials at their highest utility level and incentives in all cases. Stated differently, CE can be viewed as a global economic framework that could foster and support economic development and growth from limited resource utilization (Ellen MacArthur Foundation, 2015). In practical terms, the CE promotes a regain framework of service, where producers and vendors hold possession of their products and also go to the service providers and associated rather than a single course of utilization (Ellen MacArthur Foundation, 2015).

The most innovative idea and the building block for CE is the shift from a linear approach to the economy to a circular one. Therefore, the CE designs out of the linear business framework that transformed services into products, something that rapidly turned into an inefficient practice since, in the past, reuse and assistance results could have been better. Today, technology has jumped forward toward a step where the superiority of the products can be increased without affecting quality (Ellen MacArthur Foundation, 2015). However entirely new as a concept, previous research has already demonstrated the potential of CE; for example, some researchers have demonstrated that a circular economy can certainly provide short-term benefits as well as long-term benefits, stemming from the adoption of a feedback-oriented (i.e., circular) approach to business operations and management (Ellen MacArthur Foundation, 2015).

Today, the concept and the challenge of CE are increasingly embraced by companies, associations, and regulators worldwide. The CE not only regenerates or reproduces capital in the shape of financial, manufactured, human, social, or natural but also provides a flow of goods and services in a circular shape. The following diagram demonstrates the continuous flow of technical and biological materials through the "value circle" (Ellen MacArthur Foundation, 2013), which extends beyond a single company or the economic dimension of affairs.

Specifically, the key CE concepts can be summarized as portrayed in Fig. 2.

As shown in Fig. 2, to operationalize the idea of the CE, the Ellen MacArthur Foundation has covered it into three essential standards:

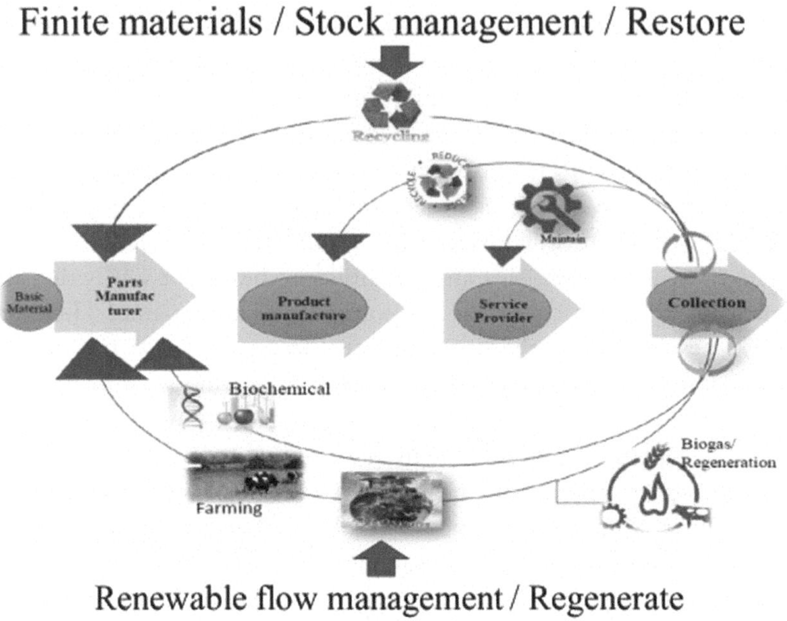

Fig. 2 Circular economy system diagram (*Source* EMF [2013, p. 24])

- preserving and upgrading characteristics of capital, for instance, utilizing sustainable power sources;
- optimizing asset yields, amplifying the use of items, parts, and materials by sharing or circling them and broadening their life expectancies;
- designing out negative externalities, for example, contamination, poisons, and negative well-being impacts (Ellen MacArthur Foundation, 2015, p. 22).

The whole process should be directed toward the generation of wealth and well-being. Moreover, in the reasoning of CE, unused does not exist. Parts of an item can be intended to fit inside a material life cycle, reasonable for dismantling and restoration, remanufacturing, or repurposing. "Waste" can be thought of as foods, the soil can treat biological foods, and specialized way of nutrients, for example, polymers and other man-finished materials, can be reused, recycled, and redesigned. (Ellen MacArthur Foundation, 2013, p. 22). To gain the maximum value from the material and recourses the life cycle of the material and resource are kept small, the materials as pure as feasible for simpler reuse and the quality as high as conceivable over the longest conceivable time (IMSA, 2013, p. 14).

Notably, the concept of CE applies to any organization and industry. It is expected to work adequately on all scales for small and large companies, associations, and people, globally and locally.

The considerations we already provided witness the necessity of accounting for the impacts generated by an organization's operations and subsequently of reporting measures and information on that.

In this context, calls from academia, regulators, and other stakeholders active and/or, for some reason, engaged in the debate on sustainability have advocated a shift toward more integrated forms of reporting.

The academic literature provides good examples of frameworks and reporting tools and techniques developed in the last two decades and used to broaden the capacity of modern organizations to report their activities and results (e.g., the balanced scorecard system, Kaplan & Norton, 1992, or the frameworks provided by GRI—Global Reporting Initiative—or other CSR—Corporate Social Responsibility—e.g., see Milne & Gray, 2013).

Within this context, integrated reporting (IIRC, 2013a) has emerged not only as an exciting and powerful novelty in the research area of corporate reporting practices but also highlighted how to disclose this information in circulars as well as CE-related information. For instance, Stewart & Niero (2018) included integrated reporting (besides other sustainability and environmental reports) in their systematic review of corporate reports in the Fast-Moving Consumer Goods Sector meant to explore how companies incorporate CE-related concepts in their sustainability agendas; Kamp-Roelands (2013) emphasizes that modern organizations have to recognize the opportunities given by circular economy and that integrated reporting may help them not only in thinking about the relationships among resources across the various sectors of the organization but also in generating new accounting information for strategic decision-making, investment decision, and performance improvement in this context.

Integrated Reporting for Circular Economy

Integrated reporting relies on a framework developed by the International Integrated Reporting Council (IIRC) to assist companies of different sizes, entities, and geographical area reports in a holistic prospect that covers all the sustainability dimensions, such as environmental, social, and economic.

Over the last few years, IIRC has issued a key-reference framework (IIRC, 2013a) as well as several other documents and papers (e.g., background papers—see IIRC [2013b, 2013c, 2013d]) available for the guidance to disclose these elements for companies values reaction process on the concept of "integrated reporting and integrated thinking," as we will underline afterward.

IR is conceived as a principle-based approach, which is not normative or prescriptive. Contrarily, IR aims to support organization in their effort to draft an integrated report, providing a core set of principles for that purpose. In detail, the list of guiding principles is the following:

- strategic focus and future orientation;
- connectivity of information;
- stakeholder relationships;
- materiality;
- conciseness;
- reliability and completeness;
- consistency and comparability.

These principles should inform the report's content and influence and facilitate how information and data are presented to stakeholders. An organization's value creation process can be defined by the organization's specific *business model* (see Fig. 3).

According to IIRC (2013a, p. 13), the business model is characterized by four key elements since it "draws on various capitals as inputs and, through its business activities, converts them to outputs (products, services, by-products, and waste), the organization's activities and its outputs lead to outcomes in terms of effects on the capitals." Although these contents have interrelationships among each other to gather these

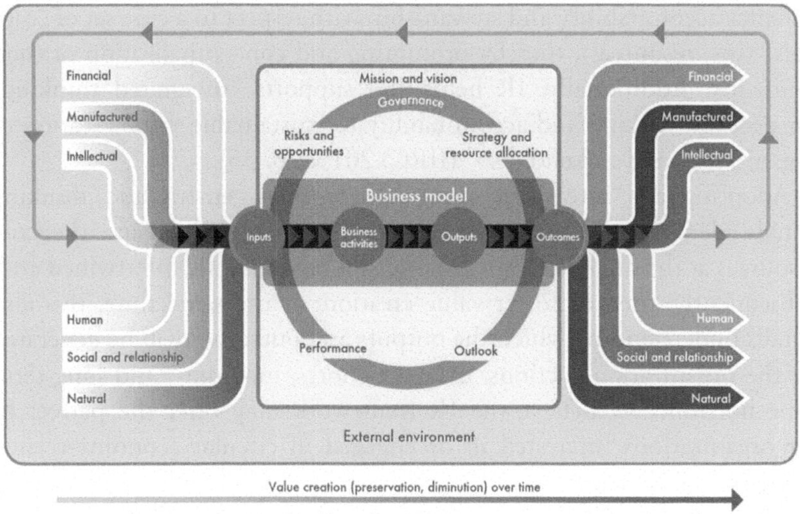

Fig. 3 IR value creation process (*Source* IIRC [2013a, p. 13], "With permission from the International Integrated Reporting Council 2020 [C]")

capitals/inputs and convert these capitals into outputs by business activities and through these established effects of outcomes by regularly examining the business model (IIRC, 2013b, p. 6).

As portrayed, according to IIRC (2013c), an organization creates *value* over the short, medium, and long term. Specifically, value creation is influenced and generated:

- by utilization of internal factors and developing resources at the organizational level;
- interplaying with the external environment through external relationships (suppliers) with other stakeholders.

Notably, a *feedback-oriented process* underpins the whole value creation process in IR, thus conveying the feature of *circularity* to IR practices.

In this regard, we have to emphasize that IR aims at being more than just a communication to the stakeholders: based on the ideas of *integrated thinking* and *integrated management*, IR has the ultimate goal to enhance accountability and stewardship with respect to a core set of "capitals" (i.e., resources), thereby promoting and conceptualization of their mutuality. Additionally, IR helps and supports "integrated thinking" for decision-making and accountability for sustainable value creation of organization and stakeholders" (IIRC, 2013a, p. 35).

Adopting an "integrated approach" to management and thinking entails identifying, understanding, and reporting which are the core resources at the organization's disposal and how they are intertwined and, subsequently, used to foster value creation; at the same time, this also entails understanding which the outputs and outcomes will be generated by the organization's actions, over the short-, medium-, and long-term time horizon. We believe the IR framework may offer the perfect fit for organizations interested in or engaged in circular economy-related activities.

The two (IR and CE) share standard features that allow exploiting their joint use. First, both build on the concept of "Capital" the key resource in any organization's operations. As stated in the IR terms Capital (see IIRC, 2013d, p. 2), "any kind of thing that has a physical or non-physical value that can be used for the company operation for the production of goods and services." In detail, IR lists six capital categories: financial, manufactured, intellectual, human, social relationship, and natural. It depicts them as intertwined and dependent upon each other to create value over time. This requires identifying where trade-offs among capital lie and how to exploit them to maximize value creation and minimize externalities, side effects, and negative consequences.

Secondly, IR and CE obviously participate in the organization value creation process over the short, medium, and long term. This leads to considering time delays and engagement with the concept that monitoring and evaluating the company's actions in circular ways can be possible, reporting over the short-, medium-, and long-term horizon. Interestingly, previous literature demonstrated that the results of the activities carried out by an organization might substantially change, taking into account a different "time horizon," that is to say, differentiating among the short, medium, and long term (e.g., Sterman, 2000).

Third, both IR and CE look at value creation as a closed-loop system: specifically, CE explicitly builds on the shift from a circular to a "circular" (i.e., closed-loop) design of economic systems, while IR grounds value creation dynamics on a feedback-oriented process (i.e., outputs and outcomes will eventually affect the capitals of the organization, closing the loop and providing the basis for future action).

This said it is noteworthy to emphasize that all the factors we have just mentioned raise a big challenge for both the organizations interested in disclosing CE-related information through their IR and for analysts interested in studying IR- and CE-related reports. Mainly, it is to emphasize that the way used to communicate data and information to relevant stakeholders may differ from company to company or depend upon several factors. In this regard, previous research confirmed (e.g., Beattie & Smith, 2013; de Villiers & Sharma, 2020; Dumay, 2016; Giorgino et al., 2016) that integrated reporting practices widely differ across companies of different sizes, industries, or geographical areas, subsequently leading to a variety of reports with heterogeneous contents, aims, and communication forms, including simultaneously reports which are definitely quantitative *and* notices drafted with a more oriented qualitative and narrative style. In terms of the disclosure of CE-related information, this may lead to a wide range of practices and technical solutions.

Subsequently, to investigate this, in this chapter, we will use content analysis and search for visual representations of relevant CE-related information in IR practices.

3 Research Design

The research design entailed searching for Circular Economy-related concepts and visual representations in integrated reporting documents. The former items (concepts) were searched through content analysis (Krippendorff, 2004) based on the use of the NVivo software; the latter were searched manually by the researchers analyzing the reports in the sample. In both cases, *codebooks* of words and images (Neuendorf, 2002) were defined as *ex-ante* (Schilling, 2006). To guide the analyses. More details are anyhow provided below.

As mentioned, this study analyzed a sample of integrated reports using *content analysis*, "a research technique for the objective, systematic and quantitative description of the manifest content of communication" (Berelson, 1952). In content analyses, frequency is usually calculated and used for measuring and communicating the relevance of the subject matter (Krippendorff, 2004). It may help evaluate the amount of disclosure about a specific concept or group of concepts (Milne & Adler, 1999). It is to emphasize that content analysis in the field of sustainability has already been used and is recognized as a reliable research method (e.g., Guthrie & Abeysekera, 2006; Milne & Adler, 1999). More specifically, this study used a sample of 12 reports drawn up by eight organizations from the basic materials industry for content analysis to determine how and to what IR discloses CE-related information. As its primary source of information and documents, the paper relies on the public IIRC database (<IR> Examples Database—http://examples.integratedreporting.org/home).

Content analysis was performed using the software NVivo. According to a top-down process, the glossary (single concepts, groups, and/or categories of concepts) was defined *ex-ante* (Schilling, 2006). To this end, the authors created a specific codebook (Neuendorf, 2002), i.e., a glossary used to perform content analysis (see Appendix 1 for more details on the Glossary). The codebook combines two primary sources (IIRC main concepts—retrieved from the Integrated Reporting Framework, IIRC, 2013a—and the Glossary of Circular Economy by the US Chamber of Commerce). Furthermore, selected terms applying a primary brainstorming method (Wilson, 2013) were added to enlarge the analysis of CE concepts. The glossary aimed to aid in developing more standardized and established terminology for CE research and IR.

As mentioned, the sample of Integrated Reports included 12 companies from the basic materials industry, as classified by the Examples Database of Integrated Reports provided by the IIRC online. The following table (Table 1) reports the key data related to the companies and their integrated reports (retrieved from the web on 2 December 2018).

Table 1 Characteristics of the sample analyzed in this study

Organizations	Anglo Gold 2016	Anglo Platinum 2017	Exxaro Resources 2017	Fresnillo plc 2016	Fresnillo 2014	Gold Fields 2017
Organization Type	Public Listed Company	Public Listed company	Public Listed Company	Public Listed Company	Public Listed Company	Public Listed Company
Year	2016	2017	2017	2016	2014	2017
Industry	Basic Material	Basic Material	Basic Material	Basic Material	Basic Material	Basic Material
Region	Africa	Africa	Africa	Europe	Europe	Africa
Document Type	Integrated Report	Integrated Report	Integrated Report	Annual Report	Annual Report	Integrated Report
Number of Pages	176	152	142	256	266	144
Number of Words	74,724	71,465	51,037	127,813	132,574	72,775
Organizations	***Gold Fields 2016**	**Implats 2017**	**Kumba Iron 2017**	**Royal Platinum 2017**	**Royal platinum 2016**	**York Timbers 2017**
Organization Type	Public Listed Company	Public Listed Company	Public Listed company	Public Listed Company	Public Listed company	Public Listed company
Year	2016	2017	2017	2017	2017	2017
Industry	Basic Material	Basic Material	Basic Material	Basic Material	Basic material	Basic Material
Region	Africa	Africa	Africa	Africa	Africa	Africa
Document Type	Integrated Report	Integrated Report	Integrated Report	Integrated Report	Integrated Report	Integrated Report
Number of Pages	132	172	112	176	186	186
Number of Words	67,869	53,111	53,572	65,550	63,417	74,732

Additionally, the study focused on the analysis of the *visual representations* included in the integrated reports. This is in line with a recent stream of literature in management accounting (e.g., Bell & Davison, 2013; Davison, 2014; Quattrone, 2017; Warren & Davison, 2017) investigating how visual representations (e.g., images, business charts, and accounting tables) may be used to disclose data and conceive information about the relationships between an organization (and/or various organizational actors) and its stakeholders, mainly external ones.

Specifically, taking into consideration the fundamental characteristics of CE and CE-related activities, we developed an *ex-ante codebook* of visual representations. Table 2 provides a brief textual description for each category of images we included in our codebook.

The researchers inspected the reports for manual identification and categorization of the images, graphs, and representations included in the codebook.

Based on these premises, the following section presents the results of our analysis.

4 Results

Content Analysis Results

As we described the research design adopted for this study, the first step of the data analysis entailed searching the integrated reports drawn-up by the organizations in our sample with the NVivo software (Table 3).

In detail, Table 3 presents the content analysis results for the category "*inputs*," as described in the 12 reports retrieved from the IIRC database operating in the essential material industry. It is noteworthy that the IR framework does not provide a comprehensive list of inputs; specifically—as mentioned by IIRC (2013a, p. 26), not only the focus on those [inputs] which belong to the material and short-medium and long-term value creation but also capital which come from the organization's operations. In broad terms, all the six categories of capital identified in the IR framework represent inputs to an organization's business model and for its value creation process.

Table 2 The codebook of visual representations used in this study

Typology of visual representation	Technical description
Business model representations	A business model describes how an organization creates and delivers value. It may include representations of resources, inputs, outputs as well as elements of the external environment
Visual representations of the main operations (also, upstream and/or downstream)	Every organization, in order to create value, carries out specific activities, referred to as "operations," which are peculiar for each company and its industry. These operations are internal to the company or carried out within the external environment (upstream or downstream operations)
Geo or spatial representations of operations	These graphs identify where the main organization's facilities are located and where its key operations are carried out, also providing details about the environment in which the organization operates
Risk Matrix and ERM charts	A risk matrix (as well as an ERM chart—Enterprise Risk Management chart) is used for risk assessment. Its main goal is to define and visualize the level of risk for specific events or actions, by considering the likelihood of those factors against the consequences that may occur
Organizational charts and Board structure charts	An organizational chart is an organigram, that is to say, a diagram that portrays the organizational structure of a company, also visualizing the relationships and roles of its departments
Causal Loop Diagrams (CLD)	A CLD consists of variables connected by arrows denoting their causal influences. Each causal link is assigned a polarity, either positive or negative to clarify how the dependent variable changes as the independent variable changes. They are used to identify circular connections (also named feedback loops) among variables
Cause maps	Cause maps identify in a graphical way how a number (two or more) of concepts are causally linked. Usually, an arrow is used to identify the causal linkage between a cause and an effect. Different typologies of these maps can be designed around this concept (e.g., causal trees)
Strategy Maps	A strategy map is a diagram that describes how an organization creates value by connecting strategic objectives that are in explicit cause-and-effect relationships with each other into the four perspectives (financial, customer, internal processes, learning & growth) of a balanced scorecard

(continued)

Table 2 (continued)

Typology of visual representation	Technical description
Balanced Scorecard (BSC)	The Balanced Scorecard is a strategic measurement and management system that provides a holistic representation of the organization. In detail, key performance indicators and critical success factors are traditionally considered across four interlinked perspectives: financial, customer, internal processes, learning and growth
Strategy representations	Maps and graphs of different forms and designs can be devoted to representing the organization's strategy, its key priorities and targets, and the fundamental resources used to create value over time
Value Stream Maps (VSM)	A VSM is a Lean Thinking image that portrays all the relevant processes used to deliver a product to a customer
LCA (Life-Cycle Assessment) Images	LCA is a technique aimed at assessing the environmental impacts associated with all the stages of a product's life cycle
Bubble diagrams	A bubble diagram (or chart) represents information in the form of a series of bubbles. Bubbles may have a different size to denote relative importance
Visual mission statement (mission, vision, and/or core values)	A mission statement is a short description or representation of why an organization exists (mission), which is its future roadmap (vision), and which are the core values at its basis
Visual representation of capitals (and their trade-offs), inputs, outputs, and outcomes	Capitals (i.e., resources) represent the fundamental input for any value creation process and the business activities carried out by an organization to generate outputs and outcomes
Value chain (or value proposition) representations	These images provide a visual representation of how and with which processes an organization creates and delivers value for its customers
Materiality matrix	Materiality is a key principle of the Integrated Reporting Framework and entails providing information that is relevant for the stakeholders and value creation

(continued)

Table 2 (continued)

Typology of visual representation	Technical description
SDG connection maps	Sustainable Development Goals (SDGs) are included in the 2030 Agenda for Sustainable Development adopted by all United Nations Member States. Within this context, a set of 17 SDGs are identified, representing global objectives to be pursued to improve sustainability and development across the world
KPIs charts (on outcomes) and scorecard indicators	Key Performance Indicators (KPIs) can be represented in various forms and with different tools, other than with accounting tables. In this context, graphs reorganizing KPIs or specific scorecards can display interesting visual solutions

In presenting the results of our content analysis, the authors believe that percentages are not particularly useful for discussing the extent of these specific terms' disclosure. Conversely, the counts offer more direct information about which inputs were most frequently cited in the 12 reports.

The inputs table also reflects the financial-related terms (i.e., financial capital, investment, Green financing) most cited in the reports we investigated. Moreover, counts are well distributed among these financial terms selected for this query, demonstrating the extent of the finance-based terms provided by the 12 Integrated reports under analysis. The input table reflects the IR reports' words, funding model, capital, investment, and financial funding contents. Overall, the financial-related times are more cited than the funding ones. As shown by Table 3, the IR reports also reflect the infrastructure terms of the companies such as infrastructure, transport, building, and equipment, which are more cited terms in these reports.

Manufactured capital-related terms such as human capital (people, Human capital, intellectual capital, automation) are more cited as compared to the term reassembled. The sharing term shows that the business model is based on the sharing of the resource between multiple people, in other to maximize the use of the product and keep it in use as long as possible. The term raw material sourcing represents the activities required to extract raw materials from their location. The number of

Table 3 Results of content analysis for "inputs"

	Anglo Gold 2016		Anglo Platinum 2017		Exxaro Resources 2017		Fresnillo plc 2016		Fresnillo 2014		Gold Fields 2017		Gold Fields 2016	
		(%)		(%)		(%)		(%)		(%)		(%)		(%)
Inputs	4	0.01	8	0.01	3	0.01	35	0.01	39	0.01	6	0.01	6	0.01
Funding model	32	0.02	34	0.02	46	0.04	70	0.02	72	0.02	22	0.01	14	0.01
Capital and Capitals	139	0.10	157	0.11	135	0.14	135	0.05	157	0.06	194	0.14	118	0.09
Investment	67	0.07	92	0.10	70	0.10	94	0.05	100	0.06	75	0.08	57	0.06
Financial	145	0.13	231	0.22	103	0.13	862	0.45	845	0.42	80	0.07	79	0.08
Funding	9	0.01	20	0.01	18	0.02	5	0.01	6	0.01	7	0.01	9	0.01
Infrastructure	28	0.04	27	0.04	42	0.09	30	0.02	25	0.02	48	0.07	26	0.04
Transport	1	0.01	8	0.01	6	0.01	2	0.01	3	0.01	3	0.01	4	0.01
Building	16	0.01	22	0.02	11	0.01	13	0.01	11	0.01	19	0.02	16	0.01
Equipment	6	0.01	22	0.02	13	0.02	91	0.05	110	0.06	32	0.03	27	0.03
Manufactured	2	0.01	5	0.01	6	0.01	0	0	0	0	2	0.01	0	0
*Re-Assembled	11	0.01	4	0.04	10	0.01	30	0.01	40	0.01	7	0.01	7	0.01
Dematerialization	0	0	0	0	0	0	0	0	0	0	0	0	0	0
People	**55**	0.03	36	0.02	42	0.04	46	0.02	35	0.01	53	0.03	63	0.04
Sharing	3	0.01	8	0.01	11	0.01	29	0.01	39	0.02	5	0.01	4	0.01
Human	62	0.03	16	0.01	19	0.01	42	0.01	20	0.01	42	0.02	30	0.02
Human capital or Human capitals	201	0.13	173	0.12	154	0.15	177	0.07	177	0.07	236	0.16	148	0.11
Intellectual property	8	0.01	21	0.02	28	0.04	44	0.02	44	0.02	5	0.01	4	0.01

	Anglo Gold 2016		Anglo Platinum 2017		Exxaro Resources 2017		Fresnillo plc 2016		Fresnillo 2014		Gold Fields 2017		Gold Fields 2016	
		(%)		(%)		(%)		(%)		(%)		(%)		(%)
Intellectual	2	0.01	4	0.01	6	0.01	0	0	0	0	1	0.01	0	0
Intellectual capital	141	0.10	158	0.12	124	0.13	135	0.05	157	0.06	193	0.14	118	0.09
Automation	0	0	1	0.01	1	0.01	1	0.01	0	0	9	0.01	11	0.01
Raw Materials	45	0.04	56	0.05	69	0.08	50	0.02	60	0.03	37	0.03	32	0.03
Raw	2	0.01	1	0.01	0	0	0	0	0	0	0	0	0	0
Raw material Sourcing	45	0.04	57	0.05	70	0.08	50	0.02	60	0.03	37	0.03	34	0.03
Alternate material	43	0.03	58	0.05	70	0.08	51	0.02	60	0.03	39	0.03	33	0.03
Eco-systems services	24	0.02	16	0.01	22	0.03	87	0.04	94	0.04	37	0.03	31	0.01
Green Financing	5	0.01	4	0.01	4	0.01	17	0.01	12	0.01	3	0.01	3	0.01
Natural	8	0.01	4	0.01	9	0.01	8	0.01	18	0.01	4	0.01	1	0.01
*Greenhouse Gases	3	0.01	4	0.01	5	0.01	13	0.01	17	0.01	2	0.01	0	0
Relationships	11	0.11	23	0.03	22	0.04	17	0.01	21	0.02	34	0.05	16	0.02
Social	58	0.03	116	0.07	64	0.06	86	0.03	74	0.02	102	0.06	93	0.06
Coordination	1	0.01	0	0	0	0	0	0	0	0	0	0	0	0
MEAN	34.07407		28.42308		35.32143		71.96429		72.21429		36.53846		26.48148	
S.D.	50.56065		44.03106		42.83478		161.7157		158.6789		57.93322		37.7148	

(continued)

Table 3 (continued)

	Implats 2017		Kumba Iron 2017		Royal Platinum 2017		Royal platinum 2016		York Timbers 2017		MEAN	S.D.
		(%)		(%)		(%)		(%)		(%)		
Inputs	11	0.01										
Funding model	53	0.04	36	0.03	39	0.03	32	0.02	48	0.03	32	13.366
Capital and Capitals	164	0.16	72	0.07	248	0.20	253	0.20	160	0.12	136.33	2.3094
Investment	71	0.10	30	0.04	55	0.06	53	0.06	86	0.09	100	35
Financial	176	0.22	102	0.13	118	0.12	44	0.04	284	0.26	603	13.07641
Funding	9	0.01	1	0.01	16	0.01	17	0.01	11	0.01	10.66	3.6545
Infrastructure	14	0.03	58	0.11	37	0.06	35	0.05	13	0.02	31.91	5.207076
Transport	1	0.01	4	0.01	6	0.01	7	0.01	14	0.01	4.91	36.2913
Building	8	0.01	16	0.02	5	0.01	6	0.01	16	0.01	13.25	5.2070
Equipment	28	0.04	14	0.02	6	0.01	13	0.01	84	0.08	37.16	36.29133
Manufactured	14	0.02	7	0.01	24	0.03	27	0.04	19	0.02	8.83	9.740574
*Re-Assembled	32	0.01	3	0.01	27	0.01	31	0.01	41	0.01	20.25	14.51723
Dematerialization	0	0	0	0	0	0	0	0	0	0	0	0
People	41	0.03	20	0.02	35	0.02	42	0.03	28	0.02	41.33	**11.89543**
Sharing	3	0.01	3	0.01	5	0.01	3	0.01	1	0.01	9.5	11.93543
Human	26	0.02	21	0.01	59	0.03	74	0.04	19	0.01	35.83	19.8074
Human capital or Human capitals	190	0.18	93	0.09	307	0.23	327	0.24	179	0.12	196.83	65.61019
Intellectual property	45	0.06	15	0.02	28	0.04	23	0.03	111	0.10	23	15.18971

	Implats 2017		Kumba Iron 2017		Royal Platinum 2017		Royal platinum 2016		York Timbers 2017		MEAN	S.D.
		(%)		(%)		(%)		(%)		(%)		
Intellectual	14	0.02	5	0.01	23	0.03	19	0.03	15	0.02	7.41	9.162646
Intellectual capital	164	0.17	70	0.07	258	0.22	245	0.22	167	0.13	160.83	52.33951
Automation	0	0	0	0	1	0.01	5	0.01	0	0	2.416	3.8690
Raw Materials	45	0.05	44	0.05	54	0.05	76	0.07	118	0.09	57.16	22.9142
Raw	0	0	1	0.01	0	0	0	0	22	0.01	2.16	6.2788
Raw material Sourcing	46	0.05	44	0.05	54	0.05	76	0.07	119	0.06	57.66	22.9597
Alternate material	48	0.05	43	0.05	56	0.05	77	0.07	96	0.08	56.16	17.8419
Eco-systems services	35	0.04	10	0.01	35	0.03	25	0.02	32	0.03	37.33	26.15455
Green Financing	12	0.01	1	0.01	3	0.01	4	0.01	6	0.01	6.166	4.83986
Natural	31	0.03	10	0.01	29	0.02	32	0.02	27	0.02	15.083	11.64207
*Greenhouse Gases	2	0.01	1	0.01	10	0.01	14	0.01	0	0	5.91	5.9765
Relationships	19	0.03	26	0.05	16	0.02	22	0.03	14	0.02	20.083	6.097068
Social	133	0.11	55	0.05	99	0.07	100	0.07	51	0.03	77.1667	31.86002
Coordination	0	0	2	0.01	0	0	0	0	0	0	0.25	0.621582
MEAN	35.62962		24.379310		43.6296		47		40.77777			
S.D.	49.03777		28.435910		73.2315		73.8582		51.4021			

citations of the raw material and alternative raw material is the same in the input table. This includes mining and oil extraction as well as forestry and some on-farm activities, same here alternative material term refers to the substituting that can be more sustainable than the material they are replaced.

On the other side, the term green financing relies on the investment in projects, initiatives, or businesses that are designed to improve society and the environment or have a business model based on sustainable or circular economy principles is a less cited term.

In the intellectual capital section, we used the term automation, which refers to the techniques, methods, or system of operating or controlling a process by highly automatic means such as electronic devices and reducing human involvement. Capitals represent the inputs for the organization's actions and activities.

Moving forward, Table 4 presents the results of the content analysis based on the terms included in the category "business activities" of the eight organizations included in our sample. In this table, we used several terms that clarify how business activities that were disclosed in the reports correlate with CE activities.

The business activities generally cover a wide range of word counts, and frequency is substantially distributed.

Notably, the most cited activities are the following: R&D, product development, design, quality and control, Production conversion, service provision, and joint venture. The term design relies on consciously creating products for longevity, reuse, and the ability to recover material at the end of its use by the first consumer. The organization designing the product may or may not be directly involved with the product or package after its first use. However, it has enabled others to reuse, refurbish, remanufacture, or recover material from the product at the end of its first helpful life. The design of the product is closely related to the circular economy activities. Because in the design phase, the producers know how the procedure is to recover the product after it is finished.

The term responsible source is more cited in the integrated reports. Responsible sourcing denotes the active effort on the part of a manufacturer to understand where the raw materials for their products are created and ensure that their production does not have negative social and

Table 4 Results of content analysis for "business activities"

	Anglo Gold 2016		Anglo Platinum 2017		Exxaro Resources 2017		Fresnillo plc 2016		Fresnillo 2014		Gold Fields 2017		Gold Fields 2016	
		(%)		(%)		(%)		(%)		(%)		(%)		(%)
Business Activities	209	0.18	226	0.18	232	0.28	276	0.14	269	0.13	173	0.15	187	0.18
Activities	70	0.07	46	0.05	39	0.06	107	0.06	120	0.07	41	0.04	32	0.04
Research	3	0.01	15	0.01	5	0.01	5	0.05	2	0.01	7	0.01	11	0.01
Development	131	0.14	112	0.13	130	0.21	188	0.12	187	0.11	159	0.18	161	0.20
Data Management	219	0.21	205	0.20	170	0.24	331	0.18	402	0.22	300	0.28	252	0.27
Planning	49	0.04	15	0.01	19	0.02	28	0.01	13	0.01	37	0.03	26	0.02
Design	20	0.01	8	0.01	3	0.01	15	0.01	4	0.01	15	0.01	16	0.01
Take Back	16	0.01	20	0.01	14	0.01	46	0.01	26	0.01	16	0.01	33	0.01
Production	221	0.22	161	0.17	66	0.10	247	0.14	274	0.15	169	0.17	173	0.20
Conversion	4	0.01	7	0.01	2	0.01	1	0.01	9	0.01	12	0.01	10	0.01
Differentiation	0	0	1	0.01	0	0	0	0	0	0	0	0	0	0
Market Segmentation	56	0.03	111	0.07	102	0.09	111	0.04	121	0.04	15	0.01	11	0.01
Durability	0	0	2	0.01	0	0	0	0	0	0	0	0	0	0
Distribution	3	0.01	6	0.01	5	0.01	6	0.01	5	0.01	25	0.03	18	0.02
Service Provision	29	0.02	26	0.02	19	0.01	77	0.04	67	0.03	17	0.01	9	0.01
Quality control	62	0.04	66	0.05	61	0.06	128	0.05	95	0.05	73	0.05	59	0.05
Control	35	0.02	47	0.03	27	0.03	79	0.03	64	0.02	35	0.03	20	0.02
Quality	27	0.02	19	0.01	34	0.03	49	0.02	31	0.01	38	0.03	39	0.03

(continued)

Table 4 (continued)

	Anglo Gold 2016		Anglo Platinum 2017		Exxaro Resources 2017		Fresnillo plc 2016		Fresnillo 2014		Gold Fields 2017		Gold Fields 2016	
		(%)		(%)		(%)		(%)		(%)		(%)		(%)
Operational improvement	127	0.14	89	0.10	96	0.15	65	0.04	64	0.04	136	0.15	102	0.13
Improvement	36	0.04	20	0.02	25	0.04	15	0.01	13	0.01	29	0.03	41	0.05
Relationship management	205	0.21	189	0.20	167	0.24	333	0.20	407	0.33	265	0.27	243	0.28
Responsible Sourcing	24	0.03	21	0.02	16	0.03	33	0.02	27	0.02	27	0.03	15	0.02
Management	198	0.20	182	0.19	158	0.23	299	0.17	376	0.21	254	0.26	229	0.26
*Joint Venture	57	0.03	57	0.03	20	0.02	13	0.01	11	0.01	23	0.01	33	0.02
After-sales service	22	0.01	106	0.06	30	0.02	88	0.03	104	0.03	26	0.01	13	0.01
Service Provider	14	0.01	21	0.02	6	0.01	27	0.01	31	0.01	8	0.01	10	0.01
After-sales	11	0.01	86	0.04	24	0.02	61	0.02	73	0.02	19	0.01	9	0.01
Sales	5	0.01	62	0.03	17	0.01	112	0.03	124	0.03	10	0.01	4	0.01
MEAN	66.17857		68.78571		53.10714		97.85714		104.25		68.89286		62.71429	
S.D.	76.03267		68.28609		63.44221		105.8667		126.6242		88.24937		81.34192	

	Implats 2017		Kumba Iron 2017		Royal Platinum 2017		Royal platinum 2016		York Timbers 2017		MEAN	S.D.
		(%)		(%)		(%)		(%)		(%)		
Business Activities	164	0.20	195	0.23	208	0.20	196	0.18	150	0.13	207.08	38.747
Activities	61	0.09	49	0.07	29	0.03	35	0.04	50	0.05	56.58	29.16866
Research	8	0.01	0	0	4	0.01	4	0.01	27	0.02	7.583	7.3417
Development	80	0.12	66	0.10	155	0.20	192	0.23	88	0.10	137.41	43.5982
Data Management	138	0.19	143	0.20	192	0.21	288	0.31	177	0.17	234.75	81.40485
Planning	10	0.01	5	0.01	11	0.01	21	0.02	12	0.01	20.5	12.69574
Design	12	0.01	5	0.01	10	0.01	10	0.01	5	0.01	10.25	5.462683
Take Back	18	0.01	14	0.01	19	0.01	27	0.01	12	0.01	21.75	9.845396
Production	197	0.28	87	0.10	96	0.11	98	0.11	35	0.04	152	75.59942
Conversion	16	0.02	10	0.01	7	0.01	6	0.01	4	0.01	7.33	4.334499
Differentiation	0	0	10	0.02	0	0	0	0	0	0	0.916	2.874918
Market Segmentation	49	0.04	72	0.06	67	0.05	73	0.05	113	0.07	75.083	37.76833
Durability	0	0	0	0	0	0	2	0.01	1	0.01	0.4166	0.792961
Distribution	10	0.02	4	0.01	3	0.01	3	0.01	17	0.02	8.75	7.28791
Service Provision	6	0.01	36	0.04	21	0.02	21	0.02	45	0.03	31.083	21.97295
Quality control	22	0.02	99	0.10	44	0.04	58	0.04	111	0.08	73.166	29.85673
Control	15	0.01	42	0.04	29	0.02	41	0.03	56	0.04	40.833	18.49734
Quality	7	0.01	57	0.06	15	0.01	17	0.01	55	0.04	32.33	16.13767
Operational improvement	111	0.17	129	0.20	84	0.11	86	0.10	42	0.05	94.25	28.71213
Improvement	24	0.04	40	0.06	21	0.03	27	0.03	20	0.025	25.91	9.159777

(continued)

Table 4 (continued)

	Implats 2017		Kumba Iron 2017		Royal Platinum 2017		Royal platinum 2016		York Timbers 2017		MEAN	S.D.
		(%)		(%)		(%)		(%)		(%)		
Relationship management	147	0.21	149	0.21	211	0.25	307	0.35	169	0.18	232.66	81.45421
Responsible Sourcing	37	0.06	50	0.08	31	0.04	39	0.05	26	0.03	28.83	9.159777
Management	132	0.18	141	0.20	181	0.21	269	0.30	156	0.16	214.58	73.38375
*Joint Venture	5	0.01	5	0.01	41	0.03	48	0.03	9	0.01	26.83	19.72923
After-sales service	61	0.04	65	0.05	34	0.02	52	0.03	73	0.04	56.16	32.0563
Service Provider	3	0.01	26	0.03	22	0.02	22	0.02	35	0.03	18.75	10.38465
After-sales	58	0.04	44	0.03	18	0.01	33	0.02	40	0.02	39.66	25.25626
Sales	6	0.01	7	0.01	5	0.01	2	0.01	27	0.01	31.75	43.63094
MEAN	49.89286		55.35714		55.64286		70.60714		55.53571			
S.D.	57.67299		53.91572		68.18179		91.23488		53.8396			

environmental impacts at the production site or in surrounding communities. This requires a certain degree of supply chain transparency so that the buyer organization can verify that their material is being sourced responsibly, especially for material without a certification scheme. It is the fundamental activity of the circular economy.

A few other words are frequently mentioned, and it is relevant to note that all terms are related to management, with key examples like planning, sales, and management terms being less cited than market segmentation. Here, market segmentation refers to dividing the market because of the potential customer and product characteristics.

The next step of the content analysis involved the category of "outputs" (Table 5).

As clarified by IIRC (2013a, p. 26) when describing the concept of "outputs," an integrated report "identifies products and services of the organizations that might include the products by-products and waste which required to discussed within the organization business model disclosures, it's depending on their materiality."

Table 5 denotes the content analysis of *Outputs* that typically belong to the products, by-products, product life cycle, redesign, refurbishment, renewable resources, closed-loop, recycling, services and waste, waste conversion, and waste division. It is the basic part of the circular economy and is more cited terms in the output table. For example, the refurbishment term involves the repair and reconditioning of the product, so that it can use another product life. Here term remanufacture involves repairing and reusing previously used a product or recovering components for a new product, it is part of a by-product. It is more cited in the IR of the organizations.

The term end of life is more cited, the term reflects the organization activities that follow the end of the first use phase of a product to its points of final disposal, and the end of life collectively contains reuse and recycling. In a circular business model, a product or its components and materials exit the end of life and re-enter another product life cycle.

The closed-loop term is less cited, the term reflects a process whereby the product or packaging comes at the end of its useful life, then recycled and reused in the circle ways which is close to the manufacturing process in the IR reports. When the producer designs the product then

Table 5 Results of content analysis for "outputs"

	Anglo Gold 2016		Anglo Platinum 2017		Exxaro Resources 2017		Fresnillo plc 2016		Fresnillo 2014		Gold Fields 2017		Gold Fields 2016	
		(%)		(%)		(%)		(%)		(%)		(%)		(%)
Outputs	2	0.01	4	0.01	0	0	3	0.01	3	0.01	2	0.01	3	0.01
Products	6	0.01	18	0.02%	14	0.02	17	0.01	21	0.01	1	0.01	0	0
*Product Life	68	0.03	41	0.02	98	0.08	74	0.02	70	0.02	78	0.03	44	0.02
*Product Life Cycle	78	0.04	56	0.03	104	0.08	86	0.02	91	0.02	83	0.04	55	0.03
*End Of life	135	0.05	74	0.03	124	0.09	96	0.02	121	0.05	96	0.04	94	0.02
Utility	4	0.01	3	0.01	4	0.01	1	0.01	1	0.01	4	0.01	3	0.01
Service	11	0.01	20	0.01	6	0.01	27	0.01	31	0.01	7	0.01	4	0.01
*Product Service System	54	0.04	42	0.03	66	0.06	105	0.04	145	0.05	29	0.02	27	0.02
Waste	19	0.01	29	0.02	8	0.01	53	0.02	49	0.01	38	0.02	44	0.02
Waste Conversion	23	0.01	36	0.02	10	0.01	54	0.02	58	0.02	50	0.03	54	0.04
Waste Diversion	20	0.01	29	0.02	8	0.01	54	0.02	49	0.01	38	0.02	44	0.02

	Anglo Gold 2016		Anglo Platinum 2017		Exxaro Resources 2017		Fresnillo plc 2016		Fresnillo 2014		Gold Fields 2017		Gold Fields 2016	
		(%)		(%)		(%)		(%)		(%)		(%)		(%)
*Recycle	0	0	0	0	1	0.01	0	0	0	0	2	0.01	0	0
*Redesign	4	0.01	0	0	0	0	0	0	0	0	1	0.01	1	0.01
By-product	14	0.01	8	0.01	46	0.01	22	0.01	19	0.01	4	0.01	4	0.01
Remanufacturing	0	0	0	0	0	0	0	0	0	0	0	0	0	0
Refurbishment	1	0.01	3	0.01	0	0	0	0	0	0	0	0	2	0.01
Renewable resource	66	0.01	131	0.12	151	0.20	209	0.11	209	0.10	102	0.09	82	0.08
Renewable	1	0.01	0	0	12	0.02	1	0.01	0	0	14	0.01	16	0.02
Resources	97	0.08	51	0.04	52	0.06	34	0.02	44	0.02	44	0.04	34	0.03
Closed-Loop	9	0.01	7	0.01	14	0.01	7	0.01	4	0.01	12	0.01	5	0.01
*Basic Material	47	0.04	70	0.05	70	0.08	60	0.03	71	0.03	45	0.03	39	0.03
MEAN	31.38095		29.619047		37.52380		43		46.952380		30.952380		26.428571	
S.D.	38.01641		33.27533		46.862158		51.44122		56.198288		33.9815776		28.620921	

(continued)

Table 5 (continued)

	Implats 2017		Kumba Iron 2017		Royal Platinum 2017		Royal Platinum 2016		York Timbers 2017		MEAN	S.D.
		(%)		(%)		(%)		(%)		(%)		
Outputs	5	0.01	0	0	2	0.01	3	0.01	1	0.01	2.3333	1.497473
Products	7	0.01	36	0.04	6	0.01	9	0.01	86	0.07	18.41667	23.5003
*Product Life	14	0.01	129	0.09	30	0.02	22	0.01	82	0.05	62.5	33.54102
*Product Life Cycle	34	0.02	138	0.10	38	0.02	23	0.01	90	0.06	73	32.96279
*End Of life	47	0.02	160	0.11	84	0.04	58	0.03	140	0.07	102.4167	34.30467
Utility	2	0.01	0	0	1	0.01	3	0.01	2	0.01	2.333	1.370689
Service	3	0.01	21	0.02	16	0.01	19	0.01	33	0.02	16.5	10.44901
*Product Service System	20	0.02	79	0.08	57	0.04	75	0.05	135	0.09	69.5	40.93565
Waste	12	0.01	36	0.03	47	0.03	52	0.03	1	0.01	32.3333	18.25244
Waste Conversion	28	0.03	46	0.04	54	0.03	58	0.04	5	0.01	39.666	18.9369
Waste Diversion	12	0.01	36	0.03	48	0.03	52	0.03	1	0.01	32.5833	18.36726
*Recycle	0	0	0	0	1	0.01	0	0	0	0	0.3333	0.651339

	Implats 2017		Kumba Iron 2017		Royal Platinum 2017		Royal Platinum 2016		York Timbers 2017		MEAN	S.D.
	(%)		(%)		(%)		(%)		(%)			
*Redesign	0	0	0	0	2	0.01	0	0	0	0	0.06666	1.230915
By-product	2	0.01	51	0.05	13	0.01	11	0.01	66	0.05	21.6666	21.04253
Remanufacturing	0	0	0	0	0	0	0	0	8	0.01	0.6666	2.3099401
Refurbishment	0	0	4	0.01	0	0	0	0	0	0	0.83333	1.40345
Renewable resource	89	0.11	98	0.12	70	0.07	79	0.08	24	0.02	109.1667	56.44117
Renewable	1	0.01	0	0	8	0.01	5	0.01	5	0.01	5.25	5.89913
Resources	30	0.03	42	0.05	32	0.03	44	0.04	11	0.01	42.91667	20.31774
Closed-Loop	12	0.01	5	0.01	8	0.01	5	0.01	9	0.01	8.08333	3.232177
*Basic Material	53	0.06	52	0.05	60	0.05	79	0.07	110	0.09	63	19.12162
MEAN	17.66666		44.42857		27.47619		28.42857		38.52380			
S.D.	22.742764		46.61508		26.783661		29.026834		48.6432102			

be cautious of the recycle or regain process, it is close to the regeneration of the product. The terms waste, waste conversion, and waste diversion in the output table are cited and mentioned as a manufacturing process. It usually exits after the waste, disposes of waste into another process that distracts material designed for landfall and alternate use that keeps the resource implanted in the material through reuse. It is closely related to CE activities. Because in the CE the waste term used as wealth. As illustrated in Table 5, all these terms are frequently mentioned, being in line with the suggestions provided by the IIRC framework (IIRC, 2013a) but it is closely related to the CE activities. Moreover, it is also significant that terms that are particularly relevant to the basic material sector are heavily cited, such as resources and natural assets.

Finally, Table 6 represents the content analysis results for "outcomes." According to the IIRC (2013a, p. 26) framework, the class of *outcomes* in IR includes both internal and external outcomes, as well as positive and negative consequences for the consumption of capital induced by business activities.

Interestingly, the asset recovery after consumption is more cited than asset consumption. On the other hand, carbon footprints are more cited; they denote the amount of greenhouse gas emissions generated across their entire life cycle through strategies such as material selection, manufacturing of use-phase energy efficiency, planned reuse, and recycling. If we see the job creation citation, it reflects the primary principal activity of the circular economy. Same here, employee development, employee engagement, and worker training are more cited in the IR reports of the organizations.

A specific framework for transitional industrial, where the product packaging material or element is used for another product itself. The packaging is called out separately because the package has its own supply chain management system that brings on the items' natural influences and life cycle. Only the Royal Platinum 2016 IR (Cited 1) and York Timbers 2017 IR (Cited 3) show the packaging term. However, the average citations are low in this term. The lease terms need to be cited in the Integrated reports. The lease terms refer to the entrepreneur model, where a producer contracts with another person or organization to use a product or service for their purpose. Still, the ownership remains with

Table 6 Results of content analysis for outcomes

	Anglo Gold 2016		Anglo Platinum 2017		Exxaro Resources 2017		Fresnillo plc 2016		Fresnillo 2014		Gold Fields 2017		Gold Fields 2016	
		(%)		(%)		(%)		(%)		(%)		(%)		(%)
Outcomes	12	0.01	15	0.01	15	0.02	13	0.01	6	0.01	10	0.01	10	0.01
Customer Satisfaction	2	0.01	10	0.01	16	0.02	11	0.01	17	0.01	1	0.01	0	0
Customers	3	0.01	5	0.01	12	0.02	20	0.02	11	0.01	2	0.01	1	0.01
Profit	13	0.01	71	0.04	18	0.02	234	0.08	240	0.08	9	0.01	15	0.01
Loss	32	0.01	88	0.04	32	0.02	120	0.03	127	0.03	32	0.01	26	0.01
Shareholder returns	67	0.07	39	0.04	28	0.04	69	0.01	63	0.03	33	0.03	27	0.03
Shareholder	45	0.05	24	0.03	13	0.02	48	0.03	38	0.02	16	0.02	17	0.02
Stakeholder	27	0.03	39	0.04	45	0.07	20	0.01	19	0.01	49	0.06	20	0.02
Asset Consumption	40	0.03	25	0.02	24	0.02	164	0.05	153	0.04	40	0.04	33	0.03
Consumption	11	0.01	6	0.01	4	0.01	12	0.01	7	0.01	24	0.03	20	0.02
Assets Recover After Consumption	43	0.03	96	0.06	36	0.03	391	0.14	389	0.13	78	0.06	63	0.05

(continued)

Table 6 (continued)

	Anglo Gold 2016		Anglo Platinum 2017		Exxaro Resources 2017		Fresnillo plc 2016		Fresnillo 2014		Gold Fields 2017		Gold Fields 2016	
		(%)		(%)		(%)		(%)		(%)		(%)		(%)
Contribution to the local economy through taxes	89	0.06	119	0.09	60	0.06	125	0.05	122	0.05	124	0.08	118	0.08
Taxes	17	0.01	35	0.02	4	0.01	31	0.01	24	0.01	19	0.01	13	0.01
Job creation	20	0.01	11	0.01	24	0.02	23	0.01	30	0.01	30	0.02	24	0.02
Employee development	183	0.19	138	0.15	139	0.22	223	0.14	224	0.13	190	0.21	207	0.24
Employee engagement	124	0.11	86	0.08	46	0.06	61	0.03	66	0.03	94	0.09	116	0.12
Employee	52	0.04	26	0.02	9	0.01	35	0.02	37	0.02	31	0.03	46	0.04
Worker Training	44	0.04	19	0.02	29	0.03	41	0.02	58	0.03	55	0.05	44	0.04
Improved Standard of Living	60	0.05	45	0.04	29	0.03	39	0.02	44	0.02	58	0.05	80	0.07
Carbon footprints	21	0.01	4	0.01	23	0.02	19	0.01	10	0.01	65	0.04	58	0.04
Living	2	0.01	5	0.01	3	0.01	3	0.01	1	0.01	7	0.01	11	0.01
Environment Impact	13	0.01	21	0.02	18	0.02	24	0.01	12	0.01	29	0.02	28	0.02

	Anglo Gold 2016		Anglo Platinum 2017		Exxaro Resources 2017		Fresnillo plc 2016		Fresnillo 2014		Gold Fields 2017		Gold Fields 2016	
		(%)		(%)		(%)		(%)		(%)		(%)		(%)
Environment	0	0	0	0	0	0	0	0	0	0	0	0	0	0
Packaging	0	0	0	0	0	0	0	0	0	0	0	0	0	0
Impact	52	0.03	66	0.04	64	0.06	126	0.04	107	0.04	71	0.04	51	0.03
License to operate	56	0.04	39	0.03	78	0.08	49	0.02	76	0.03	126	0.09	137	0.11
Lease	4	0.01	5	0.01	0	0	22	0.01	16	0.01	5	0.01	1	0.01
MEAN	38.2222		38.40741		30.76		71.2222		70.25926		44.37037		43.18519	
S.D.	41.5575		38.3278		30.01289		90.92911		91.3011		46.01016		49.84209	

(continued)

Table 6 (continued)

	Implats2017		Kumba Iron 2017		Royal Platinum 2017		Royal platinum 2016		York Timbers 2017		MEAN	S.D.
		(%)		(%)		(%)		(%)		(%)		
Outcomes	25	0.03	29	0.03	10	0.01	6	0.01	9	0.01	13.3333	7.062492
Customer Satisfaction	2	0.01	16	0.02	4	0.01	1	0.01	31	0.03	9.25	9.4496
Customers	10	0.01	13	0.02	2	0.01	3	0.01	36	0.03	9.83333	10.098
Profit	67	0.06	16	0.01	10	0.01	0	0	73	0.04	63.8333	84.99929
Loss	78	0.04	13	0.01	23	0.01	24	0.01	76	0.03	55.9166	40.03966
Shareholder returns	25	0.03	37	0.05	91	0.11	51	0.06	66	0.07	49.66667	21.26172
Shareholder	15	0.02	28	0.04	89	0.11	45	0.05	53	0.06	35.916677	22.0473
Stakeholder	44	0.07	70	0.11	47	0.06	59	0.07	25	0.03	38.6666	16.64241
Asset Consumption	18	0.02	14	0.01	44	0.05	44	0.04	95	0.05	57.83333	51.41247
Consumption	5	0.01	2	0.01	29	0.04	27	0.03	3	0.01	12.50	9.8857
Assets Recover After Consumption	58	0.05	49	0.04	48	0.05	50	0.05	196	0.012	124.75	131.0275
Contribution to the local economy through taxes	68	0.06	66	0.07	76	0.06	70	0.05	66	0.06	91.91667	27.16769

	Implats2017		Kumba Iron 2017		Royal Platinum 2017		Royal platinum 2016		York Timbers 2017		MEAN	S.D.
Taxes	13	0.01	5	0.01	2	0.01	0	0	3	0.01	13.8333	11.7072
Job creation	20	0.02	15	0.02	17	0.01	17	0.01	49	0.03	23.333	9.8749
Employee development	137	0.19	102	0.14	213	0.25	245	0.28	114	0.12	176.25	48.14962
Employee engagement	101	0.13	76	0.10	112	0.11	113	0.11	56	0.05	87.5833	26.34201
Employee	57	0.06	36	0.04	58	0.05	53	0.05	26	0.02	38.8333	14.8619
Worker Training	27	0.03	11	0.01	59	0.05	52	0.05	36	0.03	395,833	15.58821
Improved Standard of Living	33	0.04	51	0.06	42	0.04	32	0.03	65	0.05	48.1666	15.22458
Carbon footprints	3	0.01	0	0	16	0.01	20	0.01	2	0.01	20.08333	21.0301
Living	0	0	3	0.01	8	0.01	3	0.01	2	0.01	4	3.190896
Environment Impact	30	0.03	18	0.02	11	0.01	21	0.01	6	0.01	19.25	7.712151
Environment	0	0	0	0	0	0	0	0	0	0	0	0

(continued)

Table 6 (continued)

	Implats2017		Kumba Iron 2017		Royal Platinum 2017		Royal platinum 2016		York Timbers 2017		MEAN	S.D.
Packaging	0	0	0	0	0	0	1	0.01	3	0.01	0.3636	0.924416
Impact	56	0.05	63	0.05	63	0.04	100	0.07	44	0.03	71.91667	25.35012
License to operate	129	0.13	79	0.08	41	0.03	54	0.04	7	0.01	72.5833	40.30668
Lease	8	0.01	2	0.01	7	0.01	0	0	22	0.01	7.6666	7.992421
MEAN	38.1111		30.14815		41.55556		40.40741		43.1111			
S.D.	38.51307		29.19129		46.55298		51.17711		43.90491			

the producers and returns to the producers at the end of the lease period. It is the best example of PSS models of circular economy. In this term, the manufacturer assumes responsibility for the maintenance and preservation of the product, as well as the responsible end-of-life management.

The counts are well distributed among economic, social, and natural capitals. This is partly coherent with the counts related to inputs; specifically, on the one hand, financial terms are frequently used to identify the ultimate outcomes of the organization's business activities, but on the other hand, many counts also relate to natural capital, mainly to highlight (potential) environmental consequences and impacts of the taken actions.

Analysis of Visual Representations and CE in IR

As mentioned in the section of this research devoted to illustrating the research design, the second step of our analysis entailed inspecting the IR (drawn up by the organizations included in the sample) and looking for CE-related visual representations. We defined an ex-ante codebook to perform this analysis, detailed in Table 2.

The results of this analysis are portrayed in Table 7, which shows the various typologies of visual representations, providing the counts (i.e., the total number of representations identified within the reports) for each typology, as well as the values of mean and standard deviation for the organizations and the representations we considered.

It is noteworthy to stress again that the analysis was performed looking for "visual representation" and not for verbal descriptions of these concepts, which, therefore, could be contained in those reports (but are not considered in this study).

Overall, we identified 244 images of the 18 categories included ex-ante in our codebook. A residual category of "others" was also considered.

In more detail, Fig. 4 portrays the visual representations we identified in the analysis divided per organization and integrated report, while Fig. 5 identifies the counts of representations divided per category.

Table 7 Results from the visual representation analysis

Typology of visual representation	Anglo Gold 2016	Anglo Plat-inum 2017	Exxaro Resources 2017	Fresnillo plc 2016	Fresnillo 2014	Gold Fields 2017	Gold Fields 2016
Business model representations	1	1	1	1	2	1	
Value chain (or value proposition) representations			1	3	1		1
Strategy representations	1		1			1	3
Visual representation of capitals (and their trade-offs), inputs, outputs, and outcomes	1		2			1	1
Visual mission statement (mission, vision, and/or core values)	1			1			1
Geo or spatial representations of operations	3	8	5	1	1	5	5
Visual representation of the main operations (also, upstream and/or downstream)		2		2		1	
Risk Matrix or ERM charts	2	1	3	8	1	5	5

Typology of visual representation	Anglo Gold 2016	Anglo Plat-inum 2017	Exxaro Resources 2017	Fresnillo plc 2016	Fresnillo 2014	Gold Fields 2017	Gold Fields 2016
Organizational charts and Board structure charts			2	1	2	1	2
Materiality matrix				1			
Cause maps			2		6	1	
Causal Loop Diagrams (CLD)		1	6	3			3
Strategy Maps		2		1			
Balanced Scorecard			2			2	1
KPIs charts on outcomes	1	3	1	2	1		2
Value Stream Maps							
LCA (Life-Cycle Assessment) Images							
Bubble diagrams			1	1			
SDGs connection maps			1	1		1	
Total Counts per organization	***10***	***18***	***28***	***26***	***14***	***19***	***24***
Mean	0,526316	0,947368	1,473684	1,368421	0,736842	1	1,263158
S.D.	0,786796	2,507133	1,625123	1,95789	1,825742	1,66333	1,577621

(continued)

Table 7 (continued)

Typology of visual representation	Implants 2017	Kumba Iron 2017	Royal Platinum 2017	Royal platinum 2016	York Timbers 2017	Total Counts per representation	Mean	S.D.
Business model representations	7	1	1			***16***	1,333333333	1,9860625
Value chain (or value proposition) representations	2	2			2	***12***	1	0,7559289
Strategy representations	2		1	1	1	***11***	0,916666667	0,7440238
Visual representation of capitals (and their trade-offs), inputs, outputs, and outcomes	7	1	2	2	2	***19***	1,583333333	1,9002924
Visual mission statement (mission, vision, and/or core values)	1	2	1	1	1	***9***	0,75	0,3535534

Typology of visual representation	Implants 2017	Kumba Iron 2017	Royal Platinum 2017	Royal platinum 2016	York Timbers 2017	Total Counts per representation	Mean	S.D.
Geo or spatial representations of operations	2	2	6	3	1	***42***	3,5	2,2763607
Visual representation of the main operations (also, upstream and/or downstream)			3	5	2	***15***	1,25	1,3784049
Risk Matrix or ERM charts	2	2	1	2	1	***33***	2,75	2,1794495
Organizational charts and Board structure charts	2	1		3		***14***	1,166666667	07071068
Materiality matrix						***1***	0,083333333	#DIV/0!
Cause maps			4	3	1	***17***	1,416666667	1,9407902
Causal Loop Diagrams (CLD)	1		2	4		***20***	1,666666667	1,7728105
Strategy Maps						***3***	0,25	0,7071068
Balanced Scorecard	1			1		***7***	0,583333333	0,5477226
KPIs charts on outcomes		3	1	2	1	***17***	1,416666667	0,8232726

(continued)

Table 7 (continued)

Typology of visual representation	Implants 2017	Kumba Iron 2017	Royal Platinum 2017	Royal platinum 2016	York Timbers 2017	Total Counts per representation	Mean	S.D.
Value Stream Maps						*0*	0	n.d
LCA (Life-Cycle Assessment) Images						*0*	0	n.d
Bubble diagrams						**2**	0,166666667	0
SDGs connection maps			1	2		**6**	0,5	0,4472136
Total Counts per organization	***27***	***14***	***23***	***29***	***12***	**244**	20,33333333	6,7059449
Mean	1,421053	0,736842	1,210526	1,526316	0,631579			
S.D.	2,311805	0,707107	1,640399	1,240112	0,5			

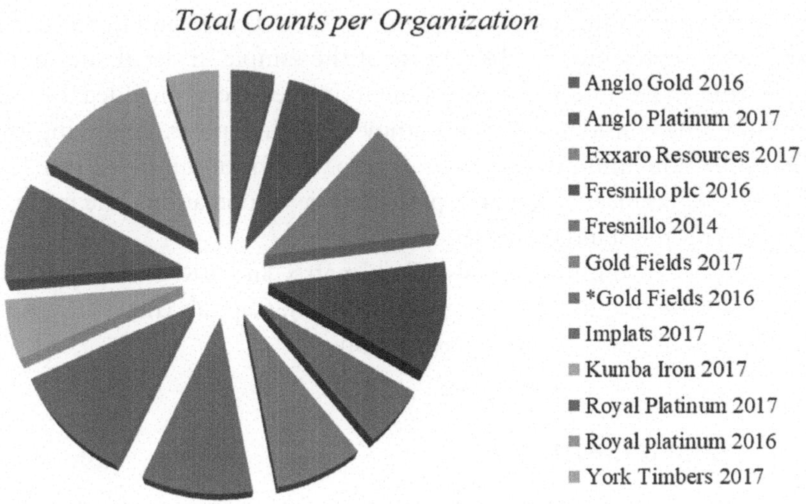

Fig. 4 Analysis of visual representations—Counts per organization and per integrated report

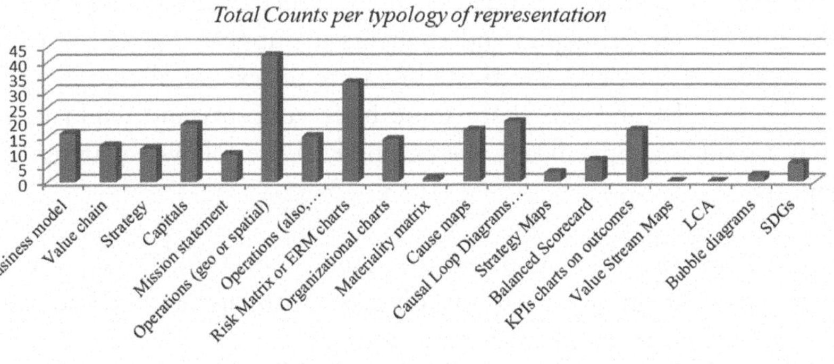

Fig. 5 Analysis of visual representations—Counts per typology of representation

All the reports inspected contained several visual representations belonging to the categories of the codebook. The mean is 12,33, with a standard deviation of 6705. The minimum number of representations (n = 10) is displayed by the 2016 integrated report drawn up by Anglo Gold, while the 2016 integrated report by Platinum provides the maximum (n = 29).

Notably, only some of the categories we included ex-ante in our code-book were represented in the reports of the sample in detail, and quite interestingly, no Life-Cycle Assessment images were provided by the organizations considered for this study in their reports. Analyzing the data, where the minimum number is zero, the maximum is 42 in reference to geographical or spatial representations of operations, the mean is 12,842, and the standard deviation is 11,006.

Highly used solutions are also Risk matrix and ERM maps (no. = 33), CLDs (no. = 20), cause maps (no. = 17), Capitals (no. = 19), and Business model (no. = 16) representations.

5 Discussion

This study focused on the potential role integrated reporting (Eccles & Krzus, 2010; IIRC, 2013a) may play in disclosing circular economy information.

As our first aim, we intended to discuss whether integrated reporting may provide the principles and elements to support the representation of CE-related activities. From the literature review we offered it is clear enough that IR and CE share some basic concepts and could benefit from a joint use. Specifically, we emphasized the following strengths of joint use.

1. First, IR and CE build on the concept of capital, i.e., the key resources at an organization's disposal. Capitals are used to create value products, by-products, and waste.
2. Second, in IR and CE, value creation is a dynamic process in which inputs are transformed to create value over the short, medium, and long term.
3. Third, IR and CE adopt a closed-loop perspective about value creation: inputs transit to outputs, and outcomes become the feedback of the inputs (i.e., the capitals).

Overall, IR and CE could fit together, and evidence is provided by the fact that further research in this area is advocated (e.g., Stewart & Niero, 2018).

This said, we can now consider the second aim of this paper, which is to discuss how and to what extent integrated reports disclose CE data and information. To this aim, we performed both content analysis and a visual representation search on a sample of IR.

The study results show that organizations incorporated some CE-related information and data in their integrated reports, though not to a great extent.

Financial-related information is the most frequently cited, and less relevance is given to other categories of terms. This said, and adopting a CE-related perspective, the analysis results show that the disclosure of relevant terms depends on the core activities carried out by each organization and its strategies.

For example, the York Timbers 2017 IR identifies the organization's different strategies (and strategy-related terms), which are closely related to its CE activities, such as remanufacturing plant, handling facilities, biogas, suppliers, customers, staff, remanufacturing capabilities, carbon footprint, by product, and intellectual capital (pages 16 and 19). Additionally, organizations describe how they create value through their business model and CE-related activities. As an example, the 2017 report drafted by Royal Platinum (pages 115 and 125) presents a closed-loop framework, renewable resources, reducing, recycling, eliminating waste, protecting biodiversity, and managing resource efficiency, which is closely related to the CE activities (Fig. 6).

The analysis showed that organizations also look at future opportunities. As an example, the 2017 IR by Exxaro (pages 5 and 127) places a definite emphasis on the business of tomorrow strategy, specifically considering a strategy of reusing, reducing, and recycling all renewable and non-renewable resources and processes that provide the goods or services that support the current and the future prosperity of the organization, and its natural resources.

The IR drafted by the organizations we considered in this study often related their CE activities to measures and parameters, quantifying their impacts. As an example, Fresnillo plc (in its 2016 Annual optimally exploiting our **mineral resources**

reducing our dependence on fossil fuels

using **renewable resources** from well-managed and restorable ecosystems whenever possible

eliminating waste by reusing or **recycling** wherever possible

protecting biodiversity and ecosystems

managing resources efficiently.

Fig. 6 Example from one Integrated Report (*Source* Royal Platinum IR [2017, p. 115])

Report) describes a system that impacts the environmental footprint, at the same time discussing concepts such as Clean Industry as well as policies to reduce and reuse non-mineral and hazardous waste and to protect and increase Health, Safety, Environment & Community Relations (HSECR).

Overall, an integrated and multifaceted approach and strategy able to make responsible use of CE-related resources is the key and most effective practice to meet the sustainability challenge and oversee the same time culture and ethics program. For example, the 2017 Integrated Annual Report by Gold Fields describes a process for the life cycle of the natural assets that also entails considering environmental issues, management practices, and community relations, therefore putting together the natural, economic, and social dimensions of CE and sustainability practices.

This said we summarized the content of the integrated reports under investigation using a *word cloud* (see Fig. 7).

A word cloud "is a special visualization of text in which the more frequently used words are effectively highlighted by occupying more prominence in the representation. (…) Word clouds can be useful for preliminary analysis and validation of previous findings" (McNaught & Lam, 2010, p. 630).

As shown in the figure, the more frequently used words in the 12 IR are management, financial, company, risk, group, report, performance, cash, value, and capital, which are closely connected to IR and the underlying rationale of an IR. Additionally, let's take a closer look at the

Fig. 7 Word cloud—Total sample word query

CE-related terms. It is noteworthy that words such as resources, asset, mineral, safety, reserves, exploration, operating, strategic, and stakeholder are also cited. Additionally, if we look at the IR side, some key terms, financial, reports, natural (Environment), performance, governance, risk, social, value, and employees are also cited. Overall, this may suggest that all the terms are considered and somehow interlinked with each other.

The second part of the analysis was devoted to searching for CE-related visual representations, especially looking for images, graphs, and maps that provide a comprehensive and interlinked visualization of CE activities.

The results from this step of the process reveal that the organizations include a variety of representations in their reports in terms of typologies (we identified 19 potential categories of representations) and overall number (we counted 244 representations of interest for this study). In particular, the organizations considered in this study seem to be more engaged with tools that have a longer and more established tradition (e.g., risk matrixes and ERM tools) or with representations that provide clear and straightforward communication to stakeholders (e.g., geo and spatial representations of the organization's operations) than with representation and maps that could better fit with CE concepts (e.g., LCA images). Additionally, we must emphasize that, quite often, the visual representations—especially those related to key operational activities—are arranged according to a linear-oriented business vision. An interesting example is provided by the 2017 IR drafted by York Timbers (2017, page 70) which provides a linear-oriented representation of its operations (see Fig. 8):

Quite interestingly, the reports also show that several other concepts—directly or potentially related to CE activities—are addressed with the use of visual representations that are of interest for this research (e.g., a risk matrix) or images devoted to capitals/resources and the representation of key operations (e.g., geospatial representation of operations). However, other typologies of images that could be more suited to present CE-related activities and issues (e.g., a CLD) were found to be not strictly related to CE.

As a last note, the authors emphasize that the organizations included in this study seem to rely more on "traditional" forms of measurement and reporting tools to communicate what they do in terms of CE and reference to the impacts generated by their operations. An example is provided in Fig. 9.

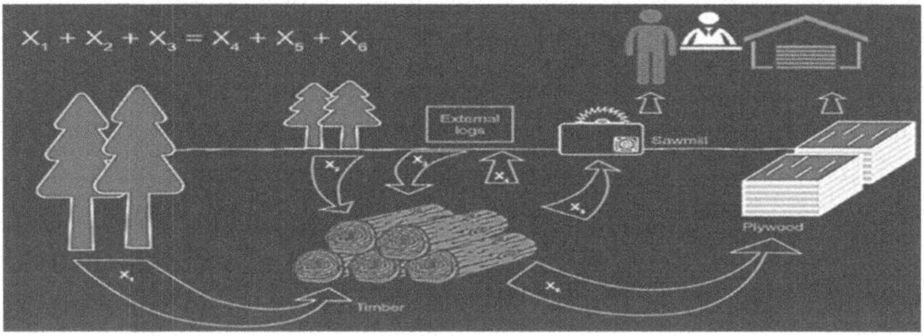

Fig. 8 Example of a visual representation from an Integrated Report (*Source* York Timbers [2017, p. 70])

	2017 R million	%	2016 R million
Value created	**65,670**		61,960
Net sales revenue	**65,670**	**6**	61,960
Value added by operations	**20,569**	**(6)**	21,991
Value distributed	**22,430**	**(7)**	24,188
Salaries, wages and other benefits	**10,093**	**(25)**	13,465
Skills development	**81**	**(27)**	112
Percentage of total payroll	**1%**		1%
Taxation and other payments to governments	**4,288**	**19**	3,594
Providers of debt capital	**1,229**	**(14)**	1,421
Minority shareholders as dividends	**272**	**518**	44
Dividend declared to shareholders	**941**	**100**	–
Community investment	**301**	**(15)**	354
Socio-economic development[1]			
Social and labour plans[2]			
Enterprise development[(including 1, 2, 3)]	**301**	**(15)**	354
Supplier development[3]			
Environmental investment	**89**	**(8)**	97
Waste disposal, emissions treatment and remediation	**27**	**9**	25
Pollution and environmental management	**62**	**(14)**	72
Total value distributed	**17,293**	**(9)**	19,086
Reinvested in the group	**5,137**	**1**	5,102
Losses from investments net of interest received	**(1,861)**	**(15)**	(2,197)

Fig. 9 Example of a "traditional" accounting table from this study (*Source* Anglo American Platinum [2017, p. 5])

6 Conclusion, Limitations, and Further Research

Conclusion

In this chapter/paper, we introduced a preliminary study of CE activities disclosure in integrated reporting practices; as mentioned, IR is assuming an increasing role in the business communication processes (e.g., Adams, 2015; Atkins, 2015b). Its actual use to effectively disclose data about CE activities still needs to be researched, thus calling for more investigation and evidence (e.g., Stewart & Niero, 2018). Specifically, we considered the framework for integrated reporting developed by the International Integrated Reporting Council (IIRC), an international coalition of regulators, investors, companies, standard setters, accounting professionals, and NGOs. The framework (IIRC, 2013a) proposes a precise and complete model of corporate reporting aimed at communicating to all stakeholders the value created by the organization in the short, medium, and long term.

This research's starting point and motivation are related to observing what happens daily in our natural world. In detail, the literature and environmental phenomena clearly demonstrate that we must act on any circular economy initiatives. For academics, this entails supporting companies in the effort of launching and managing such initiatives, measuring the impacts of the actions carried out, and reporting the key results achieved to a broad range of stakeholders. A comprehensive literature shows that CE initiatives are at the center of the modern organizations' agenda. Further research is needed to explore how (and if) those initiatives were monitored and communicated to relevant stakeholders.

Within this context, integrated reporting (alongside other sustainability and environmental reports) may offer a potentially powerful tool that companies worldwide could use to disclose their circular economy initiatives and their main results.

In more detail, starting from these considerations, this study explored the primary nexus of integrated reporting with CE issues and activities. In detail, through content analysis, the study provided data valid to investigate how and to what extent integrated reports disclose circular economy-related information. Subsequently, we inspected our sample of reports looking for CE-related visual representations.

Our preliminary findings show that the amount of disclosure of CE concepts is still relatively limited in this typology of corporate reports, and further research will be necessary to explore more in-depth how companies report CE-related data and which role is (or might be) played by accounting reports—and integrated reporting more specifically.

At the same time, our analysis showed that companies are—at least somehow—open to using images and visual representations within their integrated reports, even though they are not always tightly related to CE-related activities and concepts.

Limitations

Our study provides a preliminary analysis and certainly has some limitations. One limitation of the study may be linked to its research design and the choice of content analysis. As previous research demonstrated, content analysis's limitations have traditionally been the excessive focus on the quantity rather than the quality of disclosure (Guthrie & Abeysekera, 2006). Stated differently, the amount of exposure does not necessarily entail an organization disclosing information of high quality or relevance for its stakeholders. Another area for improvement of this study is that it draws upon a relatively limited sample or integrated reports.

Further Research

These limitations also open avenues for further research, specifically toward developing a qualitative exploratory case study (Ryan et al., 2002; Yin, 1994). Additionally, statistical analyses could be performed to correlate data emerging from the content analysis with a range of other factors considered relevant for CE (e.g., capitals or specific KPIs).

Appendix

Glossary of Circular Economy

The glossary defines many terms used in the qualitative and quantitative research guides. As mentioned in our study, this glossary aims to aid in developing more standardized and established terminology for circular economy research and Integrated reports, facilitating communication across different stakeholders and ultimately contributing to higher-quality circular economy and Integrated report Research. The paper relies on some technical terms. So, that glossary is necessary to understand the terms which are used. The U.S. Chamber of Commerce Foundation provides a glossary of the circular economy. We rely on this glossary because a report Published by the U.S. Chamber of Commerce Foundation & Corporate Citizenship Centre (CCC), in collaboration with the Ellen MacArthur Foundation, Achieving a Circular Economy: How the Private Sector is Reimagining the Future of Business, showcases companies that are contributing business solutions to society's challenges.

In this report, they are pleased to present a collection of best practices and strategies for how companies are leveraging the environmental, economic, and social opportunities that the circular economy provides and how they are doing it profitably. The Overview of the companies which are involved in this report,

U.S. Chamber of Commerce Foundation Corporate Citizenship Centre and Private Sector is Leading in the Circular Economy Revolution.

(1) The Ellen MacArthur Foundation (The Circular Economy Opportunity), (2) U.S. Chamber of Commerce Foundation Corporate Citizenship Centre (Innovative et al. Enabling the Circular Economy), (3) Accenture (Ten Disruptive Technologies), and (4) (The Dow Chemical Company).

Companies and industries involved in starting Circular Economy in this report.

1) Electronics and Information Technology Services Firms

Dell (Building a Waste-Free Tech Industry), eBay (eBay: Reuse and Redistribution at Scale), Philips North America (New Business Models for a Better Future), H.P. (Reinventing How Businesses, Supply Chains, and Whole Industries Work), IBM Corporation (Business and Environmental Benefits of Resource Efficiency at IBM).

2) Environmental Services Firms

The City of Phoenix and Arizona State University (Reimagine Phoenix, the Resource Innovation and Solutions Network, and the Resource Innovation Campus), Republic Services (Recycling—Investing in the Future), Veolia (Circular Economy in the Oil and Gas Refining Sector), Waste Management (Designing for a Circular Economy: Returning Resources to the Value Chain).

3) Finance

Closed-Loop Fund (Enabling Conditions—Financing and Influence), Rabobank Group (Refurbishing et al. and Recovering Renewable Raw Materials).

4) Manufacturing Companies

Caterpillar (Caterpillar's Remanufacturing Business Helps Make Sustainable Progress Possible), DSM (Corporate Darwinism and the Circular Economy), General Motors (G.M. Helps Launch New Trash-to-Treasure Sharing Economy), Ingersoll Rand (Reduce, Reuse, recycle ... Remanufacture), Novelis (Novelis et al.'s Unique Properties to Meet the Needs of Customers and Reduce Carbon Emissions), Steelcase Inc.(Steelcase Brings the Circular Economy to the Furniture Industry), SunPower Corporation (Rethinking Our Business Models, Products, and Factories to Become a Truly Sustainable Company), Xylem Inc. (Water Reuse: A Critical Component of a Water-Secure Future).

5) Plastics and Packaging Companies

Sealed Air Corporation (Reimagining et al.: New Approaches to a Circular Economy), Tetra Pak (Driving et al. from Renewability and Sustainable Sourcing), Walmart (Walmart Is Closing the Loop). Most of the big enterprise relies on this glossary. So, it is authenticity for our Research. https://www.uschamberfoundation.org/circular-economy-toolbox/about-circularity/glossary.

References

Adams, C. A. (2015). The international integrated reporting council: A call to action. *Critical Perspectives on Accounting, 27*, 23–28.

Adams, S., & Simnett, R. (2011). Integrated Reporting: An opportunity for Australia's not-for-profit sector. *Australian Accounting Review, 21*(3), 292–301.

Atkins, J., Atkins, B. C., Thomson, I., & Maroun, W. (2015a). "Good" news from nowhere: Imagining utopian sustainable accounting. *Accounting, Auditing & Accountability Journal, 28*(5), 651–670.

Atkins, J. F., Solomon, A., Norton, S., & Joseph, N. L. (2015b). The emergence of integrated private reporting. *Meditari Accountancy Research, 23*(1), 28–61.

Beattie, V., & Smith, S. J. (2013). Value creation and business models: Refocusing the intellectual capital debate. *The British Accounting Review, 45*(4), 243–254.

Bell, E., & Davison, J. (2013). Visual management studies: Empirical and theoretical approaches. *International Journal of Management Reviews, 15*(2), 167–184.

Berelson, B. (1952). Content analysis in communication research.

Burke, J. J., & Clark, C. E. (2016). The business case for integrated reporting: Insights from leading practitioners, regulators, and academics. *Business Horizons, 59*(3), 273–283.

Busco, C., Frigo, M. L., Riccaboni, A., & Quattrone, P. (2013). *Integrated reporting. Concepts and cases that redefine corporate accountability.*

Davison, J. (2014). Visual rhetoric and the case of intellectual capital. *Accounting, Organizations and Society, 39*(1), 20–37.

Davison, J. (2015). Visualising accounting: An interdisciplinary review and synthesis. *Accounting and Business Research, 45*(2), 121–165.

De Villiers, C., & Sharma, U. (2020). A critical reflection on the future of financial, intellectual capital, sustainability and integrated reporting. *Critical Perspectives on Accounting, 70*, 101999.

Dumay, J. (2016). A critical reflection on the future of intellectual capital: From reporting to disclosure. *Journal of Intellectual Capital, 17*(1), 168–184.

Eccles, R. G., & Krzus, M. P. (2010). *One report: Integrated reporting for a sustainable strategy*. John Wiley & Sons.

Ellen MacArthur Foundation. (2013). Opportunities for the consumer goods sector. *Towards a circular economy* (vol. 1).

Ellen MacArthur Foundation. (2015). *Delivering the circular economy—a toolkit for policymakers.*

European Commission. (2014). *Scoping study to identify potential circular economy actions, priority sectors, material flows, and value chains.*

Ellen MacArthur Foundation. (2016). *The new plastic economy: Rethinking the future of plastics & catalysing action.* https://www.ellenmacarthurfoundation.org/publications

Commission, E. (2014b). *Towards a circular economy: A Zero Waste Programme for Europe*. European Commission.

Giorgino, M., Barnabè, F., & Paolicelli, N. (2016). *Searching for the missing link between business model and strategy: The Integrated Reporting perspective*. Strategies, impact and challenges. Nova Science Publishers Inc.

Guthrie, J., & Abeysekera, I. (2006). Content analysis of social, environmental reporting: What is new? *Journal of Human Resource Costing & Accounting, 10*(2), 114–126.

International Integrated Reporting Council (IIRC). (2013a). *The International <IR> Framework*. http://www.theiirc.org/international-ir-framework/.

International Integrated Reporting Council (IIRC). (2013b). *Business model. Background paper for <IR>*. https://integratedreporting.org/wp-content/uploads/2013/03/Business_Model.pdf

International Integrated Reporting Council (IIRC). (2013c). *Value Creation. Background paper for <IR>*. http://integratedreporting.org/wp-content/uploads/2013/08/Background-Paper-Value-Creation.pdf.

International Integrated Reporting Council (IIRC). (2013d). *Capitals. Background paper for <IR>*. http://integratedreporting.org/wp-content/uploads/2013/03/IR-Background-Paper-Capitals.pdf.

Kamp-Roelands, N. (2013). A commentary on 'Integrated reporting: A review of developments and their implications for the accounting curriculum.' *Accounting Education, 22*(4), 357–359.

Kaplan, R. S., & Norton, D. (1992). The balanced scorecard: Measures that drive performance. *Harvard Business Review, 70*(1), 71–79.

Kirchherr, J., Reike, D., & Hekkert, M. (2017). Conceptualizing the circular economy: An analysis of 114 definitions. *Resources, Conservation and Recycling, 127*, 221–232.

Krippendorff, K. (2004). *Content analysis: An introduction to its methodology*. SAGE Publications.

Kraaijenhagen, C., Van Oppen, C., & Bocken, N. (2016). *Circular business. Collaborate and Circulate*.

McNaught, C., & Lam, P. (2010). Using Wordle as a supplementary research tool. *Qualitative Report, 15*(3), 630–643.

Milne, M. J., & Adler, R. W. (1999). Exploring the reliability of social and environmental disclosures content analysis. *Accounting, Auditing & Accountability Journal, 12*(2), 237–256.

Milne, M. J., & Gray, R. (2013). W (h) ither ecology? The triple bottom line, the global reporting initiative, and corporate sustainability reporting. *Journal of Business Ethics, 118*, 13–29.

Neuendorf, K. (2002). The content analysis guidebook Sage Publications, Inc. In *Library of Congress.*

Quattrone, P. (2017). Embracing ambiguity in management controls and decision-making processes: On how to design data visualisations to prompt wise judgement. *Accounting and Business Research, 47*(5), 588–612.

Ryan, B. (2002). *Research methods and methodology in finance and accounting.* Cengage Learning EMEA.

Schilling, J. (2006). On the pragmatics of qualitative assessment. *European Journal of Psychological Assessment, 22*(1), 28–37.

Stahel, W. R. (1982). Product-Life Factor. http://product-life.org/en/major-publications/the-product-life-factor

Sterman, J. D. (2000). *Business dynamics.* McGraw-Hill.

Stewart, R., & Niero, M. (2018). Circular economy in corporate sustainability strategies: A review of corporate sustainability reports in the fast-moving consumer goods sector. *Business Strategy and the Environment, 27*(7), 1005–1022.

Stewart, R., Niero, M., Murdock, K., & Olsen, S. I. (2018). Exploring the implementation of a circular economy strategy: The case of a closed-loop supply of aluminum beverage cans. *Procedia CIRP, 69*, 810–815.

Warren, S., & Davison, J. (2017). Visual methodologies for accounting and accountability. In *The Routledge companion to qualitative accounting research methods* (pp. 136–152). Routledge.

Wilson, C. (2013). *Brainstorming and beyond a user-centered design method.* Newnes.

Yin, R. K. (1994). *Case study research: Design and methods* (2nd ed.). Sage.

4

Circular Economy and Environment Disclosure

1 Introduction

During the COVID-19 global pandemic, there have been 617,579,680 confirmed cases and 6,532,705 deaths worldwide reported on 7 October 2022 (WHO, 2022). The rapid expansion of infectious medical waste generation and use of public protection equipment, laboratory specimens, pharmaceutical materials, instruments, and domestic waste increased. Most countries, particularly developing countries, are suffering from increasing medical waste due to COVID-19 (Shammi et al., 2021). This pertains to plastic-production growth is now taking place with international demand for a brand-new range of materials/resources. In response to the pandemic, the worldwide population has additionally accelerated the quantity of waste produced (Sarkar et al., 2020). Inorganic waste production is accompanied by a wide variety of environmental issues consisting of water and air pollutants, soil erosion, and deforestation (Mourad, 2016; Schanes et al., 2018).

S. Nazir and A. Capocchi, *Sustainability Reporting Practices and the Circular Economy*,
https://doi.org/10.1007/978-3-031-51845-4_4

It is an alarming situation, but with a circular economy [CE], resources are kept in a closed-loop cycle, and the reuse of resources to ensure sustainability is not only most frequently depicted as a combination of reducing, reusing, recycling, redesigning, remanufacturing, and recovering principles but also a production system that reduces the input of resources and output of waste.

United Nations [UN] (2015), sustainable development goals [SDGs] not only address measurable adjustments in the well-being of people, economic development of countries, and better environment on the earth but also provide a way to accomplish these environmental goals (Gurbo, 2017). Moving to a CE principle, all sectors of development can contribute to attaining SDG 12 of responsible consumption and production. In contrast, it can be valuable for all the other SDGs, such as SDG 9 on industrial growth and SGD 13 on climate actions, among others (Ellen MacArthur Foundation [EMF], 2020). The expansion of industry pollution is a problem exponentially developing in conjunction with the economic and demographic improvement of all industry sectors. Furthermore, the CE emphasizes the modern *principle of controlling material inputs to maximize recycling, remanufacturing, and recovery of materials, minimize waste to landfills, and seriously reduce the environmental footprint* (EMF, 2017). Several approaches have been proposed for supporting CE frameworks in an organization, for example, the stimulating framework (EMF, 2013, 2015; Stahel, 2016, 2019), product-service system (Pieroni et al., 2019), product design/redesign (Bocken et al., 2016; EMF, 2017), and sustainable development operation (Lewandowski, 2016) but not providing the relationship between CE-6RS and environment information in a closed-loop framework that covered sustainability agenda and accountability principles.

This research first contributes to understanding corporate practices and creates a bridge between non-financial information and CE reporting. Secondly, check the presence of CE-6R principles in their annual reporting practices. This research covers the environmental performance matrix (i.e., GRI-300) and provides a true picture of organizational operations and participation i.e., reducing, reusing, recycling, remanufacturing, redesigning, and recovering strategies for eliminating negative externalities and enhancing value creation, while some authors disclosed this information but not a quantitative score-wise (Barnabè & Nazir, 2021, 2022; EMF, 2013; Geissdoerfer et al., 2017; Murray et al., 2017), previously used the IIRC framework to disclosed this practice but not include the GRI-300 score-wise disclosure, the third contribution of this study, develops a codebook that could be useful for the practitioner and academic to see the practices of both manufacture and services companies as well as helpful for the creating of a new directive that will embed two practice in one form (i.e., GRI-300 series and WBCSD, 2018). Fourthly, it is the first exploratory study that explores the fundamental principle of CE i.e., reduce, reuse, recycling, redesign, remanufacturing, and recovery score-wise that could be helpful to generate a new avenue of environmental management, additionally helpful to investigating before and after Covid-19 effects. Lastly, this study may perhaps be used to see the social side (GRI 400 series) and economic side (GRI 200 series) of the companies by using this codebook and motivating top-level management to participate in CE reporting.

The research addressed whether the CE framework will be embedded into the reporting practices by close-loop and how conceivable to provide a true picture of the organization's financial and non-financial information. Environment sustainability practices are pertinent to all those activities that belong to the product operational framework (Lieder & Rashid, 2016). It is important to examine whether the business framework disclosed CE information to stakeholders for rational decision-making and participation in sustainability. However, globally most nations and companies have far to go before they can be considered to follow a CE framework (Witjes & Lozano, 2016). The study used the top 100 of the world's most sustainable corporations among 7000 public corporations to explore the practices in their reports and reveal the engagement of CE-6Rs. The study addresses two aims; (1) How and to what extent CE-6Rs principles disclosed in companies' annual reports? (2) How and to what extent do CE-6R principles engage with environmental performance? The paper is composed as follows: Sect. 2 covers a literature review and identifies gaps, Sect. 3 presents the data collection and research method, and Sect. 4 contains the findings and discussion, while Sect. 5 provides a conclusion and Sect. 6 limitations and opportunities for future research.

2 Literature Review

Circular Economy Concepts and Environment Disclosure

The CE approach usually considers various social, economic, and environmental frameworks. In Germany, in the mid-1990s, the CE concept was considered through an environmental approach (Cameron, 1997; Jacobs, 1996) addressing basic material issues and resource use for maintaining economic development, also called ecological economics. Later this was implemented with consideration of waste reusing, recycling, and the improvement of an environment-based closed circle framework for organizations or among various businesses and customers.

As indicated by Katz Gerro and Lopez Sintas (2019), reliance on CE activities should deliver better economic, social, and environmental performance. The execution of the CE-related R1-R6 principles (reduce, reuse, recycle, remanufacture, redesign, recover) inside firms is likewise comprehended as a capacity that incorporates interrelated CE practices to accomplish a shared objective (Barnabè & Nazir, 2022; Reike et al., 2018). While Ellen MacArthur Foundation (EMF, 2013a) proposed that the CE is "*an Industrial economy that is supportive and regenerative by expectation and framework*" (EMF, 2013b: 14). Webster (2021: 121) describes that "*CE is helpful to restorative by design, which expects to keep products, parts, and materials at their highest value.*"

A CE is an economic system where products and services are traded in closed-loop cycles and regenerative by design to retain as much value as possible for products, parts, and materials (EMF, 2017, 2022). Although the literature provides several definitions for the concept analyzed in this study (e.g., Kirchherr et al., 2017 analyzed 114 definitions), "a circular economy is an economic system where products and services are traded in closed-loop cycles." A CE is characterized as a framework that is regenerative by design to retain as much value as possible for products, parts, raw materials, and services. This means that the aim is to create a framework that allows for a longer life of resources, reduces material consumption, optimal reuse, and recycling of products, and recovers materials through waste (Barnabè & Nazir, 2022; EMF, 2016, 2022; Kraaijenhagen et al., 2016).

Reduce pertains to minimizing the use of pre-manufacturing, reducing the usage of resources reduction like raw material, natural resources, water consumption, carbon emissions, and greenhouse gas emissions during the manufacturing and services process (European Commission [EC], 2017) that also contains the prevention of recourses utilization. Meanwhile, reuse/resale pertains to the reusing of products, parts, materials, and natural resources after their first life cycle, while the resource should be in better shape and fulfill the demand for original products (EC, 2015). Reuse/resale of products or parts aims to decrease the consumption of virgin material, keep products and parts, and enhance the life cycle of products, parts, and resources (EMF, 2013a, 2013b, 2022). Recycling allows for the utilization of waste material, products, and resources reused again and again whenever it is possible and enhances the product life cycle by using closed-loop operations in the production and minimizing the hazardous particles in the product (EC, 2015). However, reproduction and remanufacture allow for making a new product or service using second-hand material, parts, services, and resources. Repurpose/redesign refers to the regenerative or integrated design of the old product, parts, or services designed for a next-generation product, material, resource, and services that could enhance the product life cycle and service (Jawahir & Bradley, 2016, Barnabè & Nazir, 2022). Lastly, recovery entails at the end of the usable stage intending to recollect products, parts, raw materials, and services through waste and share market (EC, 2014). It allows for emphasis on renewable resources, although non-renewable resources are converted into energy and biomass (EC, 2017).

Besides, there are no comprehensive environmental management and environment disclosure (GRI-300 series) strategies. Due to COVID-19, manufacturers and retailers have suffered remarkable issues due to the disturbance of the product's supply chain. The industries have suffered a heavy financial shot due to wasted products and materials in their stores and delivery service disturbance by lockdowns. For this, academia, regulators, and other stakeholders are actively engaged in the COVID-19 pandemic debate for sustainability and advocated moving toward more integrated forms of corporate survival.

Companies' business strategies are interlinked with business models and reporting directives which include waste recovery (GRI 306), reducing GHG emissions (GRI 305), reusing water (GRI 303), renewable energy (GRI 302), and air pollutants (GRI-300 series). However, environmental management and reporting is a guideline concept of the waste hierarchy and zero emissions which indicate circular principles in the direction of recovery to reuse (EU, 2019).

Corporate environment management and disclosure start from the product's initial phase to the ending phase and cover the product and services life cycle. Development of extended usage or reuse of products, as well as minimizing product loss during transit and storage, are all examples of environmental management that include reduce, reuse, recycle, remanufacture, redesign, and recover principles.

Nishitani et al. (2022) address a gap in the basic materials flow cost accounting relationship with environmental performance and economic performance, but still, a gap remains regarding that companies require a circular framework that supports environment performance and CE reporting practices that allow sustainability standards. However, the CE incorporates 3Rs (reduce, reuse, recycle) (Barnabè & Nazir, 2020) and 6Rs (reduce, reuse, recycle, reproduce, redesign, recover) (Barnabè & Nazir, 2022; Jawahir & Bradley, 2016) and 10Rs (refuse, reduce, reuse/resale, repair reproduce, remanufacturing, redesign, recover, recycling, recover remain) (Reike et al., 2018). From the all-industry point of view, it is very hard to measure the 10Rs principles because waste advocates the maintenance of all resources from input to output, while the services industry contains the product-service system, so the study used only those that commonly exist in the services and manufacturing industry.

Circular Economy and Sustainability Reporting

Sustainability reporting has been identified as comprising these three concepts of sustainability, i.e., social, economic, and environmental

(Burritt & Schaltegger, 2010). More precisely, Global Reporting Initiatives (GRI) and the World Business Council for Sustainable Development (WBCSD, 2018) provide an overview of the connections among CE, sustainability, and GRI requirements of different industries' disclosure indicators (GRI-300 series).

Moreover, valuable and important embedded principles are required to join GRI and WBCSD (2018), which expand a real guiding principle and a glossary on CE that would assist corporations in managing their reporting disclosure in this course (see GRI-301, 302, 03, 304, 305, 306, 307, 308 and WBCSD, 2018). Specifically, it defines a set of disclosures derived from GRI requirements and other famous frameworks. On 2 April 2021, the EC adopted a proposal for the Corporate Sustainability Reporting Directive (CSRD). This directive states that the listed companies should disclose audit (assurance), audit reports, and sustainability information to the stakeholders and present a framework that will be used to disclose these practices.

At present, corporate financial and non-financial reporting has increasing popularity that refers to in detail economic, social, and environmental perspectives in one report (Barnabè & Nazir, 2020, 2022; IIRC, 2013a; Stewart & Niero, 2018). Although the value creation of the organization is a dynamic procedure, "*an ordinary survey of every part and its associations with different segments, and an emphasis on the organisation's outlook, lead to correction and refinement to improve all the operational segments*" (Barnabè & Nazir, 2020, 2022; IIRC, 2013a, p. 14). Integrated reporting (IR) incorporates non-financial information on social and environmental measures and coordinates these with financial reporting. Non-financial disclosure is incorporated with value creation and the aim of better environmental and socially sustainable development information communication with the stakeholders (Barnabè & Nazir, 2020, 2022; IIRC, 2013b) that can be used to create new accounting information and statements.

Research is associated with integrating CE-related reporting practices with companies' disclosure practices. Furthermore, the potential of sustainability reporting strategies to the resource within the legitimization and comparison of the environmental sustainability contributions of CE strategies that yet not to be explored. Currently, CE is being promoted as a key strategy inside the "European Green Deal," suggesting CE will "modernize the EU economy" (EC, 2019, p. 7) and include measures that encourage businesses to adopt CE practices. The Non-Financial Reporting Directive (EC, 2021) is being reviewed that grow the disclosure of climate and environmental information and ensure green investments and green revenue (EC, 2019, 2021). With these reporting trends, the most effective will not only be the quantity and quality of information required to be suggested via businesses in the close to future but also the number of organizations required to publish sustainability facts.

This growing importance emphasizes the need for guiding concepts to be included inside reporting strategies, making sure that high-quality and comparable CE-relating reports may be disclosed by businesses. However, before those guiding concepts and tactics can be proposed, studies are needed to make clear the modern demanding situations concerning CE reporting issues following the steering of reporting strategies.

Institutional Theory and Hypothesis Development

The institutional theory originated in the mid-twentieth century and keeps on evolving. It has been extensively used in the research field. The basic principles of the theory relate to how people and organizations behave not only with economic efficiency but also an organization's legitimacy (Abrutyn & Turner, 2011; Campbell, 2007; DiMaggio & Powell, 1983a, 1983b; Garvare & Johansson, 2010; Scott, 2005). This research adopted institutional theory, which is a widely accepted and recognized clarification of organization practices (Abrutyn & Turner, 2011; Campbell, 2007; DiMaggio & Powell, 1983a; Li & Ding, 2013) and can explore the significance of the organization's frameworks, structures, practices, and activities (Witjes & Lozano, 2016). The research adopted institutional theory to clarify the relationship between CE and environmental performance. These hypotheses can be used to clarify the reasons for how and to what extent organizations have implemented CE principles into their reporting practices. The institutional theory refers to three institutional isomorphisms (coercive, normative, and mimetic), which are used to observe basic elements of CE-R principles in organizational practices (Li & Ding, 2013).

Coercive isomorphism can originate from either formal or informal pressure applied to organizations by different state actors that are reliant on the potential of rules, regulations, and norms wherein organizations operate, which can be seen as power or influence (DiMaggio & Powell, 1983a; Li & Ding, 2013). Coercive pressures may emerge from government, NGOs, stakeholders, and investors involved in business policies, practices, and standards setters (Adams et al., 2011; Garvare & Johansson, 2010). Investors are viewed as influential and can exceptionally impact an organization's decision-making process and can apply pressure in recommending certain practices (Li & Ding, 2013). Organizations generally have to follow and demonstrate these practices in their financial and non-financial reporting practices. The institutional theory can be helpful in recognizing the mechanism between CE practices and reporting practices and proposing a hypothesis,

> H1: How and to what extent are CE-related R1-R6 principles disclosed in companies' reports?

While normative isomorphism refers to professionalization or social commitment, in which organizations normally adopt general guidelines, SOPs (standard operating procedures), rules, and regulations (A4S, 2022; GRI, 2010; KPMG, 2008, 2010; Mathews, 2008). Nowadays, organizations are confronting ambiguity concerning social, environmental, and economic conditions. Hence the demand for sustainable financial and non-financial disclosure is increasing. Renewable resources industries adopt some standards to disclose information in their reports (i.e., GRI, G4, SDGs) and participate in green accounting standards (Llena et al., 2007). While mimetic isomorphism starts from uncertainty, or mimicking behavior that is a result of organization responses to uncertainty (DiMaggio & Powell, 1983a; Li & Ding, 2013). Mimetic isomorphism incorporates organizations acting when they face uncertainty in accomplishing objectives that are unclear or uncertain, i.e., the COVID-19 period. When the organization's objectives are complex, organizations generally look at different strategies and follow these strategies over time. Prior researchers have highlighted some points that clarify organization principles and are a critical driver for the board in building a framework that provides information to explore sustainable development issues (Schroeder et al., 2018). The CE reporting relies on sustainability, law and guidance, income and costs, carbon-reducing strategies, resources and developments that are identified with soil, groundwater, and air pollution, removal of hazardous substances, removal of waste, risk management policy, liabilities, and decision-making process for the future development of sustainability inside and outside of the firm, and strategies (Barnabè & Nazir, 2020, 2022; EMF, 2013a, 2013b, 2022). Barnabè and Nazir (2022) argue that CE has an integrated relationship with financial and non-financial related key sustainability execution indicators that are relied upon to direct organizations toward CE reporting. Naeem Farid, et al. (2021) and Naeem and Karim (2021), additionally highlight those environmentally friendly investments, together with green bonds, have safe-haven properties that substantiate the function of those bonds closer to accomplishing sustainability.

Similarly, green energy productivity (Naeem, Adekoya, et al., 2021; Taghizadeh-Hesary et al., 2019, 2021), environmental stocks (Arif et al., 2021), and ethical investments (Liu & Peifer, 2022) are highlighted as acting not sufficiently during COVID-19 pandemic. In this manner, sustainable company environmental strategies are assumed to overtake others throughout durations of economic pressure. This study has concentrated on reporting practices and explores how and to what extent CE-related R principles information is disclosed in companies' sustainability reports. How environment performance can be improved by rearranging/redesigning operations and providing good shape information to the stakeholders. To the best of our knowledge, no specific studies have previously been examined in the context of CE. The research embraced institutional theory, which incorporates mechanisms to recognize corporate environmental performance and CE principles, and proposed a second hypothesis,

> H2: How and to what extent do CE-related R1-R6 principles engage with environmental Disclosure?

3 Data Collection & Research Design

To select suitable companies for analysis, the authors first investigate the 2022 ranking of the world's top 100 corporations (With permission), which was published by Knight Cooperation on 19 January 2022 (https://www.corporateknights.com/rankings/global-100-rankings/2022-global-100-rankings/100-most-sustainable-corporations-of-2022/). Corporate knight world 100 most sustainable companies based on careful measurement of nearly 7000 public companies with revenue over US 1 billion. For a more in-depth look at the pattern of companies, the authors used only a two-year sample of 74 companies that have ranked in 2020 and 2021 years (see Appendix 1). The author considers only English language reports of the companies for analysis.

The companies' annual and sustainability reports were retrieved from companies' websites and other records that are publicly available archive records, e.g., annual reports, sustainability reports, integrated reports, within sustainability reports, companies', GRI Database, Lexis Nexis. Secondly, the research access during the COVID-19 pandemic effects on the top 100 sustainable companies, that could open a new avenue for further comparative analysis of before and after COVID-19 effects.

The study used content analysis to determine the type and extent of CE-related information disclosure on the topmost sustainable companies. The next stage in content analysis is deciding the strategy for estimating each relevant exposure. Content analysis is a method for codifying text and putting written statement content into datasets or groups, dependent on selected measures, with the ultimate objective of changing the material into quantitative scales that grant further investigation (Weber et al., 1988). It has been generally utilized in writing financial and non-financial disclosures (Campbell, 2007; de Villiers & Sharma, 2020; Gray, 2002; Moroney & Trotman, 2016).

As mentioned, this study analyzed the top 100 most sustainable corporations' annual reports using *content analysis*, which is "a research technique for the objective, systematic and qualitative description of the manifest content of communication" (Berelson, 1952). Notably, this technique can be used with either qualitative or quantitative data and allows organizing "the text of writing into various groups or categories based on selected criteria" (Guthrie et al., 2004, p. 287).

In content analyses, data are usually calculated and used for measuring and communicating the relevance of the subject matter (Krippendorff, 2004), which may help evaluate the amount of disclosure about a specific concept or group of concepts (Milne & Adler, 1999). It is to emphasize that content analysis in the field of annual reporting has already been used and is recognized as a reliable research method (e.g., Guthrie & Abeysekera, 2006; Milne & Adler, 1999). The research design entailed searching for CE-related concepts in the company's annual reports.

The former items (concepts) were searched through content analysis (Krippendorff, 2004), and according to a top-down process, the glossary (single concepts, groups, and/or categories of concepts) was defined *ex-ante* (Schilling, 2006). To this end, the authors created a specific codebook (Neuendorf, 2002) that exists both in the services and manufacturing sectors. The codebook concepts were searched through content analysis (Krippendorff, 2018) using the NVivo software—the codebook aimed to aid in the development of more standardized and established terminology for CE research. For the validation of the codebook, the authors used the US Chamber of Commerce (https://www.uschamberfoundation.org/circular-economy-toolbox/about-circularity/glossary), a leading circular economy Ellen MacArthur Foundation (https://ellenmacarthurfoundation.org/topics/circular-economy-introduction/glossary), world business council for sustainable development (https://www.ceguide.org/Glossary) glossary, different authors definition used and expert opinions on this behalf. A list of CE-related R1 to R6 principles in a codebook was created (see Appendix 2).

This coding process signifies a conceptual analysis of words. Each code in the codebook was perused to decide what range a particular variable represented. Every variable was coded for this power utilizing a scale of 0 and 1 referenced (Maroun & Prinsloo, 2020).

0 = No reference of [variable]; 1 = [variable].

Where: CED_{it}: Circular Economy Disclosure Index of R1 to R6 for company t,

N_i: Total index items, $N_i \leq 30$, X_{it}:

Content analysis,

1 = if item I is disclosed,
0 = if item I is not disclosed,
r1–r6: Reduce, Reuse, Recycle, Remanufacture, Redesign and Recover.
So that, $0 \leq \text{CED} \leq 1$.

$$\text{CED}_{it} = \sum_{r6}^{r1} X_{it}/N_i$$

Moreover, the study used environmental variables scores retrieved from Knight Cooperation (https://www.corporateknights.com/rankings/global-100-rankings/) (Copyright permission) and DataStream which covers the GRI-300 series of disclosure and also variables follow the directions of climate bonds taxonomy (Climate bonds Initiatives), European union taxonomy for sustainable activities, sustainability account standards board (SASB) reporting standards, environmental goods and services sectors (Eurostat), China Green Bond Endorsed Project Catalogue, green Bond Principles, TCFD recommended climate opportunity metrics, other private sectors rating agencies with green or sustainability taxonomy and industry experts consultation that covering all relevant industries subsectors.

Furthermore, we did the first top ten companies as a polite study. See what trends companies revealed and get some expert recommendations and suggestions. Furthermore, the authors check the sample reliability. Reliability analysis consists of data purity and consistency of a measure with no repeatability or probity of obtaining the same results again if the data were duplicated. Reliability is a technique that allows the same results to be attained repeatedly (De Vaus, 1982). Acceptable reliability is required for the validation of the sample. The reliability refers to the sample and how the dataset is free from random error. Commonly, the researchers used Cronbach's alpha coefficient ranging from 0 to 1 to check the sample reliability if higher refers to greater reliability. Usually, acceptable Cronbach's alpha is in between the range of 0.6–0.7. If Cronbach's alpha is below 0.06, that is considered poor, and above 0.8 refers to good (Nunnally, 1978). We calculated Cronbach's Alpha and found that it is 0.895, respectively. Therefore, it means that our multidimensional dataset is reliable for analysis. Additionally, the relation between the dependent and independent variables (one or more) was examined to test the hypotheses. Dependent variables consist of the CE-related R1 to R6, and independent variables consist of waste productivity (see Fig. 1) and control variables such as energy productivity, GHGs productivity, water productivity, VOC productivity, NOx productivity, Sox productivity, PM productivity, revenue, and investment while industry, year and county have fixed effects variables and the error term (see Appendix 3, independent and dependent variables).

To explore the relation between two or more variables, the coefficient examines the effects of variables on CE-related R1 to R6 principles and

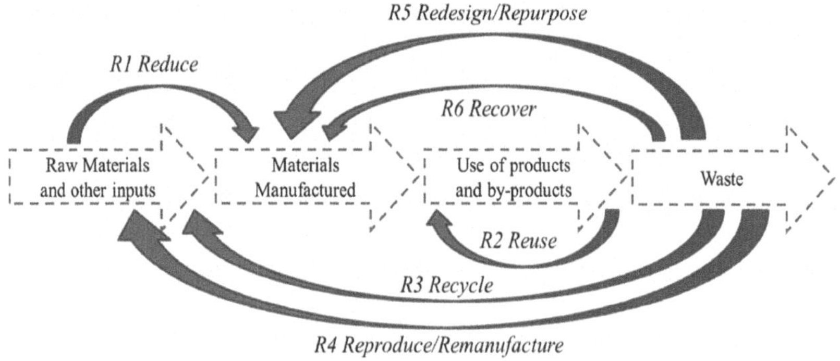

Fig. 1 Representation of the CE-6R framework (*Source* Barnabe and Nazir [2022])

has a statistically significant effect on variables. The study estimates the following CE-R1-model-1 to the CE-R6-model-6 by this equation (i.e., CED_{it} denotes R1, R2, R3, R4, R5 and R6):

$$\begin{aligned} CED_{it} = \beta_0 &+ \beta WAST_{it} + \beta ENGP_{it} + \beta GHGP_{it} \\ &+ \beta WATP_{it} + \beta VOCP_{it} + \beta NOXP_{it} \\ &+ \beta SOXP_{it} + \beta PMP_{it} + \beta REV_{it} \\ &+ \beta INV_{it} + Country_i + Year_t + Industry_i + \varepsilon \end{aligned}$$

4 Findings & Discussion

Table 1 shows the descriptive statistics for the study variables. The average minimum score of CE principles is R5, R6, and 0.2, respectively, and the maximum is 1 in all CE principles. The CE-R1 and R3 disclosure scores have a 0.6 minimum while R1 to R6 have a 1 Maximum score, while the R3 and R5 scores have a minimum score of 0.4 and 0.2, respectively. On the other side, for the investment, carbon, water, waste, VOC, NOX, SOX, and PM, the minimum score is 0 while the energy and revenue scores are 0.01 and 0.17, respectively. This finding is consistent with our first hypothesis that companies' sustainability reports disclosed CE-R1 to R6 principles in their reports.

Table 2 shows the correlation among all variables. All correlation coefficients are below 80% which indicates that there is no serious multicollinearity (reference). The highest coefficient is between firm water productivity and energy productivity. The result of the variance inflation factor (VIF) shows the maximum VIF of NOx is 2.39 and Sox 2.17, respectively, while the lowest tolerance coefficient is 0.41. Therefore, multicollinearity is not a problem in the current study.

Besides, Table 3 represents the parameter test. Model 1 states that WASTP (−1.712), VOCP (2.005), and REV (2.032) have a significant association ($p < 0.05$) and WATP (3.057) have a highly significant association (0.001) with reduce principle. While CE-R2, WATP (3.057) highly significant association, VOCP (2.081 medium $p < 0.05$) and

Table 1 Descriptive statistic

	Minimum	Maximum	Mean	Std. deviation
R1	0.80	1.00	0.84	0.08
R2	0.80	1.00	0.84	0.08
R3	0.40	1.00	0.84	0.12
R4	0.80	1.00	0.83	0.07
R5	0.20	1.00	0.72	0.15
R6	0.20	1.00	0.81	0.17
WASTP	0.00	1.00	0.44	0.30
ENGP	0.01	0.98	0.52	0.27
GHGP	0.00	1.00	0.45	0.28
WATP	0.00	1.00	0.45	0.29
VOCP	0.00	1.00	0.23	0.32
NOXP	0.00	1.00	0.24	0.30
SOXP	0.00	1.00	0.21	0.31
PMP	0.00	1.00	0.18	0.31
REV	0.17	1.00	0.82	0.19
INV	0.00	1.00	0.66	0.35

Table 2 Pearson's correlation coefficient for the full sample

	R1	R2	R3	R4	R5	R6	WASTP	ENGP	GHGP	WATP	VOCP	NOXP	SOXP	PMP	REV	INV
R1	1															
R2	0.980**	1														
R3	0.598**	0.585**	1													
R4	0.622**	0.609**	0.308**	1												
R5	0.158	0.187*	0.161	0.154	1											
R6	0.435**	0.430**	0.261**	0.195*	−0.072	1										
WASTP	−0.040	−0.026	−0.059	0.028	.280**	0.056	1									
ENGP	0.213**	0.228**	0.257**	0.188*	0.450**	−0.044	0.336**	1								
GHGP	0.111	0.128	0.161	0.050	0.278**	0.033	0.223**	0.568**	1							
WATP	0.315**	0.329**	0.205*	0.242**	0.404**	0.152	0.339**	0.557**	0.484**	1						
VOCP	0.202*	0.226**	0.179*	0.156	−0.083	0.259**	0.218**	0.121	0.032	0.210*	1					
NOXP	0.051	0.092	−0.014	−0.123	−0.050	0.169*	0.204*	−0.068	0.100	0.203*	0.486**	1				
SOXP	0.061	0.101	0.013	−0.075	−0.002	0.156	0.228**	−0.005	0.227**	0.317**	0.315**	0.670**	1			
PMP	0.105	0.127	0.098	−0.088	0.005	0.152	0.291**	0.098	0.172*	0.262**	0.534**	0.587**	0.517**	1		
REV	0.222**	0.207*	0.027	0.120	−0.216**	0.344**	−0.217**	−0.074	−0.073	−0.026	0.041	0.005	0.112	0.097	1	
INV	0.204*	0.180*	0.141	0.076	−0.085	0.375**	−0.009	0.018	−0.030	0.070	0.003	−0.009	0.028	0.094	0.267**	1

*Correlation is significant at the 0.05 level (2-tailed)
**Correlation is significant at the 0.01 level (2-tailed)

REV 1.874 ($p < 0.1$) found a significant association ($p < 0.01$). WASTP (0.017), ENGP (0.061), VOCP (0.040), and INV (0.102) are significant associations with CE-R3 respectively. On the other hand, WATP (2.758 with $p < 0.01$), VOCP (3.027 with $p < 0.01$), NOXP (−1.357 with $p < 0.01$), and PMP (−1.981, $p < 0.05$) had a significant engagement with CE-R4 principles. While CE-R5 redesign loop is a significant association with ENGP (3.011 with $p < 0.01$), WATP (2.837 with $p < 0.01$), VOCP (−2.203 with $p < 0.05$), and REV (3.659, $p < 0.05$), respectively. Lastly, the CE-R6 is closely engaged with revenue and investment ($p < 0.01$). However, all parameters have significant intercept effects.

Moreover, CE-R1 to CE-R6 principles such as reducing, reusing, recycling, remanufacturing, redesigning, and recovery have an association with the environmental performance matrix. The COVID-19 pandemic has supplied a context for firms to provoke change through sustainable practices and apply a converted framework to value creation in their operations. The European Commission (2019) has outlined numerous shifts within supply chain practices in the direction of the ecosystem structure (Mattera and Ruiz-Morales, 2020; Wang et al., 2021; Zhuo et al., 2021). To initiate modifications, a company requires infrastructure sources of different internal and external communication channels to address the demanding situations of the uncompromising environment. To reap sustainable development operations, it's essential to include corporate recognition and firm financial outcomes as sizeable keys to the ladder of implementation (Teece, 2010; Umar, Su, Rizvi, & Lobonţ, 2021; Umar, Su, Rizvi & Shao, 2021). Environmental performance has considerably changed the socio-economic shape of every company. Therefore, modern company strategies require maintaining environmental stability between sustainable reporting practices and the value creation process (Gaur et al., 2019). Given that current practices do shape the cutting-edge challenging business environment, companies and regulatory bodies that are adopting new practices to realize the sustainability approach and develop new sustainability standards (Adams & Abhayawansa, 2022; Aguilar-Rivera, 2022; Naeem et al., 2022; Tettamanzi et al., 2022). Beyond profitability, corporations need to be more knowledgeable concerning the sustainability of their companies and environmental disclosure structures (El-Kassar &

Table 3 Regression results of R1 to R6

	Model 1 R1	Model 2 R2	Model 3 R3	Model 4 R4	Model 5 R5	Model 6 R6
WASTP	−1.712**	−1.770*	−2.425***	−0.017	1.345	1.149
	(0.089)	(0.079)	(0.017)	(0.986)	(0.181)	(0.253)
ENGP	0.902	1.131	1.885**	0.329	3.011***	−2.200**
	(0.369)	(0.260)	(0.061)	(0.742)	(0.003)	(0.030)
GHGP	−0.319	−0.316	0.350	−0.433	−0.586	1.204
	(0.750)	(0.752)	(0.727)	(0.666)	(0.559)	(0.231)
WATP	3.057***	2.941***	0.899	2.758***	2.837***	1.642*
	(0.003)	(0.004)	(0.370)	(0.007)	(0.005)	(0.103)
VOCP	2.005**	2.081**	2.072**	3.027***	−2.203**	2.977**
	(0.047)	(0.039)	(0.040)	(0.003)	(0.029)	(0.003)
NOXP	−0.039	0.179	−0.964	−1.357*	0.034	0.651
	(0.969)	(0.858)	(0.337)	(0.177)	(0.973)	(0.516)
SOXP	−0.515	−0.226	0.125	−0.390	−0.314	−0.446
	(0.607)	(0.821)	(0.901)	(0.697)	(0.754)	(0.656)
PMP	−0.331	−0.412	0.498	−1.981**	0.221	−1.316
	(0.741)	(0.681)	(0.619)	(0.050)	(0.825)	(0.191)
REV	2.032**	1.874*	−0.598	1.544	−1.775**	3.659***
	(0.044)	(0.063)	(0.551)	(0.125)	(0.078)	(0.000)
INV	1.740**	1.488*	1.648*	0.464	−0.998	4.170***
	(0.084)	(0.109)	(0.102)	(0.643)	(0.320)	(0.000)
Intercept	21.126***	20.957***	14.775***	25.755***	11.695***	7.097***
	(0.000)	(0.000)	(0.000)	(0.000)	(0.000)	(0.000)
R^2	0.217	0.218	0.155	0.18	0.315	0.31
Industry fixed effects	Yes					
Year fixed effects	Yes					
Country fixed effects	Yes					
N	148					

T statistics in parentheses $*p < 0.1$, $**p < 0.05$, $***p < 0.01$

Singh, 2019). Since sustainable company strategies are based on the premise of a triple bottom line, it needs to adopt a robust commitment to those strategic movements for long-lasting advantages. The parameters Table 3 shows the companies involved the recycling waste activities and renewable energy activities. The European Green Deal represents over 73% of the EU's overall gross cost added by manufacturing and services industries (EC, 2019). Although the service industry is not energy-intensive (EMF, 2013a, 2013b), it is liable for 13% of electricity intake inside the EU28 (Eurostat, 2016). It also had a bigger expansion in electricity consumption (30%) than every other industry from 1990 to 2014 (Eurostat, 2016). Consequently, the service sector is likewise a huge contributor to greenhouse gas (GHG) emissions, contributing over 5% (310 Mt) of the total GHG emissions inside the EU (EEA, 2015). The scale of this resource (material and power) consumption and GHG emissions indicates that services-orientated companies can play a great position in enhancing resource efficiency and climate exchange mitigation. Nikseresht et al. (2022) highlight that using artificial intelligence to develop closed-loop business models in services-orientated businesses, together with asset management businesses can grow operational resource efficiency and sustainability overall performance. Similarly, the use of sustainable technologies employing service suppliers can produce reaching environmental and climate change mitigation objectives and targets on regional, national, and worldwide stages (EMF, 2020).

Additionally, the UN's (2015), agenda 2030, refers to the specific sustainable development goals (SDGs) and identifies targets that address people's prosperity in the shape of environmental, social, and economic factors. Under SDG 12 "responsible consumption and production" industries should accomplish values by applying efficient and effective utilization of materials, resources, and participation in sustainable development. However, the UN (2015) and CE follow the strategies of preservation of natural resources, using the strategy of reducing material consumption, recovery of resources through waste and implementing new business models in the organization. UN (2015) Agenda 2030 focuses on implementing different approaches to boost organization's economic, social, and environmentally sustainable practices and disclosed these practices in the organization's annual and biannual reports but still a gap remains in how GRI participates to provide well-defined information on stakeholder for rational decision-making and increase green investment. Table 3 shows that the top companies are involved in the recycling of waste, redesigning, reproduction, and recovery of energy and water which have effects on the company's revenue and investment. Besides, actions have been made by various regions and governments to encourage this, for example, the European Union's (EU) paper "Towards a circular economy: A zero waste program for Europe." Besides, the EC (2014) established frameworks for the development of CE in the EU. Among the EU's directives are those concerning plastics, energy recovery from waste and basic raw materials (EC, 2018), sustainable power resources, eco-design, and energy productivity (EC, 2015; Ghisellini et al., 2016; Mathews & Tan, 2011). Correspondingly, different nations are utilizing the CE principles among their organizations (Aranda-Usón et al., 2020).

To ensure the validity of the reported results, Table 4 shows the Robust Standard Errors in parentheses that have a significant effect on CE R principles. Whereas GHGs have engaged with the CE-R2 activity. WATP is closely associated with the reduce, reuse, redesign, remanufacturing and recover CE principles. Waste productivity is closely associated with reduce, reuse, and recycling principles. VOCP is closely associated with CE R1 to R6 principles, respectively. On the other hand, the PMP has a significant association with the R4 and R6, respectively. The robust standard error shows that REV is significantly associated with all CE-R6 principles except R3 this means that the revenue is closely associated with the reduce, reuse, redesign, remanufacturing, and recover principles. The company's investment is in close association with recycling and recovery principles. The corporate environment management principle forces us to rethink the approach to waste, renewable energy, water, and GHG emissions at their initial stage of products. At the start of the manufacturing process, the producer's responsibility to think about the recyclability of the product and its packaging. This is an essential step toward achieving a circular economic system. Waste is a natural part of the product life cycle because it's far the leftover of the completed product. Product residues have been dismantled and recycled in natural surroundings for many years, but the industrialization and enlargement of the chemical business have resulted in the emergence of a few sorts of durable materials and waste that are not effortlessly dissolved. If we take plastic as an instance, it'll stay dissolved in the natural surroundings for dozens or hundreds of years because the majority of often-used polymers aren't biodegradable (Jadaun et al., 2022). The European Commission report on Bio-inspired computing (2022) estimates that the services business accounts for approximately 1 billion tonnes of annual raw material inputs inside the European Union (EU), which is more than double the overall resource consumption of this area for twenty years in the past. Corporations may be described as agencies whose major interest is to provide service products that represent "entities over which possession rights can't be set. They cannot be traded one by one from their production" and are "produced to order and generally consist of changes inside the situations of the consuming components, due to the activities of producers on the request of the purchasers" (EU, 2021). In the measurement of CE at the small-scale level, specific indicators have been applied to check company performance (Barnabè & Nazir, 2022; Kühl et al., 2022) and customers' behaviors (Johansen, et al., 2022). A few studies have been taken to estimate the extent of CE accomplished by an organization in general (Aranda-Usón et al., 2019; Barnabè & Nazir, 2020, 2021), but there is still no consensus on the best way to measure the various CE principles environmental wise (GRI-300 series wise). Specifically, the estimation of the resource and organizations environmental capital capacities is still not analyzed.

The additional analysis provides the validation of the results. The first column shows the coefficient of the CE-6Rs. If the companies adopted all these 6Rs practices and disclosed this information in their annual reports, then it would provide a good source of information on the effects on companies' investment and revenue, on the other hand, the companies also preserve natural resources, particularly water and participate in the agenda of the UN, SDG 12 for the preservation of resources and responsible consumption. While the second column of the Table 5 shows a CE-6Rs robustness check. That also refers to the engagement of CE6-Rs with the revenue, investment, and water productivity. On the other hand, the intercept significantly has effects among all dependent variables.

Table 4 Robustness check of R1 to R6

	R1	R2	R3	R4	R5	R6
WASTP	−1.817**	−1.875**	−2.482***	−0.017	1.172	1.213
	(0.071)	(0.063)	(0.014)	(0.987)	(0.243)	(0.227)
ENGP	0.877	1.099	1.577*	0.323	2.591***	−1.891**
	(0.382)	(0.274)	(0.117)	(0.747)	(0.011)	(0.061)
GHGP	−0.301	−0.298	0.331	−0.367	−0.633	0.976
	(0.764)	(0.766)	(0.741)	(0.714)	(0.528)	(0.331)
WATP	3.080***	2.994***	0.549	2.471**	3.272***	1.868*
	(0.003)	(0.003)	(0.584)	(0.015)	(0.001)	(0.064)
VOCP	1.622*	1.693**	1.897**	2.238**	−1.994**	2.861***
	(0.107)	(0.093)	(0.060)	(0.027)	(0.048)	(0.005)
NOXP	−0.036	0.166	−1.056	−1.530	0.031	0.894
	(0.971)	(0.869)	(0.293)	(0.128)	(0.975)	(0.373)
SOXP	−0.422	−0.181	0.114	−0.324	−0.277	−0.628
	(0.673)	(0.856)	(0.910)	(0.747)	(0.782)	(0.531)
PMP	−0.289	−0.363	0.449	−1.979**	0.232	−1.653***
	(0.773)	(0.717)	(0.654)	(0.050)	(0.817)	(0.101)
REV	2.232**	2.072**	−0.611	1.688*	−1.650**	2.248**
	(0.027)	(0.040)	(0.542)	(0.094)	(0.101)	(0.026)
INV	1.954**	1.657*	1.772*	0.494	−0.973	2.786***
	(0.053)	(0.100)	(0.079)	(0.622)	(0.332)	(0.006)
Intercept	20.963***	21.232***	15.053***	25.407***	10.958***	4.778***
	(0.000)	(0.000)	(0.000)	(0.000)	(0.000)	(0.000)
Industry fixed effects	Yes					
Year fixed effects	Yes					
Country fixed effects	Yes					
N	148					

$^*p < 0.1$, $^{**}p < 0.5$, $^{***}p < .01$

Table 5 Additional analysis

	Model 7 (1)	Model 7 (2)
WASTP	−0.541 (0.589)	−0.544 (0.587)
ENGP	1.211 (0.228)	1.112 (0.268)
GHGP	0.160 (0.873)	0.135 (0.892)
WATP	3.449*** (0.001)	3.029*** (0.003)
VOCP	2.291** (0.024)	1.741** (0.084)
NOXP	−0.237 (0.813)	−0.237 (0.813)
SOXP	−0.440 (0.660)	−0.389 (0.698)
PMP	−0.736 (0.463)	−0.640 (0.523)
REV	1.596* (0.103)	1.564* (0.110)
INV	2.412*** (0.017)	2.340** (0.021)
Intercept	23.457*** (0.000)	21.446 (0.000)
Industry fixed effects	Yes	
Year fixed effects	Yes	
Country fixed effects	Yes	
N	148	

$*p < 0.1$, $**p < 0.5$, $***p < .01$

5 Conclusion

In this paper, we introduced a preliminary empirical-based study of CE-6Rs principles disclosure in companies reporting practices; as mentioned, sustainability reporting is assuming an increasing role in the business communication processes (e.g., Adams & Abhayawansa 2022; Barnabè & Nazir, 2020, 2022). Its actual use to effectively disclose data about CE principles is still under-researched, thus calling for more investigation and evidence (e.g., Barnabè & Nazir 2022; Stewart & Niero, 2018).

The starting point and the motivation of this research are related to the observation of what happens daily in our real world: in detail, the literature and environmental phenomena demonstrate that we cannot delay any more CE initiatives. For academics, this entails supporting companies in the effort of launching and managing such initiatives, but also measuring the impacts of the actions that were carried out and subsequently reporting the key results achieved to a broad range of stakeholders. A broad literature witnesses that CE initiatives are actually at the center of the modern organizations' agenda, but also that further research is needed to explore how (and somehow if) those initiatives were monitored and communicated to relevant stakeholders. Within this context, the sustainability and environmental matrix may certainly offer a potentially powerful tool that companies all over the world could use to disclose their CE initiatives and the main results stemming from them. If the GRI-300 directive and CE loops, how and to what extent do loops encircle and generate a new accounting structure while behind the law, regulation, and directive that support these sustainability reporting practices?

In more detail, and starting from these considerations, this study explored the primary nexus of environmental with CE reporting issues and activities. In detail, through content analysis, the study provided data useful to investigate how and to what extent companies' sustainability reports disclose CE-related information. Subsequently, we inspected our sample of reports looking for CE-related environmental scores.

At the same time, our analysis showed that companies are—at least somehow—open to the use of score representations within their operations, even though companies' environmental scores are closely related to CE-related principles and concepts. As Model 1 states WASTP (−1.712), WATP (3.057), REV (2.032) and INV (1.740) have a significant association with CE reduce principle and reuse principle found a significant association with WASTP (−1.770), WATP (2.941), VOCP (2.081) and REV (1.874) and INV (1.488). WASTP (−2.425), ENGP (1.812), VOCP (2.075), and INV (1.648) are significant associations with the CE recycle principle, respectively. This shows that waste is closely engaged with the reduce, reuse, and recycling principles and also impacts companies' revenue as well as investment.

WATP suggests that (2.758 with $p < 0.01$), VOCP (3.027 with $p < 0.01$), and PMP (−1.981, $p < 0.05$) had a significant engagement with CE-R4 principles. While CE-R5 redesign loop is a significant association with ENGP (3.011 with $p < 0.01$), WATP (2.837 with $p < 0.01$), VOCP (−2.203 < 0.05), and revenue (0.078 $p < 0.10$), respectively. CE-R6 loop is closely engaged with revenue and investment ($p < 0.01$).

6 Limitations

Our study provides a preliminary analysis and has certainly some limitations. One limitation of the study may be linked to its research focuses on environmental disclosure of companies within certain years effects but that could be helpful to see the before and after consequences of COVID-19. This is the first empirical base analysis of CE-6Rs based on the manufacturing and services industry but opens a new avenue of research that could be used for the comparative analysis of the manufacturing and services industry.

7 Further Research

The study also used the country-fixed effects that could open up a new research area where comparative analysis can be done by countries and see the developing and developing countries' rules and regulations on behalf of CE principles and reporting patterns. Another limitation of this study is that it draws upon a rather limited sample of companies' reports. Anyhow, these limitations also open avenues for further research, specifically for the development of a qualitative exploratory case study (Ryan, 2002; Yin, 1994). Additionally, the study develops a unison codebook of CE terms that could be used to see the social side of companies.

8 Practical Implications

Moreover, CE-R1 to CE-R6 principles such as reducing, reusing, recycling, remanufacturing, redesigning, and recovering have an association with the environmental performance matrix. If the companies adopted all these 6Rs practices and disclosed this information in their annual reports, then it would provide a good source of information on the effects on companies' investment and preservation of natural resources, particularly water and participate in the agenda of the UN (2015), SDG, 12 for the preservation of resources and responsible consumption.

Appendix 1: Dataset of Top Sustainable Companies

N	Companies	Country	*N*	Industry	*N*
1	Adidas AG	Australia	6	Appliances and lighting fixtures manufacturing	2
2	Agnico Eagle Mines Ltd	Austria	2	Asset management	2
3	Allianz SE	Brazil	4	Banks	16
4	Alphabet Inc	Canada	22	Cars and trucks manufacturing, including parts	4
5	Alstom SA	China	4	Commercial building construction	4
6	American Water Works Company Inc	Denmark	8	Computers and peripherals manufacturing	8
7	Analog Devices Inc	Finland	8	Food and beverage manufacturing	6
8	Arcelik AS	France	12	Furniture and general manufacturing N.E.C.	2
9	AstraZeneca PLC	Germany	10	Grocery stores	2

(continued)

(continued)

N	Companies	Country	N	Industry	N
10	Atlantica Sustainable Infrastructure PLC	Hong Kong	2	HVAC equipment manufacturing	2
11	Autodesk Inc	Ireland	2	Industrial Conglomerates	2
12	Banco do Brasil SA	Italy	2	Insurance companies	6
13	Bank of Montreal	Japan	6	IT services except telecom and hosting	10
14	BNP Paribas SA	Netherlands	4	Machinery manufacturing	4
15	Brambles Ltd	Norway	2	Metal and coal mining	4
16	BT Group PLC	Singapore	6	Non-road transport equipment manufacturing	2
17	Byd Co Ltd	South Korea	2	Packaging	2
18	Canadian Tire Corporation Ltd	Spain	4	Personal and business services	6
19	CapitaLand Investment Ltd	Sweden	2	Personal products (retail chemical)	6
20	Cascades Inc	Taiwan	2	Pharmaceutical & Biotech	8
21	Chr Hansen Holding A/S	Turkey	2	Plastic and rubber product manufacturing	2
22	Cisco Systems Inc	United Kingdom	10	Power generation	6
23	City Developments Ltd	United States of America	26	Power transmission and distribution	2
24	Cogeco Communications Inc			Real estate and leasing	4
25	Commerzbank AG			Refining, petrochemicals, and basic organic chemicals	2
26	Dassault Systems SE			Residential construction	2
27	Eisai Co Ltd			Retail, except grocery and auto	6

(continued)

(continued)

N	Companies	Country	N	Industry	N
28	Henkel AG & Co KgaA			Semiconductor and electronic components manufacturing	8
29	Hewlett Packard Enterprise Co			Smelters and steel-making	2
30	HP Inc			Telecom providers	8
31	Iberdrola SA			Telephones and telecom equipment manufacturing	4
32	IGM Financial Inc			Textiles and clothing manufacturing	2
33	Industria de Diseno Textil SA			Water and sewage treatment	2
34	ING Groep NV				
35	Intel Corp				
36	Intesa Sanpaolo SpA				
37	Johnson Controls International PLC				
38	Kering SA				
39	Kesko Oyj				
40	Konica Minolta Inc				
41	Koninklijke KPN NV				
42	Lenovo Group Ltd				
43	McCormick & Company Inc				
44	Metso Outotec Corp				
45	National Australia Bank Ltd				
46	Natura & Co Holding SA				
47	Neste Oyj				
48	Nordea Bank Abp				
49	Novozymes A/S				
50	Orsted A/S				
51	Pearson PLC				
52	Prologis Inc				
53	Samsung SDI Co Ltd				
54	Sanofi SA				

(continued)

(continued)

N	Companies	Country	*N*	Industry	*N*
55	SAP SE				
56	Schneider Electric SE				
57	Sekisui Chemical Co Ltd				
58	Sims Ltd				
59	Stantec Inc				
60	StarHub Ltd				
61	Storebrand ASA				
62	Sun Life Financial Inc				
63	Teck Resources Ltd				
64	Telefonaktiebolaget LM Ericsson				
65	Telus Corp				
66	Tesla Inc				
67	Transcontinental Inc				
68	TSMC				
69	Unilever PLC				
70	Verbund AG				
71	Vestas Wind Systems A/S				
72	Vitasoy International Holdings Ltd				
73	Workday Inc				
74	Xerox Holdings Corp				
Total	148				

Appendix 2: Circular Economy R1 to R6 Variable

	Items	%	Sources
Reduce (R1)	Reduce energy consumption	16.66	WBCSD Glossary, GRI, Kirchherr et al. (2017), Jawahir and Bradley (2016), Reike et al. (2018), and Fonseca et al. (2018)
	Reduce water consumption		WBCSD Glossary, GRI, Kirchherr et al. (2017), Jawahir and Bradley (2016), Reike et al. (2018), and Fonseca et al. (2018)
	Reduce plastic waste		US chamber glossary, GRI, WBCSD Glossary, Kirchherr et al. (2017), and Fonseca et al. (2018)
	Reduce material consumption		US chamber glossary, GRI, WBCSD Glossary, Kirchherr et al. (2017), Jawahir and Bradley (2016), Reike et al. (2018), and Fonseca et al. (2018)
	Reduce carbon emission		US chamber glossary, GRI, WBCSD Glossary, Kirchherr et al. (2017), Jawahir and Bradley (2016), Reike et al. (2018), and Fonseca et al. (2018)
Reuse (R2)	Renewable energy	16.66	US chamber glossary, GRI, WBCSD Glossary, Kirchherr et al. (2017), Jawahir and Bradley (2016), Reike et al. (2018), and Fonseca et al. (2018)
	Reuse products, parts, material		US chamber glossary, GRI, WBCSD Glossary, Kirchherr et al. (2017), Jawahir and Bradley (2016), Reike et al. (2018), and Fonseca et al. (2018)
	Product by product		US chamber glossary, GRI, WBCSD Glossary, Kirchherr et al. (2017), Jawahir and Bradley (2016), Reike et al. (2018), and Fonseca et al. (2018)
	Reuse water		US chamber glossary, GRI, WBCSD Glossary, Kirchherr et al. (2017), Jawahir and Bradley (2016), Reike et al. (2018), and Fonseca et al. (2018)
	Reuse plastic, packaging		US chamber glossary, GRI, WBCSD Glossary, Kirchherr et al. (2017), Jawahir and Bradley (2016), Reike et al. (2018), and Fonseca et al. (2018)
Recycle (R3)	Waste to energy productivity	16.66	US chamber glossary, GRI, WBCSD Glossary, Kirchherr et al. (2017), Jawahir and Bradley (2016), Reike et al. (2018), and Fonseca et al. (2018)

(continued)

(continued)

	Items	%	Sources
	Zero waste		US chamber glossary, GRI, WBCSD Glossary, Kirchherr et al. (2017), Jawahir and Bradley (2016), Reike et al. (2018), and Fonseca et al. (2018)
	Waste material Recycling		US chamber glossary, GRI, WBCSD Glossary, Kirchherr et al. (2017), Jawahir and Bradley (2016), Reike et al. (2018), and Fonseca et al. (2018)
	Hazardous materials recycling		US chamber glossary, GRI, WBCSD Glossary, Kirchherr et al. (2017), Jawahir and Bradley (2016), Reike et al. (2018), and Fonseca et al. (2018)
	Packaging, plastic, recycling		US chamber glossary, GRI, WBCSD Glossary, Kirchherr et al. (2017), Jawahir and Bradley (2016), Reike et al. (2018), and Fonseca et al. (2018)
Reproduce/ remanufacture (R4)	Remanufacture	16.66	US chamber glossary, GRI, WBCSD Glossary, Kirchherr et al. (2017), Jawahir and Bradley (2016), Reike et al. (2018), and Fonseca et al. (2018)
	Reproduce by original parts or material		US chamber glossary, GRI, WBCSD Glossary, Kirchherr et al. (2017), Jawahir and Bradley (2016), Reike et al. (2018), and Fonseca et al. (2018)
	Repair products and parts		US chamber glossary, GRI, WBCSD Glossary, Kirchherr et al. (2017), Jawahir and Bradley (2016), Reike et al. (2018), and Fonseca et al. (2018)
	Resource digitalization		US chamber glossary, GRI, WBCSD Glossary, Kirchherr et al. (2017), Jawahir and Bradley (2016), Reike et al. (2018), and Fonseca et al. (2018)
	Producer. Supplier responsibility		US chamber glossary, GRI, WBCSD Glossary, Kirchherr et al. (2017), Jawahir and Bradley (2016), Reike et al. (2018), and Fonseca et al. (2018)
Redesign/ repurpose (R5)	Redesign old products and parts	16.66	US chamber glossary, GRI, WBCSD Glossary, Kirchherr et al. (2017), Jawahir and Bradley (2016), Reike et al. (2018), and Fonseca et al. (2018)

(continued)

(continued)

	Items	%	Sources
	Repurpose products and parts, services		US chamber glossary, GRI, WBCSD Glossary, Kirchherr et al. (2017), Jawahir and Bradley (2016), Reike et al. (2018), and Fonseca et al. (2018)
	Extend the product life cycle		US chamber glossary, GRI, WBCSD Glossary, Kirchherr et al. (2017), Jawahir and Bradley (2016), Reike et al. (2018), and Fonseca et al. (2018)
	Eco-design		US chamber glossary, GRI, WBCSD Glossary, Kirchherr et al. (2017), Jawahir and Bradley (2016), Reike et al. (2018), and Fonseca et al. (2018)
	Regenerative energy, water, and waste productivity		US chamber glossary, GRI, WBCSD Glossary, Kirchherr et al. (2017), Jawahir and Bradley (2016), Reike et al. (2018), and Fonseca et al. (2018)
Recover (R6)	Waste recovery	16.66%	US chamber glossary, GRI, WBCSD Glossary, Kirchherr et al. (2017), Jawahir and Bradley (2016), Reike et al. (2018), and Fonseca et al. (2018)
	Waste hierarchy		US chamber glossary, GRI, WBCSD Glossary, Kirchherr et al. (2017), Jawahir and Bradley (2016), Reike et al. (2018), and Fonseca et al. (2018)
	Recover product, parts		US chamber glossary, GRI, WBCSD Glossary, Kirchherr et al. (2017), Jawahir and Bradley (2016), Reike et al. (2018), and Fonseca et al. (2018)
	Waste to the energy recovery rate		US chamber glossary, GRI, WBCSD Glossary, Kirchherr et al. (2017), Jawahir and Bradley (2016), Reike et al. (2018), and Fonseca et al. (2018)
	Recover natural resources from waste		US chamber glossary, GRI, WBCSD Glossary, Kirchherr et al. (2017), Jawahir and Bradley (2016), Reike et al. (2018), and Fonseca et al. (2018)
Total circular economy		100%	

Appendix 3: Representation of Variables

Variables	Acronyms	Definitions
Waste productivity	WASTP	Revenue (converted to USD using PPP exchange rate)/Total waste generated
Energy productivity	ENGP	Revenue (converted to USD using PPP exchange rate)/(Energy use—renewable energy generated by the company or certified RECs)
GHG productivity	GHGP	Revenue (converted to USD using PPP exchange rate)/GHG emissions: scope 1 & 2
Water productivity	WATP	Revenue (converted to USD using PPP exchange rate)/Water use
VOC productivity	VOCP	Revenue (converted to USD using PPP exchange rate)/VOC emissions
NOx productivity	NOXP	Revenue (converted to USD using PPP exchange rate)/NOx emissions
Sox productivity	SOXP	Revenue (converted to USD using PPP exchange rate)/Sox emissions
Particulate matter productivity	PMP	Revenue (converted to USD using PPP exchange rate)/Particulate matter emissions
Revenue	REV	Percentage of total revenue derived from products and services that are categorized as "clean" economy taxonomy, which is informed by a synthesis of, among others, the below sources and best practices: – Climate Bonds Taxonomy (Climate Bonds Initiative) – EU Taxonomy for Sustainable Activities – Sustainability Account Standards Board (SASB) reporting standards – Environmental Goods and Services Sector (Eurostat) – China Green Bond Endorsed Project Catalogue – Green Bond Principles – TCFD recommended climate opportunity metrics - Other private sector rating agencies with green or sustainability taxonomy

(continued)

(continued)

Variables	Acronyms	Definitions
Investment	INV	Percentage of a company's total investment (R&D, Capital expenditure, Acquisitions & Other) directed toward projects/research/ companies

References

A4S. (2022). *Accounting for sustainability*. https://www.accountingforsustainability.org/content/a4s/corporate/en/activities/reporting/response-ifrs-sustainability-disclosure-standards.html

Abrutyn, S., & Turner, J. H. (2011). The old institutionalism meets the new institutionalism. *Sociological Perspectives, 54*(3), 283–306.

Adams, C. A., & Abhayawansa, S. (2022). Connecting the COVID-19 pandemic, environmental, social and governance (ESG) investing and calls for 'harmonisation' of sustainability reporting. *Critical Perspectives on Accounting, 82*, 102309.

Adams, R. B., Licht, A. N., & Sagiv, L. (2011). Shareholders and stakeholders: How do Directors decide? *Strategic Management Journal, 32*(12), 1331–1355.

Aguilar-Rivera, N. (2022). Bioindicators for the sustainability of sugar agro-industry. *Sugar Tech, 24*(3), 651–661.

Aranda-Usón, A., Portillo-Tarragona, P., Marín-Vinuesa, L. M., & Scarpellini, S. (2019). Financial resources for the circular economy: A perspective from businesses. *Sustainability, 11*(3), 888.

Aranda-Usón, A., Portillo-Tarragona, P., Scarpellini, S., & Llena-Macarulla, F. (2020). The progressive adoption of a circular economy by businesses for cleaner production: An approach from a regional study in Spain. *Journal of Cleaner Production, 247*, 119648.

Arif, M., Hasan, M., Alawi, S. M., & Naeem, M. A. (2021). COVID-19 and time-frequency connectedness between green and conventional financial markets. *Global Finance Journal, 49*, 100650.

Barnabè, F., & Nazir, S. (2021). Investigating the interplays between integrated reporting practices and circular economy disclosure. *International Journal of Productivity and Performance Management, 70*(8), 2001–2031.

Barnabè, F., & Nazir, S. (2022). Conceptualizing and enabling circular economy through integrated thinking. *Corporate Social Responsibility and Environmental Management, 29*(2), 448–468.

Berelson, B. (1952). *Content analysis in communication research.*

Bocken, N. M., De Pauw, I., Bakker, C., & Van Der Grinten, B. (2016). Product design and business model strategies for a circular economy. *Journal of Industrial and Production Engineering, 33*(5), 308–320.

Burritt, R. L., & Schaltegger, S. (2010). Sustainability accounting and reporting: Fad or trend? *Accounting, Auditing & Accountability Journal., 23*(7), 829–846.

Cameron, E. J. (1997, July). *A formal AIN service creation, feature interactions analysis and management environment: An industrial application.* In Proceeding of Fourth Workshop on Feature Interactions in Telecommunications Systems.

Campbell, J. L. (2007). Why would corporations behave in socially responsible ways? An institutional theory of corporate social responsibility. *Academy of Management Review, 32*(3), 946–967.

De Vaus, D. (1982). The impact of geographical mobility on adolescent religious orientation: an Australian study. *Review of Religious Research, 23*(4), 391–403.

de Villiers, C., & Sharma, U. (2020). A critical reflection on the future of financial, intellectual capital, sustainability and integrated reporting. *Critical Perspectives on Accounting, 70,* 101999.

DiMaggio, P. J., & Powell, W. W. (1983a). The iron revisited; Institutional isomorphism and collective rationality in organizational fields. *American Sociological Review, 48*(2), 147–160.

DiMaggio, P. J., & Powell, W. W. (1983b). *The new institution in organizational analysis.* University of Chicago Press.

EC—European Commission. (2014*). Critical raw materials.* CRM list 2014. https://rmis.jrc.ec.europa.eu/?page=crm-list-2014-34bfe8

EC—European Commission. (2015). *First circular economy action plan.* https://ec.europa.eu/environment/topics/circular-economy/first-circular-economy-action-plan_en

EC—European Commission. (2017). *Critical raw materials.* https://ec.europa.eu/growth/sectors/raw-materials/areas-specific-interest/critical-raw-materials_en

EC—European Commission. (2018). *Regulation (EU) 2018/1999 on the governance of the energy union and climate action*. https://www.iea.org/policies/11773-regulation-eu-20181999-on-the-governance-of-the-energy-union-and-climate-action

EC—European Commission. (2021). *Proposal for a corporate sustainability reporting directive (CSRD)*. https://ec.europa.eu/info/business-economy-euro/company-reporting-and-auditing/company-reporting/corporate-sustainability-reporting_en

EEA—European Environment Agency. (2015). *Climate change impacts and adaptation*. https://www.eea.europa.eu/soer/2015/europe/climate-change-impacts-and-adaptation

El-Kassar, A. N., & Singh, S. K. (2019). Green innovation and organizational performance: The influence of big data and the moderating role of management commitment and HR practices. *Technological forecasting and social change, 144*, 483–498.

El-Kassar, A. N., Dagher, G. K., Lythreatis, S., & Azakir, M. (2022). Antecedents and consequences of knowledge hiding: The roles of HR practices, organizational support for creativity, creativity, innovative work behavior, and task performance. *Journal of Business Research, 140(c)*, 1–10.

EMF—Ellen MacArthur Foundation. (2013a). Towards the circular economy. *Journal of Industrial Ecology, 2*(1), 23–44.

EMF—Ellen MacArthur Foundation. (2013b). *Towards the circular economy, economic and business rationale for an accelerated transition*. https://ellenmacarthurfoundation.org/towards-the-circular-economy-vol-1-an-economic-and-business-rationale-for-an

EMF—Ellen MacArthur Foundation. (2015). *Delivering the circular economy: A toolkit for policymakers*. Ellen MacArthur Foundation. https://ellenmacarthurfoundation.org/a-toolkit-for-policymakers

EMF—Ellen MacArthur Foundation. (2016). *The new plastic economy: Rethinking the future of plastics & catalysing action*. https://www.ellenmacarthurfoundation.org/publications

EMF—Ellen MacArthur Foundation. (2017). *A new textile economy: redesigning fashion's future*. Ellen MacArthur Foundation. https://ellenmacarthurfoundation.org/a-new-textiles-economy

EMF—Ellen MacArthur Foundation. (2020). *Global commitment 2020 progress report*. https://emf.thirdlight.com/link/il0mcm1dqjtn-knjubr/@/preview/1?o

EMF—Ellen-Macarthur Foundation. (2022). *Circular economy introduction.* https://ellenmacarthurfoundation.org/topics/circular-economy-introduction/glossary

EU—European Union. (2019). *The European green deal*. https://ec.europa.eu/commission/presscorner/detail/en/ip_19_6691

Eurostat. (2016). https://ec.europa.eu/eurostat/data/database

Fonseca, L. M., Domingues, J. P., Pereira, M. T., Martins, F. F., & Zimon, D. (2018). Assessment of circular economy within Portuguese organizations. *Sustainability, 10*(7), 2521.

Garvare, R., & Johansson, P. (2010). Management for sustainability—A stakeholder theory. *Total Quality Management and Excellence Journal, 21*(7), 737–744.

Gaur, V. K., Regar, R. K., Dhiman, N., Gautam, K., Srivastava, J. K., Patnaik, S., ... & Manickam, N. (2019). Biosynthesis and characterization of sophorolipid biosurfactant by Candida spp.: application as food emulsifier and antibacterial agent. *Bioresource Technology, 285*, 121314.

Geissdoerfer, M., Savaget, P., Bocken, N. M., & Hultink, E. J. (2017). The circular economy—A new sustainability paradigm? *Journal of Cleaner Production, 143*, 757–768.

Ghisellini, P., Cialani, C., & Ulgiati, S. (2016). A review on circular economy: The expected transition to a balanced interplay of environmental and economic systems. *Journal of Cleaner Production, 114*, 11–32.

Gray, R. (2002). The social accounting project and accounting organizations and society Privileging engagement, imaginings, new accountings and pragmatism over critique? *Accounting, Organizations and Society, 27*(7), 687–708.

GRI. (2010). *Global conference executive brief: Rethink, rebuilt, report.* http://www.amsterdamgriconference.org/2010_GRI_Global_Conference_Executive_Briefing.pdf

Gurbo, M. (2017). *Why are sustainable development goals important: Supporting the implementation of UN sustainable development goals in Georgia project.* Institute for Development of Freedom of Information, Georgia, USA.

Guthrie, J. R., Dennerstein, L., Taffe, J. R., Lehert, P., & Burger, H. G. (2004). The menopausal transition: A 9-year prospective population-based study. The Melbourne women's midlife health project. *Climacteric, 7*(4), 375–389.

Guthrie, J., & Abeysekera, I. (2006). Content analysis of social, environmental reporting: What is new? *Journal of Human Resource Costing & Accounting., 10*(2), 114–126.

IIRC. (2013a). *The international IR framework*. International Integrated Reporting Council. https://integratedreporting.org/resource/international-ir-framework/

IIRC. (2013b). *Capitals*. International Integrated Reporting Council. https://integratedreporting.org/wp-content/uploads/2013/03/IR-Background-Paper-Capitals.pdf

Jacobs, L. F. (1996). The economy of winter: Phenotypic plasticity in behavior and brain structure. *The Biological Bulletin, 191*(1), 92–100.

Jadaun, J. S., Bansal, S., Sonthalia, A., Rai, A. K., & Singh, S. P. (2022). Biodegradation of Plastics for Sustainable Environment. *Bioresource Technology*, 126697.

Jawahir, I. S., & Bradley, R. (2016). Technological elements of circular economy and the principles of 6R-based closed-loop material flow in sustainable manufacturing. *Procedia Cirp, 40*, 103–108.

Johansen, M. R., Christensen, T. B., Ramos, T. M., & Syberg, K. (2022). A review of the plastic value chain from a circular economy perspective. *Journal of Environmental Management, 302*, 113975.

Katz-Gerro, T., & Lopez Sintas, J. (2019). Mapping circular economy activities in the European Union: Patterns of implementation and their correlates in small and medium-sized enterprises. *Business Strategy and the Environment, 28*(4), 485–496.

Kirchherr, J., Reike, D., & Hekkert, M. (2017). Conceptualizing the circular economy: An analysis of 114 definitions. *Resources, Conservation and Recycling, 127*, 221–232.

KPMG. (2008). *Climate change your business*. https://inis.iaea.org/search/search.aspx?orig_q=RN:40052557

KPMG. (2010). *KPMG promotes integration of company reports*. http://www.kpmg.com/RO/en/IssuesAndInsights/ArticlesPublications/Press-releases/Pages/Integrated-Reporting.aspx

Kraaijenhagen, C., Van Oppen, C., & Bocken, N. (2016). *Circular business: collaborate and circulate*. Circular Collaboration.

Krippendorff, K. (2004). Reliability in content analysis: Some common misconceptions and recommendations. *Human Communication Research, 30*(3), 411–433.

Krippendorff, K. (2018). *Content analysis: An introduction to its methodology*. Sage.

Kühl, C., Bourlakis, M., Aktas, E., & Skipworth, H. (2022). Product-service systems and circular supply chain practices in UK SMEs: The moderating

effect of internal environmental orientation. *Journal of Business Research, 146*, 155–165.
Lewandowski, M. (2016). Designing the business models for circular economy—Towards the conceptual framework. *Sustainability, 8*(1), 43.
Li, F., & Ding, Z. D. (2013). The effect of institutional isomorphic pressure on the internationalization of the firm in an emerging economy: Evidence from China. *Asia Pacific Business Review, 19*(4), 506–525.
Lieder, M., & Rashid, A. (2016). Towards circular economy implementation: A comprehensive review in context of manufacturing industry. *Journal of Cleaner Production, 115*, 36–51.
Liu, J., & Peifer, J. L. (2022). A moral foundations framing approach: Retail investors' investment intention in ethical mutual funds. *Business & Society, 61*(7).
Llena, F., Moneva, J. M., & Hernandez, B. (2007). Environmental disclosures and compulsory accounting standards: the case of Spanish annual reports. *Business strategy and the Environment, 16*(1), 50–63.
Maroun, W., & Prinsloo, A. (2020). Drivers of combined assurance in a sustainable development context: Evidence from integrated reports. *Business Strategy and the Environment, 29*(8), 3702–3719.
Mathews, J. A., & Tan, H. (2011). Progress toward a circular economy in China: The drivers (and inhibitors) of eco-industrial initiative. *Journal of Industrial Ecology, 15*(3), 435–457.
Mathews, M. R. (2008). Further thoughts on mega-accounting and the need for standards. *Issues in Social and Environmental Accounting, 2*(2), 158–175.
Mattera, M., & Ruiz-Morales, C. A. (2020). UNGC principles and SDGs: perception and business implementation. *Marketing Intelligence & Planning, 39*(1), 249–264.
Milne, M. J., & Adler, R. W. (1999). Exploring the reliability of social and environmental disclosures content analysis. *Accounting, Auditing & Accountability Journal, 12*(2), 237–256.
Moroney, R., & Trotman, K. T. (2016). Differences in auditors' materiality assessments when auditing financial statements and sustainability reports. *Contemporary Accounting Research, 33*(2), 551–575.
Mourad, M. (2016). Recycling, recovering and preventing "food waste": Competing solutions for food systems sustainability in the United States and France. *Journal of Cleaner Production, 126*, 461–477.
Murray, A., Skene, K., & Haynes, K. (2017). The circular economy: An interdisciplinary exploration of the concept and application in a global context. *Journal of Business Ethics, 140*(3), 369–380.

Naeem, M. A., & Karim, S. (2021). Tail dependence between bitcoin and green financial assets. *Economics Letters, 208*, 110068.
Naeem, M. A., Adekoya, O. B., & Oliyide, J. A. (2021). Asymmetric spillovers between green bonds and commodities. *Journal of Cleaner Production, 314*, 128100.
Naeem, M. A., Farid, S., Ferrer, R., & Shahzad, S. J. H. (2021). Comparative efficiency of green and conventional bonds pre-and during COVID-19: An asymmetric multifractal detrended fluctuation analysis. *Energy Policy, 153*, 112285.
Naeem, M. A., Karim, S., Nor, S. M., & Ismail, R. (2022). Sustainable corporate governance and gender diversity on corporate boards: Evidence from COVID-19. *Economic Research-Ekonomska Istraživanja, 35*(1), 5824–5842.
Neuendorf, K. A. (2002). Defining content analysis. *Content analysis guidebook*. 10–27.
Nikseresht, A., Hajipour, B., Pishva, N., & Mohammadi, H. A. (2022). Using artificial intelligence to make sustainable development decisions considering VUCA: A systematic literature review and bibliometric analysis. *Environmental Science and Pollution Research, 29*(28), 42509–42538.
Nishitani, K., Kokubu, K., Wu, Q., Kitada, H., Guenther, E., & Guenther, T. (2022). Material flow cost accounting (MFCA) for the circular economy: An empirical study of the triadic relationship between MFCA, environmental performance, and the economic performance of Japanese companies. *Journal of Environmental Management, 303*, 114219.
Nunnally, J. C. (1978). *Psychometric theory* (2nd ed.). McGraw.
Pieroni, M. P., McAloone, T. C., & Pigosso, D. C. (2019). Business model innovation for circular economy and sustainability: A review of approaches. *Journal of Cleaner Production, 215*, 198–216.
Reike, D., Vermeulen, W. J., & Witjes, S. (2018). The circular economy: New or refurbished as CE 3.0?—Exploring controversies in the conceptualization of the circular economy through a focus on history and resource value retention options. *Resources, Conservation and Recycling, 135*, 246–264.
Ryan, B. (2002). *Research methods and methodology in finance and accounting*. Cengage Learning EMEA.
Sarkar, B., Bolan, N. S., Mukhopadhyay, R., Bolan, S. S., Kirkham, M. B., & Rinklebe, J., (2020). Management of particulate plastic waste input to terrestrial and aquatic environments. In *Particulate plastics in terrestrial and aquatic environments* (pp. 397–411). CRC Press.

Schanes, K., Dobernig, K., & Gözet, B. (2018). Food waste matters—A systematic review of household food waste practices and their policy implications. *Journal of Cleaner Production, 182*, 978–991.

Schilling, J. (2006). On the pragmatics of qualitative assessment. *European Journal of Psychological Assessment, 22*(1), 28–37.

Schroeder, P., Anggraeni, K., & Weber, U. (2018). The relevance of circular economy practices to the sustainable development. *Journal of Industrial Ecology*.

Scott, W. R. (2005). *Social movement and organization movement*. Cambridge University Press.

Shammi, M., Behal, A., & Tareq, S. M. (2021). The escalating biomedical waste management to control the environmental transmission of COVID-19 pandemic: A perspective from two South Asian countries. *Environmental Science & Technology, 55*(7), 4087–4093.

Stahel, W. R. (2016). The circular economy. *Nature, 531*(7595), 435–438.

Stahel, W. R. (2019). The circular economy. *A user's guide*. Routledge.

Stewart, R., & Niero, M. (2018). Circular economy in corporate sustainability strategies: A review of corporate sustainability reports in the fast-moving consumer goods sector. *Business Strategy and the Environment, 27*(7), 1005–1022.

Taghizadeh-Hesary, F., Rasoulinezhad, E., & Yoshino, N. (2019). Energy and food security: Linkages through price volatility. *Energy Policy, 128*, 796–806.

Taghizadeh-Hesary, F., Yoshino, N., & Phoumin, H. (2021). Analyzing the characteristics of green bond markets to facilitate green finance in the post-COVID-19 world. *Sustainability, 13*(10), 5719.

Teece, D. J. (2010). Business models, business strategy and innovation. *Long range planning, 43*(2–3), 172–194.

Tettamanzi, P., Venturini, G., & Murgolo, M. (2022). Sustainability and financial accounting: A critical review on the ESG dynamics. *Environmental Science and Pollution Research, 29*(11), 16758–16761.

Umar, M., Su, C. W., Rizvi, S. K. A., & Lobonţ, O. R. (2021a). Driven by fundamentals or exploded by emotions: Detecting bubbles in oil prices. *Energy, 231*, 120873.

Umar, M., Su, C. W., Rizvi, S. K. A., & Shao, X. F. (2021b). Bitcoin: A safe haven asset and a winner amid political and economic uncertainties in the US. *Technological Forecasting and Social Change, 167*, 120680.

UN—United Nations. (2015). *Transforming our world: The 2030 agenda for sustainable development*. https://sustainabledevelopment.un.org/

Wang, Y., Yang, F., Hua, C., Hu, J., Wang, J., Zhou, J., ... Wu, R. (2021). Comparing the efficiencies of individual-scoring and complementarity-based algorithms in prioritizing existing protected areas. *Ecological Indicators, 125*, 107539.

WBCSD. (2018). *World business council for sustainable development*. https://www.ceguide.org/Glossary

Weber, M., Eisenführ, F., & Von Winterfeldt, D. (1988). The effects of splitting attributes on weights in multiattribute utility measurement. *Management Science, 34*(4), 431–445.

Webster, K. (2021). A circular economy is about the economy. *Circular Economy and Sustainability, 1*(1), 115–126.

WHO. (2022). *WHO coronavirus (COVID-19) dashboard*. https://covid19.who.int/

Witjes, S., & Lozano, R. (2016). Towards a more circular economy: Proposing a framework linking sustainable public procurement and sustainable business models. *Resources, Conservation and Recycling, 112*, 37–44.

Yin, R. K. (1994). Discovering the future of the case study. Method in evaluation research. *Evaluation Practice, 15*(3), 283–290.

Zhuo, N., Ji, C., & Yin, N. (2021). Supply chain integration and resilience in China's pig sector: Case study evidence from emerging institutional arrangements. *Environmental Science and Pollution Research, 28*(7), 8310–8322.

5

Circular Economy 6Rs and Reporting Practices: The Role of Institutional Pressures

1 Introduction

This study bridges the sustainability-related financial and non-financial information of circular economy [CE] activities, thereby providing better information to all stakeholders and investors for decision-making and promoting sustainable practices. More accurate reporting could play a significant role in supporting the apparatus of resource consumption, reduction, and recovery (Stewart & Niero, 2018). Modern companies' reporting practices cover both financial and non-financial concepts and key sustainable development performance indicators that relied upon to be move organizations toward sustainable development practices. At present, the level of information on social, economic, and environmental aspects given by firms is a subject of great interest in the literature on sustainability. Research has been focused on investigating the consideration of sustainable development information in yearly records by utilizing social, economic, and environmental procedures (Mathews, 2008), disclosure practices, and accounting in green business (Burritt &

S. Nazir and A. Capocchi, *Sustainability Reporting Practices and the Circular Economy*,
https://doi.org/10.1007/978-3-031-51845-4_5

Schaltegger, 2010; Gray & Laughlin, 2012; Llena et al., 2007) and cleaner manufacture processes (Aranda-Uson et al., 2020). While the financial and non-financial reporting information for sustainability and its quality are matters raised by CE researchers and practitioners, very few have addressed these (Stewart & Niero, 2018). Year after year, an expanding number of prominent organizations have been publishing corporate social responsibility (CSR) and sustainability reports (SR) that provide information to their internal and external stakeholders for rational decision-making and the promotion of sustainable development practices (A4S, 2010; KPMG, 2008, 2010).

Additionally, CSR reports and SR have been utilized by researchers as information sources for investigative CE-related activities regarding companies (Sihvonen & Partanen, 2017; Stewart & Niero, 2018). CSR and SR have commonly been encircled in the CE area into sustainability's "triple bottom line" (Merli et al., 2018). While studies concentrating on eco-development have shown the link between eco-innovation practices and environmental disclosure standards (de Villiers & Sharma, 2017; Ghisellini et al., 2016; Gray et al., 2014), the connection between integrated reporting [IR] and the performance of CE in organizations has not been addressed before. Nevertheless, most companies draw on a linear framework of production, which means adopting the attitude of take-make-and-waste, which depletes natural resources (Ellen MacArthur Foundation [EMF], 2012). Such economic models inhibit the effective utilization of natural resources and cannot sustain a nation's development in the long run.

Moreover, many directives for SD and CE have been passed across various geographic regions. In the European Union [EU], the documentation "Towards a circular economy: A zero waste program for Europe" and its addition (European Commission [EC], 2014) have established frameworks for the development of CE in the EU's member states. Among the EU's ongoing actions are those concerning plastics (EC, 2018a), energy extraction from waste (EC, 2017), basic materials (EC, 2018b), sustainable power sources, energy productivity, and eco-design (EC, 2015a).

In 2015, the European Commission implemented principles intended to push Europe toward CE while still creating new jobs, thereby enhancing economic and social progress (EC, 2015a). Subsequently, the EU sought to shift from a linear economy to a CE by the end of 2030 by achieving targets of 65% of municipal waste and 75% of packaging waste being recycled (EC, 2015b), along with an overall reduction of 10% in landfills. The EU Commission wants positive action by regional and national governments, customers, and stakeholders (EC, 2015c). China has led the way through its Circular Economy Act, the first time CE was put into law (Geng & Doberstein, 2008; Mathews & Tan, 2011). Even though some other nations are utilizing the standards or R principles of CE among different region organizations (Aranda-Uson et al., 2020), many have far to go before they can be considered as having wholly adopted a circular business framework (Witjes & Lozano, 2016).

Regarding previous research, only a few studies have been undertaken on CE implementation at the company level (Ghisellini et al., 2016). Lieder and Rashid (2016) highlight that the manufacturing industry plays a vital role in resource scarcity and concern for the environment, but social practices are generally neglected. Researchers and practitioners have been utilizing a range of indicators to determine the progress of CE practices at the national, regional, and international levels (Geng & Doberstein, 2008; Ghisellini et al., 2016) as well as at the product circularity level (EMF, 2015; Ghisellini et al., 2016). Regarding IR Framework (IIRC, 2013a, p. 13), which strictly follows a circular approach of strategies, resource allocation, outlook, and performance. It may represent the ideal fit not only to contribute to organizations in representing and disclosing financial and non-financial information but also to fully integrate such issues of value creation processes with a holistic approach (i.e., considering simultaneous economic, social, and environmental issues). The paper addresses the following two questions:

(Q1) How and to what extent does integrated reporting support circular economy 6Rs-related activities?

(Q2) How and to what extent do institutional pressures (coercive, normative, and mimetic) impact integrated reporting in the context of circular economy 6Rs activities?

The research highlights CE-6Rs (reduce, reuse, recycle, reproduce, redesign, recover) practices in six regions (Europe, Africa, Asia, Australasia, South America, and North America) and 13 industries. The 6R principles are drawn upon as an essential practical framework of CE (Reike et al., 2018), and research used institutional theories approach for developing hypotheses mechanism by yearly, industry and region-wise for exploring the concept. The study also contributes to CE practices in the IR and supports organizations to make better decisions to contribute to sustainable development. The chapter is organized as follows. Next is a review of the literature on CE and IR, aimed at creating a theoretical framework and developing research hypotheses. This is followed by describing the research methodology, presenting the content analysis's key findings, and testing the hypotheses. Subsequently, there is a discussion of the results, conclusion, and limitations, as well as proposals for future research being made and practical implications being outlined.

2 Literature Review and Theoretical Framework

Circular Economy Approach

The EU advanced the CE concept, and subsequently, some national governments, including China, Japan, the United Kingdom, France, and Canada, adopted the approach. The European Commission [EC] estimated that CE-type economic developments could make 600 billion euros yearly for the EU manufacturing sector alone (EMF, 2013; EC, 2015a, 2015b). Moreover, it is held that the global economy would profit by 1,000 billion US dollars annually (EMF, 2012) through the implementation of CE. In early 1980, the first Directive (85/339/EC) was issued on using liquids for human consumption, which called for producing, recycling, reusing, remanufacturing, and repackaging products intended for human consumption (EC, 2015b).

In 1994 (amended in EC, 2008), Directive 94/62/EC stated that packaging and packaging waste must be introduced harmoniously in all member states and companies. The EC 2008 plans highlight Directive

2008/98/EC of the Waste Directive Framework (WDF) and essential features of the waste management framework like reduce, reuse, recycle, redesign, reproduce, and recovery, which the companies correspond and demonstrate in their financial and non-financial reporting. Business models utilizing CE-6Rs practices that retain the products and materials being used include reproducing (Gray & Charter, 2007; Nasr & Thurston, 2006), reduce (Lacy & Rutqvist, 2015), reuse (Stahel, 2014a), redesign (EMF, 2017), and recovery (see Fig. 1).

As indicated by the EMF (2013, p. 33), CE is beneficial through having a framework that intends to keep products, parts, and materials at their highest utility and incentive in all cases. At the same time, the study explored how IR practices support CE activities by using the essential operationalized R principles. These R-principles recommend value creation options (Rs) for the business. These pertain to R1 (Reduce), R2 (Reuse), R3 (Recycle), R4 (Reproduce/Re-manufactured), R5 (Redesign), and R6 (Recover) (Reike et al., 2018). In the CE-6R, reduction mainly emphasizes the initial three product life-cycle phases. It indicates the reduced utilization of resources in premanufacturing, reduced energy utilization, materials, and different resources during production, and decreased emissions and waste during the utilization phase (Reike et al., 2018). Reuse indicates the reuse of the product many times or its parts after its first life cycle, reducing the use of virgin

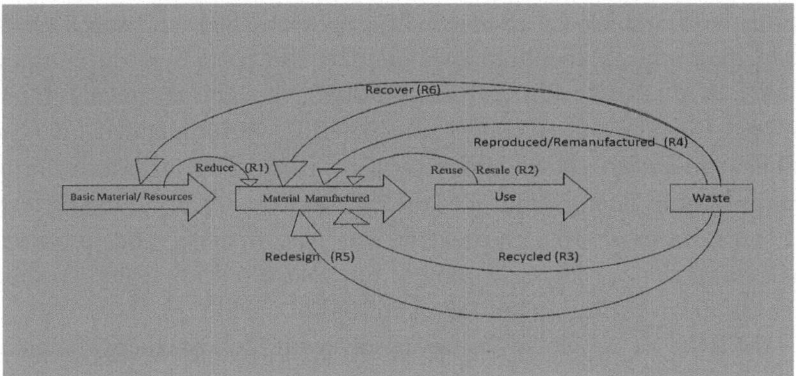

Fig. 1 CE-6Rs framework (*Source* EMF, 2013, p. 33)

materials and bringing it into more advanced products and parts (Kirchherr et al., 2017). Recycling includes moving over material that would, in some way or another, be a restrained waste into new materials or products (Kirchherr et al., 2017; Reike et al., 2018). The process of remanufacturing products at the end of the utilization stage, categorization, disassembling, and cleaning for use in the different product life cycles is indicated as recovery (Gray & Charter, 2007). The redesign process includes updating products for next-generation products, which would utilize parts, materials, and assets recovered from the past life-cycle or past age of consequences. In contrast, remanufacture includes reprocessing products effectively used for recovery to their novel phase or a like-new structure by reusing as many components as could be expected under the circumstances without loss of practicality (EMF, 2015).

Integrated Reporting Approach

There have been increasing concerns that more than conventional corporate reporting is needed for providing information to the stakeholders (Adams et al., 2011; Cohen et al., 2012). Acknowledging such concerns, several organizations have tried to improve the information accessible to stakeholders through enhancing their financial and non-financial reporting (Cohen et al., 2012). The non-financial information is commonly revealed using an instrument, including intellectual capital reports, corporate social responsibility reports (CSR), and social, environmental, ethical, and human rights that also pertain to the business (Cohen et al., 2012). Furthermore, in 2010, the recently formed International Integrated Reporting Council (IIRC) recommended financial and non-financial related information by permitting an evaluation of the continuous demonstration of the organization. IR not only discloses the organization's strategy, governance, performance, and prospects concerning the outside environment but also shows the value creation over the short, medium, and long term (IIRC, 2013d, p. 7).

The IIRC is a "global collaboration with policymakers, financial specialists, organizations, standard setters, the accounting researchers/

scholars and NGOs" that provides "the important and up-to-date information for individuals and organizations" (IIRC, 2013a) engaged with corporate reporting, to set up a practical framework to disclosed financial and non-financial information into one report. Recently, the European Union (EU, 2014) stepped forward to address financial consultants' and investors' information needs, inspecting non-financial in the context of natural and social. Specifically, the EU's Directive 2014/95/ (EU Directive) requires the fundamental willingness to disclose financial information, and the EU Guidelines 2017/C215/01 (EUG) are aimed at helping firms to disclose financial and non-financial information appropriately. Also, the EU (2017, p. 4) is to "assist organizations with revealing high standard, pertinent, valuable, predictable and progressively similar non-financial (natural, social and management related) info that encourages versatile, sustainable business and gives an openness to all organizational stakeholders."

> The intention of IR is not only better communication in the internal environment to achieve short-, medium-, and long-term value creation of the organization, for it is also about establishing concise communication regarding organization strategy, governance, performance, and prospects, with regards to its outside environment. This will lead to the production of significant worth over the short, medium, and long term. (IIRC, 2013)

In doing so, IR builds on the disclosure that seeks to add capacity of companies to give records with suppliers of financial capital, investors, stakeholders, and the more extensive society in a report, and succinctly, covering material connections between different business activities, operational units, and resource nature they use or influence (Giorgino et al., 2016; IIRC, 2013) (see Fig. 2).

The IIRC exploits the term "capitals" to indicate these different resources, with the six types identified being financial, manufactured, intellectual, human, social and relationship, and natural (IIRC, 2013b). Moreover, the framework holds that the representation of the organization's business model should be combined, with specific accentuation on how this business model and the procedures coordinate with the six capitals (IIRC, 2013c). Further, the IIRC (2013b) framework shows the

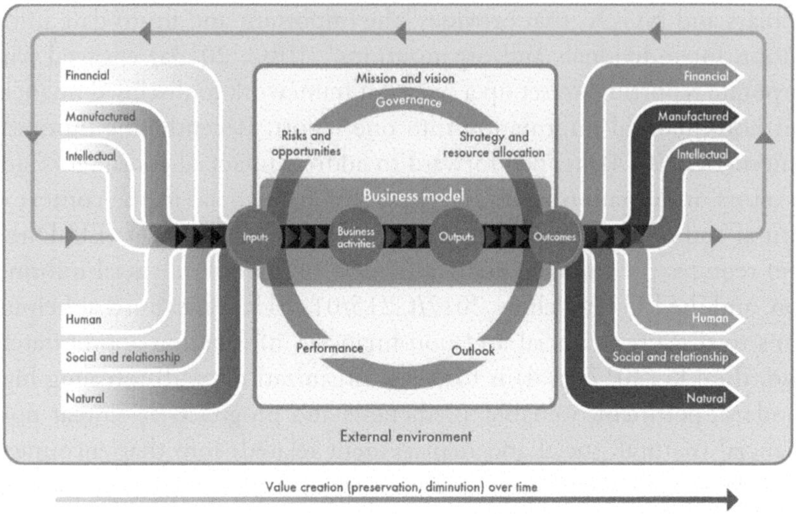

Fig. 2 IR value creation process (*Source* IIRC, 2013a, p. 13) (With permission from the International Integrated Reporting Council 2020 (C))

business model's "association with the inputs, business activities, outputs and outcomes to create the value creation over the short, medium and long term." Moreover, it sets out the strategic objective to achieve maximum opportunities and reduce the risk factors of the organization.

The Covered Practice of Circular Economy 6Rs and Integrated Reporting

Accounting has been recognized as a tool for corporate management profiles (Burritt & Schaltegger, 2010; EC, 2000a, 2000b). Accordingly, sustainability accounting practices are pertinent in the board operational development (Gray, 2002) and dynamic procedures inside organizations planning to accomplish a circular model in the decision-making process. This research also involves exploring the connection between specific practices of IR and the CE-related activities that firms present. This investigation gives new insight into the selection of CE at the microscale level by utilizing a transversal methodology, as this research creates connections among the social, economic, and environmental fields as one report (Integrated report) embeds with CE.

Moreover, the term CE is utilized by governments, scientists, researchers, scholars, and organizations to depict a framework for dealing with sustainable development that constrains economic development (OECD, 2015a, 2015b). In the CE framework, firms are attaining a framework at all phases of their manufacturing operations, intending to reduce the utilization rate of natural resources, reduce waste and emissions, enhance resource efficiency, and upgrade manufacturing operations. These principles and frameworks provide financial and non-financial information and disclose missing links between business models and strategy in the IR perspectives (Giorgino et al., 2016), especially when firms assume circular business models. Simultaneously, the general sustainable development in material manufacturers is appealing more consideration by investors, specialists, and stakeholders.

Moroney and Trotman (2016, p. 553) noticed that "sustainability disclosure can identify with one specific set of revelations (i.e., Water and energy) or can comprise of a full sustainability report covering financial (i.e., Economic development, investment), environment (e.g., Energy, water, gas emissions, waste) and social revelation (e.g., Work practices, worker rights, gender equality, participation in the community)."

Kamp-Roelands (2013, p. 358) notices that modern organizations have to receive the opportunities of CE that can be helpful in integrated reporting to think about the relationships among different resource across the different sectors of the organization and generating new accounting information for stakeholder participation in sustainable development, rational investment decision and can improve organization performance. Non-financial and costs recognized interest in carbon-reducing strategies, resources, groundwater, air pollution, minimizing harmful substances, and waste dumping should be recorded in reports specifically for stakeholders. Research assumes that CE-related 6Rs activities include essential processes that may be incorporated in IR practices like product life cycle costing, cost accounting, natural, financial, and non-financial measurements, and community development.

IR and CE frameworks emphasize resource utilization and inform all stakeholders on the decision-making and participation in the sustainable development agenda. These frameworks emphasize firms' value creation and have adopted the concept of corporate sector outcomes needing to be scrutinized through reporting over the short-, medium-, and long-term perspectives for strategic decision-making (Busco et al., 2013). CE and IR diagrams work circularly (EMF, 2013, p. 33; IIRC, 2013a, p. 13). CE frameworks represent a shift from a linear to a circular (i.e., closed-loop) design of economic systems (EMF, 2013, p. 33). The IR framework pertains to value creation dynamics on a feedback-oriented basis (i.e., inputs become outputs, and outputs and outcomes will eventually affect the organization's capital, thus being closed-loop and providing the basis for future action) (IIRC, 2013). This reflects significant evidence that all the factors are interlinked with each other and have a significant opportunity for the organization's interest in disclosing the financial and non-financial information and remarkable emphasis on the process used for communicating information to all relevant stakeholders.

Institutional Theory and Hypothesis Development

During the 1970s, the organization's structure changed (Abrutyn & Turner, 2011). The first organizations were treated as separate entities, as a part of their internal environment. This refers to the change in the organization's behavior, whereby this was not just seen as about the internal or external environment, for it also was seen to have come to depend on the social norms and governance systems (Scott, 2005). Subsequently, institutional pressure connected with sustainability capacities (abilities applied to the sustainable development activities of firms) about organizations needing to figure out how to implement CE activities in their operations (Lieder & Rashid, 2016; Ranta et al., 2018; Stewart & Niero, 2018). The institutional pressure covers numerous aspects, more association between various firms and the organized area that exists of multiple organizations with comparative lines of business. (DiMaggio & Powell, 1983a). Research has shown that institutional pressures like the rules and regulations of different regions and industries influence sustainable development proactivity and the adoption of CE activities (Witjes & Lozano, 2016) into IR for the organization's value creation (IIRC, 2013d). These pressures are called isomorphisms, with three distinct types identified: coercive, normative, and mimetic (Li & Ding, 2013). These are considered formal and informal pressures regarding companies' conduct and reporting practices (de Villiers & Sharma, 2017; DiMaggio & Powell, 1983a).

Coercive isomorphism refers to political and legal impacts created by the need for legitimacy (Li & Ding, 2013). These are shaped by the views as well as the rules and regulations forged by the powerful, including governments, NGOs, policymakers, industrial standards, trendsetters, patent organizations, and rating agencies, among others, who can apply coercive pressures on companies to follow sustainability development practices (Campbell, 2007; de Villiers & Sharma, 2017). However, coercive isomorphism's explicit and implicit aspects are operationalized mainly through government policies. In their theoretical research, Boiral and Gendron (2011) raise the possibility of the variability of sustainability practices and regional implementation of regulations as a key determinant of coercive isomorphism. Coercive isomorphism activities by governments include, for example, the EC waste Directive Framework (EC, 2008), national waste plans, and the EU demanding positive action by federal governments, customers, corporate organizations, and stakeholders (EC, 2015a)—subsequently, legislative impacts on CE-6Rs and integrated reporting practices. In 1994, (EU, 1994) Directive 94/62/EC stated that packaging and packaging waste must be handled in a coordinated way in all the member states.

Moreover, it sets the safety standard to be followed by the companies for recycling and product quality in the remanufacturing procedure. These operations directly persuade with the companies' policies (DiMaggio & Powell, 1983b), as every region has different standards (Aranda-Uson et al., 2020), and the companies of every region follow different rules and regulations for disclosing financial and non-financial related information for the stakeholders. The literature expands on the CE-6Rs, and IR practices in the region are more dominant and efficient with solid mechanisms.

Hypothesis 1: CE-6Rs-related integrated reports are more prevalent in regions implementing a more vital coercive mechanism for the circular economy.

The normative isomorphism pertains to standards delineating an organization's conduct (Li & Ding, 2013), determined by each industry's directives. This can be implemented by professionalism. Professional skills are the aggregated meaning of individuals in an occupation regarding the conditions of their activity (DiMaggio & Powell, 1983b). The development of CE-6Rs practices in different industries through expert systems in an organization's reporting system, experts adopted different directives, standards, or practices for the organization's sustainability like global reporting index. This makes a domain of compatible sectors, which thus fortifies the authenticity of the expected standards. Moreover, it alludes to the different rules and regulations, a typical understanding of varying industry reporting cultures, and what an authentic activity about shared view and comprehension is (Li & Ding, 2013). Normative isomorphism involves the pursuit of internal and external professionalism to develop the organization's sustainable performance in the long run and its value creation (Campbell, 2007; de Villiers & Sharma, 2017). CE-6Rs activities and IR practices refer to the economic, environmental, and social development that would be able to observe the essential sustainable development by the CE in different industries, which influences the organization reporting (Garvare & Johansson, 2010). The literature expands on the CE-6Rs and IR practices in the different industries, which are more dominant and influential in solid mechanisms.

Hypothesis 2: CE-6Rs-related integrated reports are more prevalent in industries implementing a more robust normative mechanism for the circular economy.

Mimetic isomorphism refers to changes originating from company vagueness and vulnerability (DiMaggio & Powell, 1983a; Li & Ding, 2013). The vulnerability can emerge from more comprehension of innovation, precise objectives, and uncertainty in the organization over time.

In response to this vulnerability, companies aim to emulate what appears to be progressive, legitimate, or first that seems to stay ahead of the competition (Li & Ding, 2013). Hence, mimetic isomorphism refers to companies' response against uncertainty and market competition, which involves adopting strategies for long-term survival in the market (Li & Ding, 2013). What companies adopted the strategy for survival in the market over the years, and what response did companies get after adopting the CE-6Rs-related reporting practices? Mimetic isomorphism also alludes to the high-value creation of the organization, which organizations are bound to imitate in ambiguous circumstances (Li & Ding, 2013). Mimetic isomorphism refers to observed market trends that have been changing daily, organizing a successful market competition strategy over the years, and getting strategies response. The literature expands the CE-6Rs and IR practices by years to be more leading and influential in solid mechanisms.

Hypothesis 3: CE-6Rs-related integrated reports are more prevalent in years that implement a more vital mimetic mechanism for the circular economy.

3 Research Design

Content Analysis

Content analysis is used for this study, which is "a research technique for the objective, systematic and quantitative description of the manifest content of communication" (Krippendorff, 1989, p. 403). This technique can be used with either qualitative or quantitative data and allows for organizing "the text of writing into various groups or categories based on selected criteria" (Guthrie et al., 2004, p. 287). With content analysis, frequency is usually calculated and used for measuring and communicating the relevance of the subject matter (Krippendorff, 2004, p. 418) and pertinent to the context of the current study. This can help evaluate the amount of disclosure about a specific concept or group of concepts

(Milne & Adler, 1999). It needs to be emphasized that content analysis in the field of sustainability has already been utilized, being recognized as a reliable research method (e.g., Guthrie & Abeysekera, 2006; Milne & Adler, 1999). For this paper, the public IIRC database (<IR>Examples Database—http://examples.integratedreporting.org/home) reports were retrieved on 22 August 2019 (see Table 1).

More specifically, for this study, content analysis was utilized to determine the type and extent of disclosure of CE-6Rs-related information. A sample of 84 reports (see Table 2), drawn from six regions (Europe, South America, North America, Asia, Africa, and Australia) and 13 industries (basic materials, consumer goods, consumer services, financial services, health care, industrials, professional service, public sector, oil and gas, real estate, technology, telecommunications, and the utility industry) for the years 2011 to 2018 of 74 leading organizations, were utilized. The aim is the development of more standardized terminology for CE and IR research, which would facilitate communication across different stakeholders and, ultimately, contribute to higher-quality scholarship in this field. The research design entailed searching for CE-6Rs-related concepts in integrated reports (see Table 3).

The 6Rs concepts were searched through content analysis (Krippendorff, 1989, p. 403) by using the NVivo software. Subsequently, these results, with the inclusion of synonyms for the 6Rs elements, were exported onto an Excel spreadsheet.

Statistical Methods

For the testing of the hypotheses, the relation between the dependent and independent variable one or more was examined. To explore the relation between two or more variables, one widely utilized way is to apply the regression (ANOVA for hypothesis testing) approach. Explicitly, the hypothesis recognized by the authors is deduced as upheld by the proof if the statistically substantial relationship is determined by p-value $< \alpha$, where α means a significant level. To test the hypothesis, the author used SPSS software to analyze the hypothesis, either the variable has

Table 1 Overview of the dataset

Year	Integrated reports	%	Industries	Integrated reports	%	Region	Integrated reports	%
2011	1	1.19	BASIC MATERIALS	12	14.28	EUROPE	36	42.85
2013	1	1.19	CONSUMER GOODS	7	8.33	SOUTH AMERICA	2	2.38
2014	3	3.57	CONSUMER SERVICES	8	9.52	NORTH AMERICA	1	1.19
2015	3	3.57	FINANCIAL SERVICES	23	27.38	ASIA	12	14.28
2016	30	35.71	HEALTH CARE	4	4.761	AFRICA	29	34.52
2017	45	53.57	INDUSTRIALS	9	10.71	AUSTRASIA	4	4.76
2018	1	1.19	PROFESSIONAL SERVICES	3	3.57	Total	84	100
Total	84	100	PUBLIC SECTOR	1	1.19			
			OIL AND GAS	1	1.19			
			REAL ESTATE	5	5.59			
			TECHNOLOGY	3	3.57			
			TELECOMMUNICATION	4	4.76			
			UTILITIES	4	4.76			
			Total	84	100			

Table 2 Companies dataset

No	Companies	Years	Regions	Industries
1	THE CROWN ESTATE	2018	EUROPE	REAL ESTATE
2	TRUWORTH	2017	AFRICA	CONSUMER GOODS
3	CEMEX	2017	NORTH AMERICA	INDUSTRIAL
4	IMPLATS PLATINUM	2017	AFRICA	BSAIC MATERIAL
5	BT GROUP	2017	EUROPE	TELECOMMUNICATION
6	BROWN AND COMPANY PLC	2017	ASIA	CONSUMER GOODS
7	HALFORDS	2017	EUROPE	CONSUMER SERVICE
8	ESKOM	2017	AFRICA	UTILITIES
9	GENERALI	2017	EUROPE	FINANCIAL SERVICES
10	MTN	2017	AFRICA	TELECOMMUNICATION
11	ABSA	2017	EUROPE	FINANCIAL SERVICE
12	ENBW	2017	EUROPE	UTILITIES
13	MARKS AND SPENCER	2017	EUROPE	CONSUMER GOODS
14	UNITED UTILITIES	2017	EUROPE	UTILITIES
15	DSM	2017	EUROPE	HEALTH CARE
16	VODACOM	2017	AFRICA	TELECOMMUNICATION
17	ADAPT IT	2017	AFRICA	TECHNOLOGY
18	CBUS	2017	AUSTRALASIA	PUBLIC SECTOR
19	STRATE	2017	AFRICA	FINANCIAL SERVICE
20	SANTOVA	2017	AFRICA	PROFESSIONAL SERVICE
21	ROYAL BAFOKENG PLATINUM LTD	2017	AFRICA	BASIC MATERIAL
22	DENTSU	2017	ASIA	CONSUMER SERVICE
23	ROSNEFT	2017	ASIA	OIL AND GAS
24	SANFORD	2017	AUSTRALASIA	CONSUMER GOODS
25	MERIDIAN ENERGY	2017	AUSTRALASIA	UTILITIES
26	YORK TIMBER	2017	AFRICA	BASIC MATERIAL
27	DUCHY OF CORNWALL	2017	EUROPE	REAL ESTATE
28	LLOYDS BANKING GROUP	2017	EUROPE	FINANCIAL SERVICE
29	KUMBA IRON ORE	2017	AFRICA	BASIC MATERIAL
30	MEDICLINIC	2017	EUROPE	HEALTHCARE
31	BRITISH LAND	2017	EUROPE	FINANCIAL SERVICE
32	ITAÚ UNIBANCO HOLDING S. A	2017	SOUTH AMERICA	FINANCIAL SERVICE
33	INTERCONTINENTAL HOTEL GROUP	2017	EUROPE	CONSUMER SERVICE
34	GO-AHEAD	2017	EUROPE	CONSUMER SERVICE

(continued)

Table 2 (continued)

No	Companies	Years	Regions	Industries
35	FMO	2017	EUROPE	FINANCIALSERVICE
36	GOLDFIELD	2017	AFRICA	BASIC MATERIAL
37	DIMO	2017	ASIA	INDUSTRIAL
38	EXXARO	2017	AFRICA	BASIC MATERIAL
39	ANGLO PLATINUM	2017	AFRICA	BASIC MATERIAL
40	BAE SYSTEM	2017	EUROPE	INDUSTRIAL
41	DBS	2017	ASIA	FINANCIAL SERVICE
42	BRITISH AMERICAN TOBACCO	2017	EUROPE	CONSUMER SERVICE
43	LENDLEASE	2017	AUSTRALASIA	REAL ESTATE
44	TRANSNET	2017	AFRICA	CONSUMER SERVICE
45	AEGON	2017	EUROPE	FINANCIAL SERVICE
46	BARCLAYS AFRICA GROUP	2017	AFRICA	FINANCIAL SERVICE
47	DBS	2016	ASIA	FINANCIAL SERVICE
48	EURAZEO	2016	EUROPE	FINANCIAL SERVICE
49	STAFER	2016	EUROPE	INDUSTRIALS
50	WACO INTERNATIONAL	2016	AFRICA	INDUSTRIALS
51	ARGUDEN GOVERNANCE ACADEMY	2016	EUROPE	PROFESSIONAL SERVICE
52	FRESNILLO	2016	EUROPE	BASIC MATERIAL
53	ITAÚ UNIBANCO HOLDING S.A	2016	SOUTH AMERICA	FINANCIAL SERVICE
54	EOH HOLDINGS	2016	AFRICA	TECHNOLOGY
55	SAICA	2016	AFRICA	PROFESSIONAL SERVICE
56	DBSA	2016	AFRICA	FINANCIAL SERVICE
57	PEOPLE LEASE AND FINANCE	2016	ASIA	FINANCIAL SERVICE
58	CREST NICHOLSON	2016	EUROPE	REAL ESTATE
59	GOLDFIELDS	2016	AFRICA	BASIC MATERIAL
60	HULAMIN LTD	2016	AFRICA	INDUSTRIALS
61	ROYAL BAFOKENG PLATINUM LTD	2016	AFRICA	BASIC MATERIAL
62	MARUI GROUP	2016	ASIA	CONSUMER SERVICE
63	COCA-COLA HELLENIC BOTTLING COMPANY	2016	EUROPE	CONSUMER GOODS
64	TATA STEEL	2016	ASIA	INDUSTRIALS
65	NOVO NORDISK	2016	EUROPE	HEALTHCARE

(continued)

Table 2 (continued)

No	Companies	Years	Regions	Industries
66	ASPIAG SERVICE S.R.L. DESPAR NORD EST	2016	EUROPE	CONSUMER GOODS
67	NEDBANK	2016	AFRICA	FINANCIAL SERVICE
68	DSM	2016	EUROPE	HEALTHCARE
69	MITUSI & CO	2016	ASIA	FINANCIAL SERVICE
70	REDEFINE PROPERTIES	2016	AFRICA	REAL ESTATE
71	STANDARD BANK GROUP	2016	AFRICA	FINANCIAL SERVICE
72	DELLAS	2016	EUROPE	INDUSTRIAL
73	ING	2016	EUROPE	FINANCIAL SERVICE
74	AEGON	2016	EUROPE	FINANCIAL SERVICE
75	ANGLOGOLD ASHANTI	2016	AFRICA	BASIC MATERIAL
76	TALAWAKELLE TEA ESTATES	2016	ASIA	CONSUMER GOODS
77	SANLAM LTD	2015	AFRICA	FINANCIAL SERVICE
78	ING	2015	EUROPE	FINANCIAL SERVICE
79	BRITISH AMERICAN TOBACCO	2015	EUROPE	CONSUMER SERVICE
80	FRESNILLO	2014	EUROPE	BASIC MATERIAL
81	HAMMERSON	2014	EUROPE	FINANCIAL SERVICE
82	SAGE	2014	EUROPE	TECHNOLOGY
83	DIMO	2013	ASIA	INDUSTRIALS
84	VODAFONE	2011	EUROPE	TELECOMMUNICATIONS

significant effects or non-significant effects, as well as test the hypothesis rejects or fails to reject the hypothesis by using the *p*-value. More details are provided below.

Results

As mentioned above, 84 reports from 2011 to 2018 in 14 industries of six regions, as classified by the database of the IIRC online website were probed. The following tables show the key-related data of the CE-6Rs in integrated reports, years, regions, and industries. Additionally, the tables show the key terms cited in the retrieved data by reference and frequencies (percentages).

Table 3 CE-6Rs in integrated reporting variables code for content analysis

Categories	Description
Reduce (R1)	– Reduce natural resources consumption (EMF, 2013) – Reduce CO_2 emissions (EC, 2015a); EC (2015b) – Reduce water consumption and energy (EC, 2015a); EC (2015b) – Less material per unit of production (EC, 2018b) – The ratio of reduced packaging waste (EC, 2018a) – Reduce packaging and plastic usage (EMF, 2016)
Resell/Reuse(R2)	– Reusing part of the products (EMF, 2017; Stahel, 2014b) – Reuse by purpose (EMF, 2016; Stahel, 2014b) – The ratio of parts repair/refurbishment for sale (EMF, 2012; Stahel, 2014a) – Sales turnover on second-hand products – Reuse product (EMF, 2012)
Recycle (R3)	– Number of products recycled – Post-consumer product waste/post-producer product waste (EMF, 2013; EC, 2015) – Quality of product maintained (EC, 2015a); EC (2015b) – Technology transfer in recycling for low-carbon energy (Kirchherr et al., 2017) – Control over harmful substances (EMF, 2012; EC (Action plan), 2015b) – Number of recycling technologies used (EMF, 2017) – High-quality recycling – Participation in job creation by recycling – Quantity of recycled material (EMF, 2015)

(continued)

Table 3 (continued)

Categories	Description
Re-Manufactured/Reproduce (R4)	– Multi-component product disassembled and reconstructed a new product – Reprocessing (Linder & Williander, 2017) – Recycling used for the new product (EMF, 2013; Jayal et al., 2010) – Upgrade products by using more advanced components (Stahel, 2014a) – Number of reconditioned products (EMF, 2013) – Numbers of product by product (Jayal et al., 2010) – The ratio of restoration (Jayal et al., 2010) – Number of old parts used in the new product – Number of products re-furbished by using new components (Jayal et al., 2010) – Extent product life by repair
Redesign (R5)	– Rethink for upgrading (EMF, 2015) – New product with old parts (EMF, 2015) – Reproduce for a new function (EMF, 2013) – Extend the product life by redesign – Make the product in a new form (EMF, 2013) – Recreated for an original function (Stahel, 2014b) – Number of redesigned products with a new function (Jayal et al., 2010) – Number of old parts used for the new product – Number of defective product repairs – Number of second-hand product repairs
Recover/Energy (R6)	– Energy recovery (EMF, 2012) – Basic material recovery – Energy Recovery – Use of biomass and recovery (EMF, 2012) – Quantity of basic material recovered – Quantity of electricity produced

Table 4, year-wise, reflects that the reduced term is more cited in the 84 IRs and the designing term less cited, even in 2013 and 2018 reports redesign (R5) term zero cited. The percentages of cited terms in 2017 and 2016 were higher compared to the other years because most of the reports in this dataset contained these two years. Move forward to the industry-wise (see Table 5).

It is notable that the industry-wise most referenced with R principles, e.g., the financial services and basic materials industries, are more cited reference terms. In contrast, the professional services reports are less cited according to word reference and percentage-wise. Regarding the oil and gas sector, only one report was cited, but the average of reference and the percentage is high as compared to other reports. If overall mentioned that the reduce term is the most cited and less cited term redesign, for example, in consumer goods, real estate, and professional service the redesign term is zero cited referenced. Move forward to Table 6.

Table 6 presents the results of the region-wise content analysis of IRs for Europe, South America, North America, Asia, Africa, and Australasia. Europe comprises 42.84% of reports taken from the dataset. In general, the European region covers a wide range of frequencies that are substantially distributed. Regarding the African region, the dataset contains 29 reports, Asia even having a small sample size large cited CE-6Rs term denotes a high level of CE-6Rs practices in integrated reports.

Testing of Hypotheses

The paper elects causal variables as independent and outcome variables as dependent. Independent variables are also predictor variables or explanatory variables, dependent variables may be called results or responses (Winer, 1971, pp. 435–436). The integrated reports, region-wise reporting, industry-wise reporting, and year-wise reporting are independent variables in this research, while CE-6Rs (R1, R2, R3, R4, R5, R6) are the dependent variables.

Table 4 Results of year-wise content analysis regarding evidence of CE-6Rs activities in IR practices

Year-wise frequencies (%)

Years	R1 (%)	R2 (%)	R3 (%)	R4 (%)	R5 (%)	R6 (%)	Total/6Rs (%)	Mean	SD
2011	254 (1.17)	4 (0.45)	4 (0.44)	44 (1.59)	1 (1.85)	9 (0.728)	316 (1.56)	52.66	99.92
2013	79 (0.54)	28 (3.2)	28 (3.1)	26 (0.94)	0 (0)	8 (0.647)	169 (0.83)	28.16	27.52
2014	792 (5.49)	37 (4.2)	43 (4.76)	143 (5.19)	2 (3.70)	59 (4.77)	1,076 (5.31)	179.33	303.79
2015	1,200 (8.32)	21 (2.4)	21 (2.32)	251 (9.11)	4 (7.40)	111 (8.98)	1,608 (7.94)	268	465.89
2016	4,286 (29.72)	370 (42.4)	383 (42.46)	867 (31.47)	12 (22.22)	413 (33.44)	6,331 (31.2)	1,055.16	1,605.95
2017	7,761 (53.82)	399 (45.7)	410 (45.45)	1,398 (50.74)	35 (64.81)	619 (50.12)	10,622 (52.4)	1,770.33	2,969.67
2018	46 (0.319)	13 (1.49)	13 (1.44)	26 (0.943)	0 (0)	16 (1.29)	114 (0.56)	19	15.62
Total/ 6RS %	14,418 (100)	872 (100)	902 (100)	2,755 (100)	54 (100)	1,235 (100)	20,236 (100)		
Mean	1,802.25	109	112.75	344.375	6.75	154.375			
SD	2,796.891	170.642	175.803	513.263	12.1037	232.772			

Table 5 Results of content analysis by industries regarding CE-6Rs integrated reporting practices

Industry-wise frequencies (%)

Industries	R1 (%)	R2 (%)	R3 (%)	R4 (%)	R5 (%)	R6 (%)	Total/ 6Rs (%)	Mean	SD
BASIC MATERIALS	2,943 (20.4)	232 (26.6)	240 (26.6)	339 (12.3)	9 (16.6)	198 (16)	3,961 (19.5)	660.16	1,123.56
CONSUMER GOODS	952 (6.6)	75 (8.6)	82 (9.09)	223 (8.09)	0 (0)	82 (6.6)	1,414 (6.9)	235.66	358.29
CONSUMER SERVICES	1,747 (12.1)	56 (6.4)	0 (0)	296 (10.7)	3 (5.5)	133 (10.7)	2,235 (11)	372.5	682.33
FINANCIAL SERVICES	3,664 (25.4)	120 (13.76)	123 (13.6)	884 (32.08)	23 (42.59)	348 (28.1)	5,162 (25.5)	860.33	1,408.29
HEALTH CARE	747 (5.18)	56 (6.4)	62 (6.87)	201 (7.29)	9 (16.6)	91 (7.3)	1,166 (5.76)	194.33	278.26
INDUSTRIALS	1,701 (11.8)	248 (28.4)	251 (27.8)	256 (9.29)	2 (3.7)	97 (7.8)	2,555 (12.6)	425.83	633.22
PROFESSIONAL SERVICES	107 (0.742)	1 (0.1)	1 (0.11)	34 (1.23)	0 (0)	14 (1.13)	157 (0.77)	26.16	41.70
PUBLIC SECTOR	41 (0.28)	1 (0.11)	1 (0.11)	7 (0.254)	3 (5.5)	4 (0.323)	57 (0.28)	9.5	15.59
OIL AND GAS	302 (2.09)	1 (0.11)	58 (6.43)	62 (2.25)	1 (1.8)	52 (4.2)	476 (2.3)	79.33	112.56
REAL ESTATE	430 (2.9)	45 (5.16)	45 (4.98)	122 (4.42)	0 (0)	47 (3.8)	689 (3.4)	114.83	159.32
TECHNOLOGY	284 (1.96)	15 (1.7)	16 (1.77)	85 (3.08)	1 (1.8)	36 (2.9)	437 (2.15)	72.83	107.54
TELECOMMUNICATION	878 (6.08)	14 (1.6)	15 (1.166)	151 (5.48)	2 (3.7)	82 (6.6)	1,142 (5.6)	190.33	341.60

(continued)

Table 5 (continued)

Industry-wise frequencies (%)

Industries	R1 (%)	R2 (%)	R3 (%)	R4 (%)	R5 (%)	R6 (%)	Total/ 6Rs (%)	Mean	SD
UTILITIES	622 (4.31)	8 (0.9)	8 (0.88)	95 (3.44)	1 (1.85)	51 (4.1)	785 (3.87)	130.83	243.28
Total/6RS	*14,418* (100)	*872* (100)	*902* (100)	*2,755* (100)	*54* (100)	*1,235* (100)	*20,236* (100)		
Mean	1,109.07	67.07	69.384	211.923	4.153	95			
SD	1,119.25	84.482	86.433	226.346	6.427	91.666			

Table 6 Results of content analysis by region regarding CE-6Rs-related integrated reporting practices

Region-wise frequencies (%)									
Regions	R1 (%)	R2 (%)	R3 (%)	R4 (%)	R5 (%)	R6 (%)	Total/ 6Rs (%)	Mean	SD
EUROPE	7,931 (55.04)	243 (27.86)	260 (28.82)	1,537 (55.78)	26 (48.14)	659 (53.3)	10,656 (52.65)	1,776	3,062.668
SOUTH AMERICA	133 (0.92)	12 (1.37)	12 (1.33)	37 (1.343)	0 (0)	13 (1.05)	207 (1.02)	34.5	49.74636
NORTH AMERICA	303 (2.10)	27 (3.09)	27 (2.99)	45 (1.633)	2 (3.70)	29 (3.3)	433 (2.13)	72.166	113.92
ASIA	1,708 (11.8)	256 (29.35)	265 (29.37)	418 (15.71)	8 (14.81)	200 (16.1)	2855 (14.10)	475.83	617.9496
AFRICA	3,902 (27.9)	316 (36.23)	320 (35.47)	653 (23.70)	15 (27.77)	311 (25.1)	5,517 (27.26)	919.5	1,475.014
AUSTRIASIA	441 (3.06)	18 (2.064)	18 (1.99)	65 (2.35)	3 (5.55)	23 (1.86)	568 (2.80)	94.666	170.9511
Total/6RS (%)	14,418 (100)	872 (100)	902 (100)	2755 (100)	54 (100)	1235 (100)	20,236 (100)		
Mean	2,403	145.333	150.333	459.166	9	205.833			
SD	3,056.179	140.646	145.479	584.143	9.919	252.323			

To test hypothesis 1, CE-6Rs-related integrated reports are more prevalent in regions that implement a stronger coercive mechanism for the circular economy.
H_0: There is no association between regions and CE-6Rs integrated reports practices.
H_1: There is an association between regions and CE-6Rs and integrated reports practices.

The ANOVA Table 7 shows the null hypothesis failed to reject, as a *p*-value $0.035 < 0.05$ was determined, variables have statistically significant effects. All the regions involved in CE-6Rs activities into their integrated reports.

Hypothesis 2: CE-6Rs-related integrated reports are more prevalent in industries that implement a stronger normative mechanism for the circular economy.
H_0: There is no association between industries and CE-6Rs integrated reports practices.
H_1: There is an association between industries and CE-6Rs integrated reports practices.

The experiment of Hypothesis 2 shows that the null hypothesis failed to be rejected as the *p*-value was $0.001 < 0.05$ (Table 8). This indicates an association between industries and CE-6Rs integrated reports. Moving on to testing Hypothesis 3 (Table 9).

Hypothesis 3: CE-6Rs-related integrated reports are more prevalent in years that implement a stronger mimetic mechanism for the circular economy.

Table 7 ANOVA for hypothesis testing

Model	Sum of squares	Df	Mean square	F	Sig
Regression	13,620,218.456	2	6,810,109.228	3.723	0.035
Residual	60,364,209.099	33	1,829,218.458		
Total	73,984,427.556	35			

Table 8 ANOVA for hypothesis testing

Model	Sum of squares	Df	Mean Square	F	Sig
Regression	4,420,783.909	2	2,210,391.954	7.187	0.001
Residual	23,066,689.271	75	307,555.857		
Total	27,487,473.179	77			

Table 9 ANOVA for testing Hypothesis 3

Model	Sum of squares	Df	Mean Square	F	Sig
Regression	17,392,415.777	2	8,696,207.889	6.655	0.003
Residual	58,800,559.889	45	1,306,679.109		
Total	76,192,975.667	47			

H_0: There is no association between years and CE-6Rs integrated reporting practices.
H_1: There is an association between years and CE-6Rs integrated reporting practices.

The statistical analysis shows that the *p*-value $0.003 < 0.05$, and hence, the null hypothesis failed to reject. This means that year-wise CE-6Rs into IR practices are highly significantly related.

4 Discussion

This study reveals the association between CE-6Rs and IRs for different years, industries, and geographical regions. Addressing RQ1 (How and to what extent does integrated reporting support the circular economy 6Rs-related activities?). Regarding the emphasis on the CE-6Rs, it has emerged that CE-related information was widely cited among the scrutinized IRs. Subsequently, a few IRs from different regions, like South America with zero references and North America with only two cited concerns, have revealed concerns about redesigning terms. Even though the EU convincingly established the regional CE practice (EC, 2015a, 2015b) for preserving natural resources and disclosing these elements in financial and non-financial reporting (EU, 2014, 2017) (see Fig. 3).

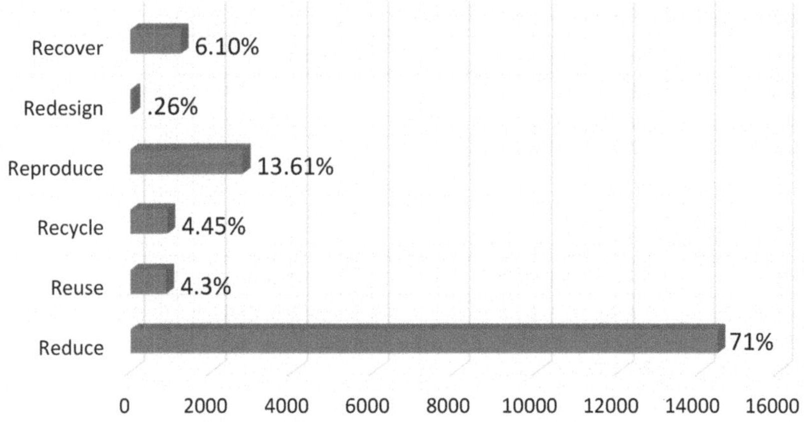

Fig. 3 Percentages intensity of CE-6Rs variables in IRs

Figure 3 provides a holistic view of CE6-Rs-related IR practices; according to percentage, the reduced term is most cited, and the redesign term is less cited. The paper recognized that CE-related activities in IR unequivocally influenced sustainable development and provided form information to stakeholders (Busco et al., 2018; Garvare & Johansson, 2010) for rational investment decision-making. The paper provides state-of-the-art research for academia, business, industry, practitioners, and policymakers, i.e., internal and external stakeholders. Moreover, organizations' consciousness of sustainable development issues, for example, environmental change, GHG effects, landfill site use, land and water pollution, health standards, job creation, reduced resource consumption, recycling of products, and reuse has been expanded (Stahel, 2014b). Under CE, fewer materials are required to manufacture a product, either through reduced material usage or recycled materials being employed (Stahel, 2014b).

However, the role of investors and stakeholders is an issue that crosses with the following of a CE at the small-scale level, only considered as cost savings, interests in the development of innovation, improved client connections, and the resourcefulness of firms (Adams et al., 2011; Stahel, 2014b), can be helpful study for both potential of stakeholder, either cost or sustainability. Although the study concentrates on assessment, is IR close-fitting with the CE-related activities and embedding with IR practice? The results of Tables 2–4 show that, to a large extent, IR practices support CE-6Rs-related activities.

Concerning RQ2 (How and to what extent do institutional pressures (coercive, normative, and mimetic) impact integrated reporting in the context of circular economy 6Rs activities?), the theoretical underpinnings of institutional theory research (DiMaggio & Powell, 1983; Scott, 2005) are drawn upon. Additionally, results demonstrate that CE-related IR practices significantly affect the region, industry, and year-wise. For instance, the European, Asian, and African may have reasonable IR practices regarding formal, obligatory, and classified principles and laws. In contrast, both regions have various potential practices concerning rules, sustainability standards, models, and frameworks (Boiral & Gendron, 2011).

Hypothesis 1 (CE-6Rs-related integrated reports are more prevalent in regions that implement a stronger coercive mechanism for the circular economy) has been supported with statistically significant effects. The Europe and Africa regions are most effectively involved in IR practice. In line with past research on regional sustainability (de Villiers & Sharma, 2017), it has been found that companies in different regions have to represent sustainability reporting and fellow guideline procedures (i.e., A4S, 2010; EU, 2014, 2017; GRI, 2010; KPMG, 2010), in general, disclosed at least amount of information about the CE activities in their reports. Regarding the guidelines of CE, it is argued that if stricter regulative key performance indicators were to exist in the regions, this would lead to more sustainable development through such practices. Accordingly, the European Commission (2015a, 2015b) has issued some CE directives that all member countries must follow. While in Africa, directives have been issued on IR, these do not pertain to CE-related activities at the organization level, but Table 5 pertains to statistically significant effects. Formal law instituted by the EC described the European context.

Similarly, Africa's (IIRC, 2011) contextual investigation was portrayed by casual law incited by expert associations, which seemed to get a more elevated level of conceiving. Moreover, the industry standards and framework enhance sustainability and manage the behaviors, like the guidance of GRI sustainable practice, UN (2015) Agenda 2030 guidance (Goal 12, Consumption of resources), A4S industry disclosures for corporate sustainability performance, and EU (2017) non-financial reporting. According to the coercive isomorphism perspective, sustainability laws impact CE-related information in regions like the EU (EC, 2015a, 2016). Directive 94/62/EC stated that packaging and packaging waste introduced with the harmonious way of consumption influence the CE-6Rs-related practices. In addition, the EU has issued Directive 2014/95/ (EU Directive), which requires the disclosure of all non-financial information, and the EU Guidelines 2017/C215/01 (EUG) to help firms provide this information. All regions' regulative instruments may be noteworthy in implementing CE activities into IR practices. Regarding the regulation of the CE, the research found that some areas like the EU and Africa act stricter regulative IR to disclose qualitative and quantitative information about CE activities into IR practices.

Regarding Hypothesis 2 (CE-6Rs-related integrated reports are more prevalent in industries that implement a more vital normative mechanism for the circular economy). Normative isomorphism pertains to there being a range of sustainable reporting rules, frameworks, and acceptable standards that may be significant in IR for all industries (A4S, 2010; DiMaggio & Powell, 1983a; GRI, 2010; KPMG, 2010; Li & Ding, 2013; UN, 2015). It has been found that CE-6Rs-related IR practices are already used in different industries, but not at large scale. For example, reducing the production of waste or reusing recycled waste already exists across various industries. As normative isomorphism refers to, CE-6Rs in IR practices refer to the professionalism that would be able to observe the essential stakeholders (Govt.) and provide a good shape financial and non-financial information, which influences the organization and society for the development in industries (DiMaggio & Powell, 1983b; Garvare & Johansson, 2010; Li & Ding, 2013). However, government legislation has a high impact on CE-related activities and corporate reporting practices in different industries, which change with the passage of time. These practices reflect significant evidence and have an ample opportunity for the organization's interest in adopting and disclosing the CE-related information in the IR to communicate information to the relevant stakeholder (Busco et al., 2018) that may differ from organization to organization. This combined practice of CE and IR presents various inside and outside advantages. According to the author, a broad investigation of IR practices about the CE has yet to be done. Moreover, findings pertain to every industry IR demonstrates a sum of CE-related activities in their reports. Besides, the study could give the beginning step to assist in exploring CE-6Rs activities in IR.

For estimating best practices, the study examines the year-wise practice of IR that verifies the business has been getting consideration for quite a while by trying to make unparalleled/accepted procedures by creating division explicit sustainability rules. Hypothesis 3 (CE-6Rs-related integrated reports are more prevalent in the year that implements a more vital mimetic mechanism for the circular economy) refers to year by year the IR practices increasing. Statistically, there is a significant effect. This means that the companies' practices are growing year by year. Most of the integrated reports exist from 2016 to 2017 years in this dataset. This may not be clarified that the CE-6Rs-related IR practices are increasing year-wise.

Environmental performance has considerably changed the socio-economic shape of every company. Therefore, modern company strategies require maintaining environmental stability between sustainable reporting practices and the value creation process (Barnabè & Nazir, 2022). Given that current practices do shape the cutting-edge, challenging business environment, companies, and regulatory bodies that are adopting new practices to realize the sustainability approach and develop new sustainability standards. Beyond profitability, corporations need to be more knowledgeable concerning the sustainability of their companies and environmental disclosure structures (Barnabè & Nazir, 2021). Since sustainable company strategies are based on the premise of a triple bottom line, it needs to adopt a robust commitment to those strategic movements for long-lasting advantages. This study proposes a framework covering a massive range of sustainability operations to evaluate sustainability. This framework can contribute to the linkage of operations, management and decision analysis areas, sustainability, and related ethical elements of the organization. Concerning social, environmental, economic, and manufacturing implications, this paper highlights exploited subjects in academia and practitioners that have obtained increasing interest and visibility in a practical context. The CE-6Rs-related framework embraces corporate potential toward an increasingly circular management framework. A combined framework for the value creation of organizations by adopting CE-6Rs practices in IR is proposed (Fig. 4).

The framework allows for a comprehensive picture of CE activities in IR practice regarding the degree to which the organization is pursuing value creation and contributing to sustainable development. Hence, the contribution of this paper is a comprehensive CE and IR framework, which is a pragmatic technique for a regenerative economy, environmental issues, and contributing to the social side of society. The combined framework accentuates a mutual perspective of resources, business activities, outputs, and outcomes. It emphasizes providing all stakeholders with information for participation in investment decision-making and enhancing sustainable development.

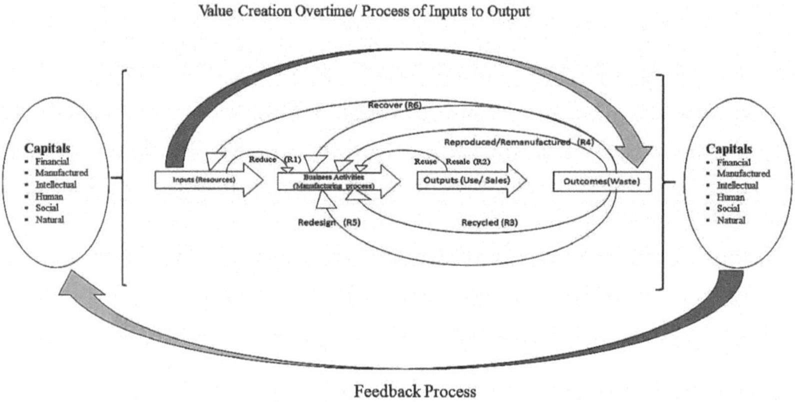

Fig. 4 Combined framework of CE-6Rs and IIRC (*Source* EMF, 2013, p. 33; IIRC, 2013, p. 13)

5 Conclusion

The study highlights how the CE-6Rs relate to IR practice in all industries and geographical areas. Subsequently, research led to various reports on heterogeneous industries and regions. This paper has provided an investigation into the IR practices from 2011 to 2018 in relation to CE-6Rs activities across six areas in 13 industries. It emerged that 84 IRs demonstrated CE-6Rs-related activities at a large scale. The findings indicate that most IRs include the closed-loop cycle (reduce) high-referenced term as most of the integrated reports focused on the emission of GHGs, material, water-reducing practices, and the least reference term redesign. The research discloses the existing IR practices and CE activities in different regions and industries. Evidence and institutional pressure revealed that coercive, normative, and mimetic isomorphism specifically impact CE-6Rs-related IR practices. For instance, the European, Asian, and African regions may have reasonable IR practices regarding formal, obligatory, and classified principles and laws. In contrast, both regions have various potential practices concerning rules, sustainability standards, models, and frameworks (Boiral & Gendron, 2011), while the impact of mimetic isomorphisms needs further investigation because many reports are present from 2016 to 2017 in IIRC.

6 Limitations

Certain limitations exist with this study. The most significant limitations of the research, which open doors for further research, are as follows. First, the primary quantitative restriction of the study is related to the years. The year 2012 IIRC provides no IR, same as in 2018. Only one report is contained in the IIRC. Most of the reports belong to 2016 and 2017. The sample mainly relies on the 2016- and 2017-year reports; information may be needed to demonstrate the full critical effect of the CE-related strategy and enactment in the IR.

7 Future Research

In any case, the connection between industry standards (e.g., G4, GRI, UN 2030, EU directives) for sustainable development (accepted as best practices) and CE-related IR practices should be additionally investigated to determine whether any other patterns of CE can be identified. Hence, a comprehensive investigation is required through expert surveys, interviews, and case studies.

8 Practical Implications

From the practical perspective, the findings of this study could be used by corporate managers and stakeholders to deploy CE-related practices in the organization and society to enhance sustainable consumption practices. The study provides an accurate picture and shapes information to all the stakeholders for managerial decision-making, policymakers, and trendsetters for developing new standards and regulations for adequately implementing CE activities into their organization reporting. It would create indicators to measure the CE and its role in the sustainable development performance of the organization and companies. A combined framework helps minimize resource consumption, promote regenerative activities in the business, and generate new accounting information for stakeholders.

References

A4S. (2010). *Accounting for sustainability*. http://www.accountingforsustainability.org/output/page186.asp

Abrutyn., S., & Turner, J. H. (2011). The old institutionalism meets the new institutionalism. *Sociological Perspectives, 54*(3), 283–306.

Adams, R. B., Licht, A. N., & Sagiv, L. (2011). Shareholders and stakeholders: How do directors decide? *Strategic Management Journal, 32*(12), 1331–1355.

Aranda-Uson, A., Portillo-Tarragona, P., Scarpellini, S. & Llena-Macarulla. F. (2020). The progressive adoption of a circular economy by businesses for cleaner production: An approach from a regional study in Spain. *Journal of Cleaner Production*, 247, 119648.

Barnabè, F., & Nazir, S. (2021). Investigating the interplays between integrated reporting practices and circular economy disclosure. *International Journal of Productivity and Performance Management, 70*(8), 2001–2031.

Barnabè, F., & Nazir, S. (2022). Conceptualizing and enabling circular economy through integrated thinking. *Corporate Social Responsibility and Environmental Management, 29*(2), 448–468.

Boiral, O., & Gendron, Y. (2011). Sustainable development and certification practices: Lessons learned and prospects. *Business Strategy and the Environment, 20*(5), 331–347.

Burritt, S., & Schaltegger, S. (2010). Sustainability accounting and reporting: Fad or trend? *Accounting, Auditing & Accountability Journal, 23*(7), 829–846.

Busco, C., Frigo, M. L., Riccaboni, A., & Quattrone, P. (2013). *Integrated reporting: Concepts and cases that redefine corporate accountability*. Switzerland.

Busco, C., Malafronte, I., Pereira, J., & Starita, M. G. (2018). The determinants of companies' levels of integration: Does one size fit all? *The British Accounting Review, 51*(3), 277–298.

Campbell, L. J. (2007). Why would corporation behave in socially responsible ways? An institutional theory of corporate social responsibility. *The Academy of Management Review, 32*(3), 946–967.

Cohen, J. L., Holder-Webb, L., Nath, L., & Wood, D. (2012). Corporate reporting on nonfinancial leading indicators of economic performance and sustainability. *Accounting Horizons, 26*(1), 65–90.

de Villiers, C., & Sharma, U. (2020). A critical reflection on the future of financial, intellectual capital, sustainability and integrated reporting. *Critical Perspectives on Accounting, 70*, 101999. https://www.sciencedirect.com/science/article/pii/S1045235417300606

DiMaggio, P. J., & Powell, W. W. (1983a). The iron revisited; Institutional isomorphism and collective rationality in organizational fields. *American Sociological Review, 48*(2), 147–160.

DiMaggio, P. J., & Powell, W. W. (1983b). *The new institution in organizational analysis*. University of Chicago Press.

EMF. (2012). *Economic and business rationale for an accelerated transition: Towards a circular economy* (Vol. 2). Ellen MacArthur Foundation. https://www.ellenmacarthurfoundation.org/publications

EMF. (2013). *Opportunities for the consumer goods sector: Towards a circular economy* (Vol. 1). Ellen MacArthur Foundation. https://www.ellenmacarthurfoundation.org/publications

EMF. (2015). *Delivering the circular economy—A toolkit for policymakers*. Ellen MacArthur Foundation. https://www.ellenmacarthurfoundation.org/publications

EMF. (2016). *The new plastic economy: Rethinking the future of plastics & catalysing action*. https://www.ellenmacarthurfoundation.org/publications

EMF. (2017). *A new textile economy, redesigning fashion's future*. Ellen MacArthur Foundation. https://www.ellenmacarthurfoundation.org/publications

EU, (1994). *Directive 94/62/EC on packaging and packaging waste*. http://eur-lex.europa.eu/LexUriServ/LexUriServ.do?uri=CELEX:31994L0062:EN:HTML

European Commission. (2000a). *EU financial reporting strategy: The way forward*. https://eur-lex.europa.eu/legal-content/en/ALL/?uri=CELEX:52000DCO359

European Commission (2000b). *Company reporting*. https://ec.europa.eu/info/business-economy-euro/company-reporting-and-auditing/company-reporting_en

European Commission. (2008). *Directive 2008/98/EC of the European Parliament and the Council*. https://eur-lex.europa.eu/legal-content/EN/TXT/?uri=CELEX:32008L0098

European Commission. (2014). *Towards a circular economy: A zero waste programme for Europe, COM (2014)398*. https://www.eumonitor.eu/9353000/1/j9vvik7m1c3gyxp/vjl4tamjogxb

European Commission. (2015a). *EU resource efficiency scoreboard*. https://ec.europa.eu/environment/resource_efficiency/targets_indicators/scoreboard/index_en.htm

European Commission. (2015b). *Closing the loops—An EU action plan for the circular economy*. COM/2015/0614 final. https://eur-lex.europa.eu/legal-content/EN/TXT/?uri=CELEX:52015DC0614

European Commission. (2015c). *Communication from the commission to the European Parliament, the council, the European Economic and Social Committee and the committee of the regions*. COM (2015) 614/2.

European Commission. (2017). *The role of waste-to-energy in the circular economy*. https://ec.europa.eu/environment/waste/waste-to-energy.pdf
European Commission. (2018a). *A European strategy for plastics in a circular economy*. https://ec.europa.eu/environment/circular-economy/pdf/plastics-strategy.pdf
European Commission. (2018b). *EU raw material week 2018—Closing the loop on critical raw materials*. https://ec.europa.eu/easme/en/news/eu-raw-materials-week-2018-closing-loop-critical-raw-materials
European Union. (2014). *Non-financial reporting*. https://ec.europa.eu/info/business-economy-euro/company-reporting-and-auditing/company-reporting/non-financial-reporting_en
European Union. (2017). *Guidelines on non-financial reporting*. https://ec.europa.eu/anti-trafficking/sites/antitrafficking/files/guidelines_on_non-financial_reporting.pdf
Garvare, R., & Johansson, P. (2010). Management for sustainability—A stakeholder theory. *Total Quality Management and Excellence Journal, 21*(7), 737–744.
Geng, Y., & Doberstein, B. (2008). Development of the circular economy in China: Challenges and opportunities for achieving 'leapfrog' development. *International Journal of Sustainable Development, 3*, 231–239.
Ghisellini, P., Cialani, C., & Ulgiati, S. (2016). A review on circular economy: The expected transition to a balance interplay of environmental and economic systems. *Journal of Cleaner Production, 114*, 11–32.
Giorgino, M. C., Barnabe, F., & Paoicelli, N. (2016). Searching for the missing link between business model and strategy: *The Integrated Reporting Perspective*. In A. Jablonski (Ed.), *Business models: Strategies, impact and challenges*. Nova Science Publisher.
Gray, C., & Charter, M. (2007). *Remanufacturing and product design designing of the 7th generation*. The Centre for Sustainable Design, University College for the Creative Arts and SEEDA.
Gray, R., & Laughlin, R. (2012). It was 20 years ago today Sgt Pepper, accounting, auditing & accountability journal, green accounting and the blue meanies. *Accounting Auditing & Accountability Journal, 25*(2), 228–255.
Gray, R. (2002). Of messiness, systems, and sustainability: Towards more social and environmental finance and accounting. *The British Accounting Review, 34*, 357–386.

Gray, R., Adams, C. A., & Owen, D. (2014). Accounting, social responsibility and sustainability: Accounting for the society and the environment. *Social and Environmental Accountability Journal, 34*(3), 193–194.

GRI. (2010). *Global conference executive brief: Rethink, rebuilt, report*. http://www.amsterdamgriconference.org/2010_GRI_Global_Conference_Executive_Briefing.pdf

Guthrie, J., & Abeysekera, I. (2006). Content analysis of social, environmental reporting: What is new? *Journal of Human Resource Costing and Accounting, 10*(2), 114–126.

Guthrie, J., Petty, R., Yongvanich, K., & Ricceri, F. (2004). Using content analysis as a research method to inquire into intellectual capital reporting. *Journal of Intellectual Capital, 5*(2), 282–293.

IIRC. (2011). *Discussion paper. Towards integrated reporting. Communicating value in the 21st century*. International Integrated Reporting Council. https://integratedreporting.org/wp-content/uploads/2011/09/IR-Discussion-Paper-2011_spreads.pdf

IIRC. (2013a). *The international IR framework*. International Integrated Reporting Council. https://integratedreporting.org/resource/international-ir-framework/

IIRC. (2013b). *Business model: Background paper for IR*. International Integrated Reporting Council. https://integratedreporting.org/wp-content/uploads/2013/03/Business_Model.pdf

IIRC. (2013c). *Capitals: Background paper for IR*. International Integrated Reporting Council. https://integratedreporting.org/wp-content/uploads/2013/03/IR-Background-Paper-Capitals.pdf

IIRC. (2013d). *Value creation: Background paper*. International Integrated Reporting Council. https://integratedreporting.org/wp-content/uploads/2013/08/Background-Paper-Value-Creation.pdf

Jayal, A. D., Badurdeen, F., Dillon, O. W., Jr., & Jawahir, I. S. (2010). Sustainable manufacturing, modeling and optimization challenges at the product, process and system levels. *CIRP Journal of Manufacturing Science and Technology, 3*, 144–152.

Kamp-Roelands, N. (2013). *A commentary on integrated reporting*: A review of developments and their implications for the accounting curriculum. *Accounting Education, 22*(4), 357–359.

Kirchherr, J., Reike, D., & Hekkert, M. (2017). Conceptualizing the circular economy: An analysis of 144 definitions. *Resources, Conservation & Recycling, 128*, 221–232.

KPMG. (2008). *Climate change your business*. https://inis.iaea.org/search/search.aspx?orig_q=RN:40052557

KPMG. (2010). *KPMG promotes integration of company reports*. http://www.kpmg.com/RO/en/IssuesAndInsights/ArticlesPublications/Press-releases/Pages/Integrated-Reporting.aspx

Krippendorff, K. (1989). Content analysis. In E. Barnouw, G. Gerbner, W. Schramm, T. L. Worth, & L. Gross (Eds.), *International encyclopaedia of communication* (Vol. 1, pp. 403–407). Oxford University Press.

Krippendorff, K. (2004). Reliability in content analysis some common misconceptions and recommendations. *Human Communication Research, 30*(3), 411–433.

Lacy, P., & Rutqvist, J. (2015). *Waste to wealth: The circular economy advantage*. Macmillan.

Li, F., & Ding, Z. D. (2013). The effect of institutional isomorphic pressure on the internationalization of the firm in an emerging economy: Evidence from China. *Asia Pacific Business Review, 19*(4), 506–525.

Lieder, M., & Rashid, A. (2016). Towards circular economy implementation: A comprehensive review in the context of manufacturing industry. *Journal of Cleaner Production., 115*, 36–51.

Linder, M., & Williander, M. (2017). Circular business model innovation: Inherent uncertainties. *Business Strategy and the Environment, 26*(2), 182–196.

Llena, F., Moneva, J. M., & Hernandez, B. (2007). Environmental disclosures and compulsory accounting standards: The case of Spanish annual reports. *Business Strategy and the Environment., 16*, 50–63.

Mathews, M. R. (2008). Further thoughts on mega-accounting and the need for standards. *Issues in Social and Environmental Accounting, 2*(2), 158–175.

Mathews, J. A., & Tan, H. (2011). Progress toward a circular economy in China, the drivers (and inhibitors) of eco-industrial initiative. *Journal of Industrial Ecology, 15*(3), 435–457.

Merli, R., Preziosi, M., & Acampora, A. (2018). How do scholars approach the circular economy? A systematic literature review. *Journal of Cleaner Production, 178*, 703–722.

Milne, M. J., & Adler, R. W. (1999). Exploring the reliability of social and environmental disclosures content analysis. *Accounting, Auditing & Accountability Journal, 12*(2), 237–256.

Moroney, R., & Trotman, K. T. (2016). Differences in auditors' materiality assessment when auditing financial statement and sustainability reports. *Contemporary Accounting Research, 33*(2), 551–575.

Nasr, M., & Thurston, M. (2006). Remanufacturing: A key enable to sustainable product systems. In *13th CIRP International Conference of Life Cycle Engineering* (pp. 15–18).

OECD. (2015a). *Enable the next production revolution.* https://www.oecd.org/officialdocuments/publicdisplaydocumentpdf/?cote=DSTI/IND(2015)2&docLanguage=En

OECD. (2015b). *Compendium of productivity indicators.* https://www.oecd-ilibrary.org/industry-and-services/oecd-compendium-of-productivity-indicators_22252126

Ranta, V., Stenroos, A. L., & Makinen, J. S. (2018). Creating value in the circular economy: A structured multiple-case analysis of business models. *Journal of Cleaner Production, 201*, 998–1000.

Reike, D., Vermeulen, W. J. V., & Witjes, S. (2018). The circular economy; New or refurbished as CE 3.0? Exploring controversies in the conceptualization of the circular economy through a focus on history and resource value retention options. *Journal of Cleaner Production, 135*, 246–264.

Scott, W. R. (2005). *Social movement and organization movement.* Cambridge University Press.

Sihvonen, S., & Partanen, J. (2017). Eco-design practices with a focus on quantitative environmental targets: An exploratory content analysis within ICT sector. *Journal of Cleaner Production, 143*, 769–783.

Stahel, W. R. (2014a). *Reuse is the key to the circular economy.* European Commission. http://ec.europa.eu/environment/ecoap/about-eco-innovation/experts-interviews/reuse-is-the-key-to-the-circular-economy

Stahel, W. R. (2014b). *The business angle of a circular economy—Higher competitiveness, higher resource security and material efficiency.* The Product-Life Institute. www.product-life.org

Stewart, R., & Niero, M. (2018). Circular economy incorporates sustainability strategies: A review of corporate sustainability reports in the fast-moving consumer goods sector. *Business Strategy and the Environment, 27*(7), 1005–1022.

Winer, B. J. (1971). *Statistical principles in experimental design* (2th ed.). McGraw-Hill: Kogakusha Ltd.

Witjes, S., & Lozano, R. (2016). Towards a more circular economy: Proposing a framework linking sustainable public procurement and sustainable business models. *Resource, Conservation, Recycling, 112*, 37–44.

UN. (2015). *United Nations Sustainable Development Agenda (2030).* https://www.un.org/sustainabledevelopment/development-agenda/

6

Circular Economy and Balanced Scorecard

1 Introduction

Global warming, pollution, and declining soil fertility have increased environmental issues as well as increased the demand for raw materials. The concept of sustainability was first considered as the substitute/solution for social improvement, and the most effective environmental and economic issue for people to rethink their ideas about resource recovery and productivity, which concerned in the late twentieth century (Gacser & Szoka, 2021). Linking the principles of sustainability and development has truly been large because in the 1980s, a milestone turned into the work of the World Commission on Environment and Development, more known as the Brundtland Commission, which provided its report in 1987 entitled "Our Common Future." As the Brundtland Commission stated in 1987, "development that meets the needs of the present without compromising the ability of future generations to meet their very own demands." The concept explains sustainable economic, environmental, and social development in cohesion (WCED, 1987). Criticism of this has additionally emerged, with conservative critics interpreting sustainability as stagnation, which isn't always

S. Nazir and A. Capocchi, *Sustainability Reporting Practices and the Circular Economy*,
https://doi.org/10.1007/978-3-031-51845-4_6

sufficient to meet the demands of a significantly growing population (Gacser & Szoka, 2021).

Although the discussion on circular economy (CE) was initiated in early 2000, in the last decades, the concept has attracted a lot of attention from researchers, policymakers, and practitioners to enforce initiatives that allow the transition from a linear to a CE. Besides, the successful CE framework is expected to contribute to all three dimensions of sustainable development: environmental, social, and economic (Lamba et al., 2023). Thus, it is possible to reduce the environmental, social, and economic effects of intense industrialization and increase consumption (Zarbakhshnia et al., 2023). Balancing and intertwining environmental and social concerns is a vital concern with sustainability issues (de Oliveira & Oliveira, 2023). The CE framework is in line with the proposals of the United Nations Agenda 2030 for Sustainable Development. Mainly related to Sustainable Development 17 Goals and 169 targets, which intend to allow resilient infrastructures, sustainable industrialization, promote innovation, and ensure sustainable production and consumption flows. Also, associated with the social aspects, sustainable development goals 1, 5, and 8 goals to minimize and reduce poverty level, offer proper work and economic progress, and improve gender equality (Crespo-Rosas & Franco-García, 2023; de Oliveira & Oliveira, 2023).

Despite the enormous literature that has been published on the circular economy in the last decade, in addition, theoretical and empirical work is still required (Barnabè & Nazir, 2021; 2022). Studies introducing a new circular economy balanced scorecard by using key overall performance indicators [KPIs] and their respective dimension are nonetheless scarce in literature (Calzolari et al., 2022; Sassanelli et al., 2019). In this context, research proposes a new concept tool of a balanced scorecard (Kaplan, 2009). Few researchers have taken into consideration social and environmental aspects (Duman et al., 2018), and a gap remains that a comprehensive balanced scorecard is still required which includes the social, environmental, economic, and governance aspects of the organization. This study presented and used key performance indicators (KPIs) that are associated with social, economic, environmental, and governance impact on companies' performance as well as assessment to complement the companies' performance by using this framework (Kaplan & Norton, 1996); KPIs related to the social, environmental, economic, and governance dimension of sustainability are used for this purpose. For this purpose, the study retrieved data from the Knight top 100 corporations.

In this context, we examine the top 100 more sustainable companies that belong to the manufacturing and services sectors. In addition, the framework not only supports supply chain management but also highlights diverse stakeholders concerned. Stakeholders are concerned with the organization's economic, social, environmental, and governance for the rational decision-making process and economic improvement (Duman et al., 2018; Hernández-Arzaba et al., 2022). Considering the above, this paper proposes a framework to evaluate social, economic, and environmental aspects to promote circular economy in their organizations and disclosed in their reports. This balanced scorecard framework may be used to enhance the model proposed by using Kaplan and Norton (1996) and other contexts. To validate the framework, we researched the top 100 most sustainable corporations.

The contributions of this look are twofold: (i) How are companies reporting practices disclosing circular economy practices? How does circular economy engage and support four dimensions of sustainability (social, economy, governance, and environmental)? The study exploited sustainability subjects that can be beneficial to managers and practitioners to provide systematized aspects to the decision-making related to the circular economy, explicitly concerning social, environmental, governance, and economic issues. This paper is established as follows: Sect. 1 provides the concerned historical past, the study gaps and problems, the incentive and relevance of the look, the overall objective, and the primary contributions of the paper. Section 2 presents the literature overview, with the main topics approached within the paper. Section 3 describes in detail the methodological processes observed. Section 4 presents the results. Section 5 discusses the findings of the paper in the context of literature and findings. Finally, Sect. 6 confirms the concluding remarks, the limitations, and further studies.

2 Literature Review

Balanced Scorecard

A balanced scorecard is a management technique that permits the measurement of the overall performance of an organizations strategy that uses financial and non-financial aspects. In 1991, Kaplan and Norton introduced the concept of a balanced scorecard and expanded it in addition to the balanced scorecard (1996).

The usual model has four components that can be linked to the company's approaches and values. These dimensions consist of economic, consumer, internal business processes, and organizational learning and growth. In general, many managers and companies' policymakers consult with a "balanced scorecard" as a linking of financial and non-financial measures with companies' performance and goals (Kaplan & Norton, 1996). The balanced scorecard's four perspectives have been used to analyze the company's performance: first, the economic perspective emphasizes revenue and investment that demonstrate and link with strategic and financial goals; second, the customer perspective emphasizes all those activities that demonstrate the company's strategy and actions to provide organization value creation; third, measures that show the overall performance of the organization in importance with internal elements that are covered inside the internal organization process; fourth and lastly, the learning and growth perspective that emphasizes how company properly deals with future demanding situations by using maximum organizational resources.

Some authors highlight social and environmental elements on the balanced scorecard (Duman et al., 2018). Economic and governance aspects have been associated or incorporated with organization management control and are necessary to consider for the organizations' value creation process and attract stakeholders for investment purposes. Economic social environmental and governance aspects have strong links with highlighted companies' sustainability issues that could be obviously necessary for the companies' values creation and image. Hockerts (2001) addressed the strategy to disclose social, economic, and environmental concerns into the traditional aspects of the "BSC." Key performance indicators (KPIs) are used the measure an organization's goals and strategies that cover the social, economic, and environmental aspects of the organization and other dimensions of the organization.

According to Kaplan and Norton (2000), the potential of business should be a basic element of performance measurement and represented through the presence of social indicators in the "internal process," additionally prospective "customer" perspective belongs to environmental aspects that sustain all the organization's operations. Hansen and Schaltegger (2016) proposed a "sustainability balanced scorecard" method, which adds a financial/economic perspective and states that sustainable revenue and sustainable investment need to protect the economic sustainability as well as the company's sustainability. In general, each economic and social component must be addressed at an identical time and in an identical way. Learning and growth perspectives arise from the use of balanced scorecards in complicated business governance that is turning into an increasing number of substantial, and the need to connect and apply such governance structures employee's participation that mainly introduces tools and decision-making processes which enhance the sustainability practice within the organization. Business customers need to be capable of better visualizing the analysis of big totals of complicated statistics.

Balanced Scorecard and Circular Economy

Company managers make decisions on data and records that consist of a variety of decisions and decisive issues, subsequently, creating a wide range of extract and intangible business-related values (Wixom et al., 2013). A fundamental assumption of "BSC" formations identifies their basic plan to achieve and the techniques of communication by which these facts are received. The circular economy (CE) idea often entails treating the economic and environmental ramifications with extreme importance. It aims to maintain an infinite flow of value in goods, resources, and materials. However, there is a significant decrease in product waste (Lihong, 2011; Witjes et al., 2016). In other words, it aims to shift people's behaviors from a linear economic model (extraction, manufacture, use, and disposal) toward a new, circular one that modifies the conventional life cycle of goods, materials, and resources (including water and energy) by reintroducing them in subsequent production cycles (Witjes et al., 2016). Utilizing resources more effectively results in a greater balance and harmony between the economy, environment, and society (Hopwood et al., 2005; Reh, 2013; Scheel, 2016). Additionally, it is a concept that is relevant to businesses in all industries (Hopwood et al., 2005; Janubová & Grešš, 2016; Reh, 2013; Scheel, 2016) and consequently to the building sector (Janubová & Grešš, 2016; Witjes & Lozano, 2016). It is important to highlight that there have been virtually no attempts to quantify it (Pask et al., 2017). The "BSC" and "CE" have interconnections for delivering and achieving strategic objectives, BSC focuses on gathering and analysis while CE enhances business value.

- CE encourages the KPIs of the balanced scorecard to disclose relevant information.
- CE activities and plans are aligned with strategic goals.
- Integration of "BSC with CE" is usually recommended when there is a foundation for a circular design business model.
- BSC is employed in circular design as a precious tool to discover more business possibilities, as "BSC" makes a field of collecting vital records and categorizing them based on their connections.

There may be a common set of correlations among "CE" and "BSC," which allows the necessary foundations represented in strategic goal alignment, and "KPI," this alignment being translated and interpreted via "CE" principles. Strategy presentation and overall performance measurement is the basic tool of BSC while "CE" is performed as an important part of overall performance translation which uses circularity form and consolidation with the performance aspect. The most important steps are accompanied that allow the put together of the overall performance dimension via CE, which involves facts series, statistics consolidation, and exploitation.

Balanced Scorecard and Circular Economy and Sustainability Reporting

In recent years, pressure from external stakeholders, new regulatory requirements for regulatory compliance, and new rules and regulations from the company management have extended the importance of sustainability accounting and reporting. The company management corresponds with sustainability principles in decision-making procedures and business operations. The concept of accounting and sustainability goes back in a protracted manner, which clearly defines that sustainable accounting can be separated and interpreted in many approaches. To date, there is no generally accepted definition of sustainability accounting. By consensus, three elements have emerged in sustainability accounting: the environmental, social, and economic dimensions (see also the triple bottom lines, or TBL) (Elkington & Rowlands, 1999). According to Steen-Olsen et al. (2016), TBL accounting mainly uses quantitative, financial, non-financial, social, and environmental key performance indicators for the measurement of companies' performance and decision-making. Based on the studies of Gacser and Szoka (2021), sustainability accounting includes two parts. It is mainly used to measure, analyze, and record the social and environmental effects and economic sustainability of the business, and secondly, it sets standards and regulations for the financial implementation of environmental perception and social justice. Annual financial reports have a long history compared to sustainability reporting. Although there are some early examples, most reports on the social and environmental aspects have existed since the 1980s, and in fact, environmental screw-ups have extended their range and importance.

The formal policies for sustainability reporting have been started in the past decades. The Global Reporting Initiative (GRI) was founded in 1997 by the Coalition for Environmentally Responsible Economies (CERES) and the United Nations Environment Program (UNEP) to create guidelines for reporting on the economic, environmental, and social dimensions of companies. The European Union has developed a ranking system for listing companies' economic principles that are categorized as sustainable to prompt the flow of financial resources for sustainable activities across the EU which is called EU taxonomy. It is part of the European Green Deal Action Plan, which aims to ensure zero carbon emissions and restoration of the natural environment within the EU by 2050. This is the beginning point for measuring sustainability, and companies can be used to summarize, determine, and report sustainability indicators. The European Union has contributed to the enhancement of the regulatory framework for sustainability reporting, with the adoption in 2014 of a directive (2014/Directive 95/EC, also known as the Non-Financial Reporting Directive (NFRD)) requiring a massive number of companies groups (11,700) to disclose the financial and non-financial information to their stakeholders.

The European Commission issued a guide in June 2017 to assist organizations in disclosing social, economic, and environmental information in a report, supplemented by the 2019 Climate Change Guidelines. In 2022, the European Commission standard a proposal for a Corporate Sustainability Reporting Directive, which changed the reporting patterns and guidance of the Non-Financial Reporting Directive. These directives mainly aim to disclose the financial and non-financial information of the listed companies which highlights the auditing and accounting information in a detailed report. The European Financial Reporting Advisory Group will expand a necessary Community Sustainability Reporting Standard. The first draft widely evolved in 2022 as well as keeping EU policies (Gacser & Szoka, 2021). The CSRD (Corporate Sustainability Reporting Directive) will enter into force in 2023, changing the NFRD. Thus, the scope of reporting is expected to be extended to all large corporations operating in the EU that engage greater than 250 people or have a turnover of greater than EUR 40 million or a balance sheet of more than EUR 20 million. Moreover, the companies used multiple and cross-sector indicators to evaluate the economic, social, governance, and environmental overall performance. For instance, the water indicator is determined by the manufacturing plant that can offer the most manufacturing goods with the least water or reduce natural resource consumption, reuse natural resources, waste reduction, reduce product cost, and redesign product packaging. For comparability, companies want to analyze by using relative indicators (e.g., companies divide the quantity of water used by the wide variety of products) to understand the absolute cost. Move forward to Fig. 1.

- *Financial/economic perspective*

In the balanced scorecard, the financial perspective serves two purposes. The first is referred to as a method's financial overall performance, and the second one is referred to as the endpoint of the fundamental impact on supply chain management, which suggests BSC's other perspectives; the business recognizes the financial alignment (Kaplan, 2009). These techniques intend to enhance asset management, product cost, and product recovery and grow turnover. In addition, a sustainability balanced scorecard enhances the product cost savings, return on capital, return on investment, return on assets, and return on equity; these companies used the indicators to access information and future decisions

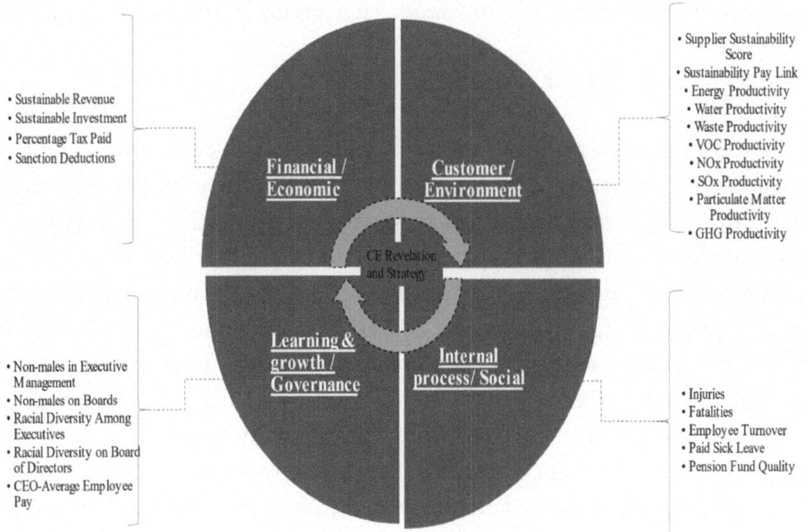

Fig. 1 Balanced scorecard and circular economy (*Source* Kaplan, 2009)

developed to get organization goals (Sassanelli et al., 2019). Manufacturing and services industries want to undertake circular economic frameworks that can be used to measure product costs and strong stakeholder engagement (Hernández-Arzaba et al., 2022; Torgautov et al., 2022). Manufacturing industries refer to reducing product costs and landfill which were identified the waste reduction and waste recycling (Hernández-Arzaba et al., 2022). On the contrary, the recycling expenses of waste are a big problem for countries and companies (Tsai et al., 2020) and affect the companies' revenue and investment. However, in certain European nations, recycling costs are equally important for the reason that they lead to significant commercial losses. Moreover, the stakeholder's engagement in general plays a vital role in reducing the companies' waste by using circular ways and is useful financially. Although the circular economic framework is an exceedingly new idea globally, key stakeholders appear to realize its importance (Torgautov et al., 2022).

RQ1: To what extent do companies disclose financial/economic perspectives and support CE principles by the balanced scorecard framework?

- *Customer/environment perspectives*

From the customer point of view, it specifies that companies identify customers' demands and be focused on the way to obtain the desired economic outcomes, in addition to how the corporation intends to be economical inside the marketplace. It has to be evident how all measures and targets are engaged to the success of the objectives of the financial prospects (Torgautov et al., 2022). For consumers, the firm has a definite plan to emerge as its favored supplier. This approach has two primary objectives: (1) reducing consumer wait time by responding quickly to those requests, which are measured by delay time; and (2) stopping and decreasing consumer complaints by measuring the number of customers complaining. Torgautov et al., 2022 and Hernández-Arzaba et al., 2022 state that observed contracting with suppliers to employ their waste ranked as a great operational practice for handling on-site waste. Secondly, the redesign of waste practices is used in manufacturing operations although it requires a lot of circular practices. Minimizing excess waste is one of the excellent practices of circular economy inside the production unit (Torgautov et al., 2022). Tsai et al. (2020) have rated collaboration and relationships among stakeholders (value chain) at their highest in terms of stakeholder engagement issues and waste management context.

CE builds remedy and recovery platforms for industrial and home-based waste, as well as the surrounding areas with reduced water consumption industry. The company ambitions to reduce water consumption, reduce NOx emissions, reduce SOx emissions, reduce CO_2, and recycle waste with the aim to reduce its environmental footprint as well as moves to endorse CE framework and environmental protection, that is why the company pursuits to reduce water, reduce NOx emissions, lessen dirt emissions, lessen CO_2, and recycle waste. Water consumption, NOx emissions, dust and CO_2 emissions, and recycling rates are used to determine how nicely to meet environmental sustainability objectives. This could enable the assessment of the effectiveness and feasibility of the proposed method with the aid of small and medium organizations in rising economics.

RQ2: To what extent do companies disclose customer/environment perspectives and support CE principles by the balanced scorecard framework?

- *Internal business process/social perspective*

It's about comparing the important approaches that contribute to the long-term uncompromising benefit of the business and figuring out whether innovation and protection are the closest processes for delivering exquisite solutions. However, introducing a new product in the market is the primary objective of the organization and fulfills the demand of customers by adopting innovation. The companies mainly focus on the reduction of material costs as well as material consumption. For this, the companies adopt circular economy-related principles. The performance of those goals is measured by using key performance indicators. Within this study, we embed internal processes with the social responsibility of the companies. Companies have created maximum measures for high-significance rankings and secure inter-agreements such as employee turnover, paid sick leave, and pension fund quality scores.

RQ 3: To what extent do companies disclose internal business processes/ social perspectives and support CE principles by the balanced scorecard framework?

- *Learning and growth perspectives/governance*

The infrastructure that is required for the accomplishment of the company's goals from other perspectives is described through the learning and growth perspectives. "How to control and manage change inside the organization?" is the question in this situation. It all states the strategic goals: Employee abilities, protection, and skill enhancement are the principal components of the learning and growth perspective.

The company's abilities in the skills development process are split into two desires: (1) skill development and (2) information gain access to facilitation. For this a number of training hours consistent with the employee and the disposal of records were used to evaluate the method's effectiveness. Business safety and protection are generally associated with achieving zero fatal accidents, with misplaced time accidents and the number of work accidents getting used to assess the strategy's effectiveness.

Internal knowledge sharing is arranged as a priority over such factors as getting admittance to new strategies and information change in the industry, which are outside knowledge sharing and employee training (governance factors). As most of the organizations surveyed are big-sized (i.e., own an abundance of branch offices throughout several international locations), expertise sharing and distribution may additionally seem logical and appropriate in this context. The personnel's training and supplier experience are crucial factors in waste reduction and measured training and education as the second most efficient approach to measuring and executing waste management plans (Begum et al., 2009; Kirchherr & Piscicelli, 2019). In this research, the balanced scorecard also rated the significance of circular economy principles that could enhance the stakeholder decision-making process and organization value creation. However, making a circular balanced scorecard could be effective in measuring the company's performance (Esmaeilian et al., 2018).

The business has carried out employee skill development plans, shared security practices, and supported approaches to the local community.

RQ 4: To what extent do companies disclose learning and growth perspectives/governance perspectives and support CE principles by the balanced scorecard framework?

3 Research Methodology

The study used content analysis to calculate the circular economy principles data from the companies' annual reports and check the hypotheses. In qualitative studies, various analysis techniques can be used, for example, phenomenology, hermeneutics, grounded theory, ethnography, phenomenography, and content analysis (Burnard, 1995). In comparison with qualitative research strategies, qualitative content analysis is not linked to any unique science, and there are fewer guidelines to follow. During the entire manner, the researcher needs to adhere to a qualitative approach, and the main challenge is to attain the rigor and credibility that make the results as authentic as possible. However, in content analysis, extraordinary standards of credibility may be chosen within the discussion of reliability. The researcher can apply identical concepts as in quantitative research, an alternative not widely used across the board when appearing in analysis, and use other qualitative techniques (Long & Johnson, 2000). In 1952, Berelson defined content analysis as "a studies method for the objective, systematic and quantitative description of the take place content material of statement" (1952, p. 18). To make the technique relevant in both a quantitative approach and a qualitative approach, and without specifying the depth of analysis, Krippendorff (2004) described the content analysis as "a research approach for making replicable and legitimate inferences from texts (or other significant matter) to the contexts of their use" (p. 18). Downe-Wamboldt (1992) underlines that content material evaluation is greater than a counting procedure, as the goal is to hyperlink the results to their context or to the environment in which they had been produced: "Content analysis is a research approach that offers a systematic and goal method to make legitimate inferences from verbal, visual, or written facts so that you can describe and quantify particular phenomena" (p. 314).

It is to emphasize that content analysis in the field of sustainability has been already used and is recognized as a reliable research method (e.g., Guthrie & Abeysekera, 2006; Milne & Adler, 1999). Additionally, the authors created a codebook (Neuendorf, 2010) to perform content analysis (see Appendix 1 for more details on the Glossary). The codebook aimed to aid more standardized and established terminology for CE research. For the authentication of the codebook, the authors used the US Chamber of Commerce (https://www.uschamberfoundation.org/circular-economy-toolbox/about-circularity/glossary), a leading circular economy Ellen-Macarthur Foundation (https://ellenmacarthurfoundation.org/topics/circular-economy-introduction/glossary), world business council for sustainable development (https://www.ceguide.org/Glossary) glossary and different authors definition used, expert opinion and a list of R1 to R6 CE principles codebook were created (see Appendix 1).

Additional terms, selected by the two researchers applying a basic brainstorming method (Wilson, 2013), were added to enlarge the analysis of CE concepts and additionally, performed a pilot study of the top 10 companies. The glossary aimed to aid in the development of more standardized and established terminology for CE research, reporting, and governance practices. To select suitable companies for analysis, the authors first investigate the 2022 list of the world's top 100 corporations list which was published on 19 January 2022 (https://www.corporateknights.com/rankings/global-100-rankings/2022-global-100-rankings/100-most-sustainable-corporations-of-2022/), provided by the knight cooperation (with permission). Corporate Knight world 100 most sustainable companies based on careful measurement of nearly 7000 public companies with revenue over US 1 billion (see Appendix 2). The dataset consists of 33 sectors, 23 countries of 74 companies. The (see Appendix 2) key data related to the companies and their annual reports for 2020 to 2021 (which were retrieved from the company's website).

This research considers only English language reports of the companies for analysis. We used only a two-year sample of 2020 and 2021 reports for different reasons. Firstly, these 74 companies are commonly available in both years; secondly, the research can access the COVID-19 pandemic effects on the top 100 sustainable companies; thirdly, this research could open a new avenue for further comparative analysis of before and after COVID-19 effects. Content analysis is a strategy for dividing and estimating each relevant term for reporting disclosure (Wine, 1971). Content analysis is a method for codifying text and putting the content of written statements into datasets or groups, dependent on selected measures, with the ultimate objective of changing the material into quantitative scales that grant further investigation (Weber, 1990). The research design entailed searching for CE-related concepts in the annual reports. This coding process signifies a conceptual analysis of words. Each code in the codebook was perused to decide what range a particular variable represented. Every variable was coded for this power utilizing a scale of 0 and 1 referenced (Maroun & Prinsloo, 2020) (i.e., 0 = No reference of [variable]; 1 = available if reference [variable]). Moreover, the researchers used KPIs scores that were provided by Knight Cooperation (https://www.corporateknights.com/rankings/global-100-rankings/) (Copyright permission). The Corporate Knight developed these variables after an all-inclusive analysis of research, papers, meetings, and annual reports of observed companies. (See Appendix 3 for independent variables).

4 Finding and Discussions

As mentioned above, companies disclose their information in annual and biannual reports by using different economic, environmental, social, and governance standards. Within the balanced scorecard framework, these financial, customer, and internal processes and learning and growth perspectives are referred to as economic, environmental, social, and governance pillars and reports should cover these pillars. The purpose of the economic, environmental, social, and governance is to monitor the financial and non-financial risk and create opportunities inherent inside the company's operations. The reporting practices represent the first level of economic, environmental, social, and governance responsibility. There are several ranges of compliance with the economic, environmental, social, and governance. First, when companies report on sustainability indicators, the next is while companies already set targets/goals and objectives related to sustainability indicators and companies frequently measure the fulfillment of these objectives. When companies consider whether to develop a product, companies' objective is to measure greenhouse emissions when producing a new product and what sort of margin it's going to produce. Companies constantly look at how to reduce CO_2 emissions and product costs, which means that sustainability is incorporated into corporate governance. Move forward to Table 1.

Table 1 represents the descriptive statistics for the study variables. The average minimum score of CE principles is R5 and R6, respectively, and the maximum is 1 in all CE principles, while other variable minimum scores are 0 except for revenue and energy productivity. The finding shows that companies disclosed a minimum of 1 time-cited CE-related principles.

Table 2 shows the correlation among all variables of our model. All correlation coefficients are below 80% which indicates that there is no serious multicollinearity (Alin, 2010). The highest coefficient is between the firm water variable and INV variable 0.324% and 0.238%. The result of the variance inflation factor (VIF) shows the maximum VIF of NOx 2.43 and Sox 2.19, respectively. While the lowest tolerance coefficient is 0.41 of Sox, therefore, multicollinearity is not an issue in the current study.

The correct estimation of materials is a crucial procedure and may lead to a substantial technology for waste reduction and redundant materials resulting in financial overspending; however, the procurement-related concerns have uncertain consequences (Steen-Olsen et al., 2016). Further, the circular economy and balanced scorecard are tools for waste management and measurement which can potentially benefit the waste management collaboration among stakeholders, waste-pushed design, product life cycle, cycle waste generating plans, complex waste management analytics, and because of progressed waste-associated documentation/programs. Perhaps de Oliveira and Oliveira (2023) have recognized a production site for a waste management plan which is one of the high-quality environmental control practices that is closely associated with the BSC customer perspectives. It includes every waste class prevention plan,

Table 1 Descriptive statistics

	Minimum	Maximum	Mean	Std. Deviation
R1	0.80	1.00	0.84	0.08
R2	0.80	1.00	0.84	0.08
R3	0.40	1.00	0.84	0.12
R4	0.80	1.00	0.83	0.07
R5	0.20	1.00	0.72	0.15
R6	0.20	1.00	0.81	0.17
REV	0.17	1.00	0.82	0.19
INV	0.00	1.00	0.66	0.35
PTP	0.00	1.00	0.51	0.27
F-Ded	0.00	0.05	0.01	0.02
SUP-S	0.00	0.83	0.23	0.27
SPL	0.00	1.00	0.88	0.33
ENG-P	0.01	0.98	0.52	0.27
WAT-P	0.00	1.00	0.45	0.29
WAST-p	0.00	1.00	0.44	0.30
VOC-P	0.00	1.00	0.23	0.32
NOX-P	0.00	1.00	0.24	0.30
SOX-P	0.00	1.00	0.21	0.31
PM-P	0.00	1.00	0.18	0.31
GHG-P	0.00	1.00	0.45	0.28
ING	0.00	1.00	0.49	0.35
FAT	0.00	1.00	0.76	0.40
EMP	0.00	1.00	0.46	0.30
PSL	0.00	1.00	0.86	0.34
PFQ	0.00	0.98	0.48	0.26
N-MEX	0.00	1.00	0.69	0.28

(continued)

Table 1 (continued)

	Minimum	Maximum	Mean	Std. Deviation
N-MOB	0.04	1.00	0.72	0.23
R-DEX	0.00	0.99	0.39	0.41
R-DBOD	0.00	0.99	0.42	0.41
CEO-P	0.00	1.00	0.39	0.31
Valid *N* (list-wise)	148.00			

Table 2 Correlation matrix

	R1	R2	R3	R4	R5	R6	REV	INV	PTP	F-DED	SUP-S	SPL	ENG-P	WAT-P	WAST-P
R1	1														
R2	0.980**	1													
R3	0.598**	0.585**	1												
R4	0.622**	0.609**	0.308**	1											
R5	0.158	0.187*	0.161	0.154	1										
R6	0.435**	0.430**	0.261**	0.195*	−0.072	1									
REV	0.222**	0.207*	0.027	0.120	−0.216**	0.344**	1								
INV	0.204*	0.180*	0.141	0.076	−0.085	0.375**	0.267**	1							
PTP	−0.184*	−0.205*	−0.036	−0.081	0.065	−0.226**	−0.150	−0.119	1						
F-DED	−0.206*	−0.167*	−0.189*	−0.145	−0.041	−0.093	−0.039	−0.045	0.233**	1					
SUP-S	0.120	0.133	0.113	−0.036	−0.143	0.118	0.035	0.100	0.079	−0.101	1				
SPL	0.039	0.045	0.068	−0.095	0.054	0.093	0.001	−0.031	0.107	−0.048	0.143	1			
ENG-P	0.213**	0.228**	0.257**	0.188*	0.450**	−0.044	−0.074	0.018	0.167*	−0.040	0.069	0.030	1		
WAT-P	0.315**	0.329**	0.205*	0.242**	0.404**	0.152	−0.026	0.070	0.002	0.009	0.059	−0.025	0.557**	1	
WAST-P	−0.040	−0.026	−0.059	0.028	0.280**	0.056	−0.217**	−0.009	0.157	−0.014	0.020	0.145	0.336**	0.339**	1

(continued)

Table 2 (continued)

	VOC-P	NOX-P	SOX-P	PM-P	GHG-P	ING	FAT	EMP	PSL	PFQ	N-MEX	N-MOB	R-DEX	R-DBOD	CEO-P
VOC-P	1														
NOX-P	0.486**	1													
SOX-P	0.315**	0.670**	1												
PM-P	0.534**	0.587**	0.517**	1											
GHG-P	0.032	0.100	0.227**	0.172*	1										
ING	0.148	0.048	0.110	0.219**	0.189*	1									
FAT	0.105	0.029	0.095	0.145	0.108	0.171*	1								
EMP	0.022	0.024	0.011	0.053	0.206*	0.150	0.084	1							
PSL	−0.009	0.006	−0.009	0.112	0.085	0.123	0.111	0.135	1						
PFQ	0.172*	0.022	0.044	0.135	0.189*	0.008	−0.041	0.172*	0.217**	1					
N-MEX	−0.003	−0.176*	−0.135	−0.053	0.270**	0.036	0.206*	0.002	0.229**	0.140	1				
N-MOB	−0.015	−0.128	−0.123	0.009	0.250**	−0.077	0.013	0.000	0.012	0.081	0.246**	1			
R-DEX	0.050	−0.035	−0.012	−0.004	0.066	0.013	0.003	−0.023	−0.053	0.097	0.204*	−0.145	1		
R-DBOD	0.146	0.024	−0.022	0.090	−0.035	0.163*	0.030	−0.065	0.077	0.079	0.145	−0.090	0.504**	1	
CEO-P	−0.051	−0.038	−0.086	−0.036	−0.031	0.122	−0.003	0.107	0.191*	0.145	0.091	0.003	−0.246**	−0.300**	1

*Correlation is significant at the 0.05 level (2-tailed)
**Correlation is significant at the 0.01 level (2-tailed)

forecasting of generated waste quantity, allocation of resources/assets, expenses, and responsibilities (Oliveira & Oliveira, 2023). Notably, manufactured and industrialized modules are one of the most efficient practices for minimizing waste (Sassanelli et al., 2019). The KPIs associated with recycled content reused and refurbished bio-based and natural substances with revenue and investment.

This can be read from Table 3 of the financial wise BSC-CE that revenue found a significant association with R1 (1.983 $p < 0.05$), R2 (1.803 $p < 0.1$), R5 (−2.399 $p < 0.01$), and R6 (3.164 $p < 0.01$), but the companies' investment in R1 and R6 is significantly associated respectively while the total CE-6Rs is closely associated with an investment. On the other hand, the percentage of tax payable is closely associated with the CE reuse and recover principle. If we see the fine deduction, R1, R3, and TCE-6Rs are closely associated with the financial/economic perspective of BSC.

The financial part of indicators is related to the value creation of the organization. The financial/economic perspective represents the operational aspect that closely links and impacts sustainable investment and attracts stakeholder (Oliveira & Oliveira, 2023). The financial indicators and perspective could permit decision-makers to manipulate some actions/techniques associated with organization problems (Sassanelli et al., 2019). Therefore, this study offering a framework with this line of concept will become possible to systematize the subjectivity inherent to the decision-making approach and recognize its multidimensional nature. Moreover, the study suggests that this framework is used to harmonize among the sustainability components like environment, social, governance, and economics. This new visualization method offers the assessment of new circular models underneath the four dimensions of sustainability: economic, environmental, governance, and social (Witjes & Lozano, 2016). Then, the usual framework proposed in this paper may be used to assess the economic impact of corporations and supply chains in other segments (Table 4).

Robustness error-wise CE activity reduce (2.396), R2 (2.199), R5 (0.031), and R6 (0.065) found a significant association with revenue whereas other activities did not associate significantly, while investment

Table 3 Financial/economic perspectives

	R1	R2	R3	R4	R5	R6	TCE-6Rs
Parameter	T Sig	t Sig	T Sig	t Sig	t Sig	t Sig	t Sig
Intercept	23.775 (0.000)	23.635 (0.000)	16.034 (0.000)	27.560 (0.000)	13.469 (0.000)	9.401 (0.000)	26.005 (0.000)
REV	1.983** (0.049)	1.803* (0.073)	−0.167 (0.868)	1.158 (0.249)	−2.399*** (0.018)	3.164*** (0.002)	1.113 (0.268)
INV	1.722* (0.087)	1.431 (0.155)	1.635 (0.104)	0.462 (0.645)	−0.332 (0.740)	3.813*** (0.000)	2.359** (0.020)
PTP	−1.260 (0.210)	−1.691* (0.093)	0.268 (0.789)	−0.363 (0.717)	0.534 (0.594)	−1.914** (0.058)	−1.018 (0.310)
F-Ded	−2.096** (0.038)	−1.518 (0.131)	−2.258** (0.025)	−1.567 (0.119)	−0.723 (0.471)	−0.485 (0.628)	−2.005** (0.047)
R^2	0.119	0.102	0.054	0.037	0.052	0.229	0.106
Adj R^2	0.094	0.076	0.028	0.010	0.025	0.208	0.081
N	148						
Year	Yes						
Industry	Yes						
Country	Yes						

Table 4 Robustness analysis of financial perspectives

	R1	R2	R3	R4	R5	R6	T6CER
Parameter	T Sig	t Sig	t Sig	t Sig	t Sig	t Sig	t Sig
Intercept	30.385 (0.000)	27.828 (0.000)	16.565 (0.000)	34.760 (0.000)	12.630 (0.000)	6.263 (0.000)	25.934 0.000
REV	2.396** (0.018)	2.199** (0.029)	−0.177 (0.860)	1.389 (0.167)	−2.177** (0.031)	1.856* (0.065)	1.100 (0.273)
INV	1.986* (0.049)	1.602 (0.111)	1.735* (0.085)	0.539 (0.591)	−0.311 (0.756)	2.469** (0.015)	2.339** (0.021)
PTP	−1.168 (0.245)	−1.453 (0.148)	0.207 (0.837)	−0.350 (0.727)	0.542 (0.589)	−1.882* (0.062)	−0.963 (0.337)
F-Ded	−2.748*** (0.007)	−1.640* (0.103)	−2.193** (0.030)	−2.120** (0.036)	−0.619 (0.537)	−0.421 (0.674)	−2.203** (0.029)

is significantly associated with the R1, R3, R6, and 6E-6Rs activities. Sustainability reports require indicators that quantify the extent to which it has met its intentions. The GRI provides a series of financial, social, environmental, and governance indicators to measure the companies' performance, but in general, indicators are not sufficient for all the industry. In many cases, indicators and quantitative information are not sufficient to inform the entire story, so sustainability reports should additionally include remarks to interpret activities that are difficult to quantify or require further explanation. Thus, quantitative and qualitative indicators together reveal overall performance. Economic key performance indicators, e.g., economic value created, the proportion of goods bought locally, percentage of taxes paid and proportion of independent directors on the board.

A sustainability report not only includes all the aspect of environmental social and economic aspects of companies but also provides the governance aspect of companies (Barnabè & Nazir, 2022). It is characterized by way of the information disclosed by the directives of content material and formal requirements of sustainability reviews, and alternatively, disclosure continues to be not mandatory. The sustainability report is a mechanism (report) for accountability and access to the companies' position. Without the report, the company's stakeholders will not recognize what the organization's sustainability direction is, what activities it desires to achieve, and what challenging situations companies face to implement sustainability within the organization, i.e., financial reporting; a company must report how to use social and environmental resources and its effects on society and the economy. Companies inclined to publish use the recommendations and frameworks approved by international corporations (i.e., GRI, IIRC, and SASB) for company reporting that provides standardized and detailed information in their reports (Crespo-Rosas et al., 2023).

This can be seen from Table 5 that CE reduces principle is found a significant association with WAT-P (3.301 $p < 0.01$), WAST (−2.396 $p < 0.01$), and VOC-P (1.688 $p < 0.05$), but the SUP-S is only significantly associated with R5 respectively. On the other hand, the sustainability pay link variable is not associated with any R principle. On the other hand, water productivity and VOC-P are closely related or associated with TCE-6Rs principles as well as all intercepts have a significant association with each R principle. On the other hand, investors and consumers are committed to paying attention to circular economy reduce, reuse, and recycle principles. It is mostly a tough objective to compile the facts and information into a framework. Environmental key performance indicators, e.g., quantities of CO_2 emitted, quantity or extent of pollution, the quantity of waste, kilowatts of energy used, and tonnes of water used. It takes time to expand information systems, but often the right facts are already to be maintained; however, companies think it's important information (i.e., water and energy use, waste charges, costs).

Table 6 represents the robustness analysis of the customer perspective. Waste and water are found significant associations with R1, R2, R4, and R5 principles, while the VOC-P is closely related to R3, R4, R5, R6, and TCE-6Rs. This can be shown that the waste is closely associated with the basic 3Rs CE principles like reduce, reuse, and recycle principles. Companies were recognizing and considering this information and communicating these facts and figures to stakeholders for a rational decision-making process as well as participating in the sustainability agenda. Companies slowly built up their appropriate information systems to satisfy their needs and disclosed this information—becoming independent from the year to financial statements—started to appear, with a strong emphasis on the environmental aspects that include quantifiable indicators for measuring environmental issues including air pollution, CO_2 pollutants, or polluted water. Companies identify green initiates that will make a massive contribution to the environmental goals of the regulation, climate change mitigation, sustainable use and protection of water and marine resources, transition to a CE framework, prevention and reduction of pollutants, protection, restoration of biodiversity and ecosystems, and reduction of GHGs.

Table 7 highlights the internal social process of the organization which has a significant influence on social sustainability. The EMP was significantly engaged with circular economy remanufacturing and recovery activities while the paid sick leave is significantly engaged with the R5, R6, and total circular economy activities, considering the corporate social responsibility communicated with the companies' internal process and the employee's treatment by the companies. On the other

Table 5 Customer perspectives

	R1	R2	R3	R4	R5	R6	TCE-6Rs
Parameter	T Sig	T Sig	T Sig	t Sig	t Sig	T Sig	t Sig
Intercept	34.966*** (0.000)	34.606*** (0.000)	22.109*** (0.000)	42.756*** (0.000)	14.762*** (0.000)	15.532*** (0.000)	37.814*** (0.000)
SUP-S	1.269 (0.207)	1.384 (0.169)	0.780 (0.437)	−0.558 (0.577)	−2.316** (0.022)	0.942 (0.348)	0.284 (0.777)
SPL	0.717 (0.475)	0.727 (0.468)	0.919 (0.360)	−0.847 (0.398)	0.993 (0.322)	0.947 (0.345)	1.113 (0.268)
ENG-P	1.083 (0.281)	1.318 (0.190)	1.950** (0.053)	0.324 (0.747)	2.696*** (0.008)	−1.696* (0.092)	1.268 (0.207)
WAT-P	3.301*** (0.001)	3.200*** (0.002)	1.183 (0.239)	2.639*** (0.009)	2.674*** (0.008)	1.957** (0.052)	3.676*** (0.000)
WAST-p	−2.396*** (0.018)	−2.420*** (0.017)	−2.499*** (0.014)	−0.351 (0.726)	1.730* (0.086)	−0.114 (0.910)	−1.205 (0.230)
VOC-P	1.688* (0.094)	1.767* (0.079)	1.798* (0.074)	3.107** (0.002)	−1.867** (0.064)	2.332** (0.021)	2.038** (0.043)
NOX-P	−0.284 (0.777)	−0.023 (0.982)	−0.890 (0.375)	−1.675** (0.096)	0.156 (0.876)	0.002 (0.999)	−0.541 (0.590)
SOX	−0.258 (0.797)	−0.011 (0.991)	−0.043 (0.966)	−0.042 (0.966)	−0.526 (0.600)	0.114 (0.909)	−0.194 (0.846)

	R1	R2	R3	R4	R5	R6	TCE-6Rs
PM-P	0.163	0.032	0.620	−1.703*	−0.232	−0.272	−0.241
	(0.871)	(0.975)	(0.536)	(0.091)	(0.817)	(0.786)	(0.810)
GHG-P	−1.047	−1.054	−0.061	−0.337	0.356	0.094	−0.324
	(0.297)	(0.294)	(0.951)	(0.737)	(0.722)	(0.926)	(0.747)
R^2	0.177	0.190	0.148	0.169	0.317	0.117	0.225
Adj R^2	0.117	0.131	0.086	0.108	0.267	0.052	0.169
N	148						
Year	Included						
Industry	Included						
Country	Included						

Table 6 Robustness analysis of customer perspective

	R1	R2	R3	R4	R5	R6	TCE-6Rs
Parameter	t Sig	t Sig	t Sig	T Sig	t Sig	t Sig	t Sig
Intercept	39.487 (0.000)	38.295 (0.000)	23.861 (0.000)	38.447 (0.000)	11.288 (0.000)	15.424 (0.000)	36.435 (0.000)
SUP-S	1.069 (0.287)	1.179 (0.240)	0.742 (0.459)	−0.624 (0.534)	−2.417 (0.017)	1.151 (0.252)	0.267 (0.790)
SPL	0.843 (0.401)	0.836 (0.405)	0.979 (0.329)	−0.752 (0.453)	0.751 (0.454)	0.683 (0.496)	1.058 (0.292)
ENG-P	1.127 (0.262)	1.362 (0.175)	1.653* (0.101)	0.328 (0.743)	2.382** (0.019)	−1.499 (0.136)	1.200 (0.232)
WAT-P	3.270*** (0.001)	3.198*** (0.002)	0.727 (0.469)	2.481*** (0.014)	3.087*** (0.002)	2.343** (0.021)	3.191*** (0.002)
WAST-p	−2.504*** (0.013)	−2.500*** (0.014)	−2.721*** (0.007)	−0.370 (0.712)	1.477* (0.142)	−0.127 (0.899)	−1.260 (0.210)
VOC-P	1.359 (0.176)	1.422 (0.157)	1.664** (0.098)	2.332*** (0.021)	−1.792** (0.075)	2.731*** (0.007)	1.660** (0.099)
NOX-P	−0.271 (0.787)	−0.021 (0.983)	−0.959 (0.339)	−1.882* (0.062)	0.143 (0.887)	0.003 (0.997)	−0.553 (0.581)
SOX	−0.214 (0.831)	−0.009 (0.993)	−0.038 (0.970)	−0.035 (0.972)	−0.503 (0.616)	0.180 (0.857)	−0.170 (0.865)
PM-P	0.146 (0.884)	0.028 (0.977)	0.573 (0.568)	−1.716 (0.088)	−0.246 (0.806)	−0.448 (0.655)	−0.222 (0.824)
GHG-P	−0.951 (0.343)	−0.944 (0.347)	−0.056 (0.956)	−0.311 (0.757)	0.391 (0.696)	0.079 (0.937)	−0.266 (0.791)

hand, studies used a list of social indicators and analyzed the prioritizing of those indicators that use multicriteria choice assistance and statistics methods. However, the authors argue how these indicators are used for social-related company issues. Although the study offers the inclusion of environmental and social indicators within the balanced scorecard from the Kaplan and Norton structure, it no longer cites what form of indicators may be used and does not involve their particular size. According to Hansen and Schaltegger (2016), the sustainability-oriented balanced scorecard (SBSC) is an open idea that can be used to include environmental and social factors into the standard company strategies. However, based on a broad literature review, there is no consensus related to the structure of the BSC and CE to include indications related to environmental, social, economic, and governance dimensions of sustainability. The authors argue that a sustainability CE and BSC is considered a framework to integrate sustainability in strategic components in organizations and emphasize that other performance management frameworks that can be used for the management decision-making process. Our paper proposes a framework primarily based on the CE activities as well as containing the strategic factors that are integrated with the balanced scorecard method. The balanced scorecard gives a valuable shape to analyze the social indicators in operational measures.

Considering that the studies deal with the identification and assessment of the companies' performance, Table 8 states that all parameter intercepts are significantly associated with the social indicators. As mentioned above, we identify the social economic environment and governance sustainability by using the top 100 companies' KPIs, which includes the categories of social indicators, proposing the inclusion of corporations of labor conditions and welfare. The different research handling social indicators recommend using corporate employees' positions for the assessment of social sustainability. However, social indicators' weak point is associated with collecting quantitative records, which are not often available at a company level and may be available on the websites of companies. The studied organizations have the availability of all information that will be necessary for a comprehensive analysis covering sustainability information.

Table 7 Internal process/social perspectives

	R1	R2	R3	R4	R5	R6	T6CE
Parameter	t	t	t	t	t	T	t
	Sig	Sig	Sig	Sig	Sig	Sig	Sig
Intercept	17.693***	16.946***	8.960***	12.875***	4.065***	7.207***	14.855***
	(0.000)	(0.000)	(0.000)	(0.000)	(0.000)	(0.000)	(0.000)
ING	−0.279	−0.318	2.189**	−0.554	1.100	0.704	1.097
	(0.781)	(0.751)	(0.031)	(0.581)	(0.274)	(0.483)	(0.275)
FAT	1.181	1.303	0.574	1.315	0.326	0.227	1.029
	(0.241)	(0.196)	(0.567)	(0.192)	(0.745)	(0.821)	(0.306)
EMP	1.878**	1.555	0.237	2.436***	−0.223	1.672**	1.577
	(0.064)	(0.123)	(0.813)	(0.017)	(0.824)	(0.098)	(0.118)
PSL	1.209	1.062	0.513	0.792	2.462***	3.443***	2.677***
	(0.230)	(0.291)	(0.609)	(0.430)	(0.016)	(0.001)	(0.009)
PFQ	−0.885	−1.162	−0.280	0.565	0.441	0.540	−0.014
	(0.379)	(0.248)	(0.780)	(0.573)	(0.661)	(0.590)	(0.989)
R^2	0.725	0.701	0.576	0.573	0.669	0.740	0.664
Adj R^2	0.551	0.512	0.307	0.302	0.460	0.576	0.451
N	148						
Year	Included						
Industry	Included						
Country	Included						

Table 8 Robustness analysis of internal process/social perspectives

	R1	R2	R3	R4	R5	R6	TCE-6Rs
Parameter	t Sig	t Sig	t Sig	t Sig	t Sig	t Sig	t Sig
Intercept	17.834*** (0.000)	17.123*** (0.000)	11.416*** (0.000)	13.051*** (0.000)	4.671*** (0.000)	5.454*** (0.000)	14.853*** (0.000)
ING	−0.238 (0.813)	−0.281 (0.779)	1.728** (0.088)	−0.458 (0.648)	0.728 (0.468)	0.495 (0.622)	0.847 (0.399)
FAT	1.080 (0.283)	1.183 (0.240)	0.535 (0.594)	1.069 (0.288)	0.240 (0.811)	0.164 (0.870)	0.925 (0.358)
EMP	1.551 (0.125)	1.276 (0.205)	0.191 (0.849)	1.922** (0.058)	−0.174 (0.862)	1.216 (0.227)	1.226 (0.223)
PSL	0.936 (0.352)	0.874 (0.384)	0.398 (0.691)	0.630 (0.530)	1.760** (0.082)	1.736** (0.086)	1.933** (0.056)
PFQ	−0.703 (0.484)	−0.916 (0.362)	−0.258 (0.797)	0.522 (0.603)	0.365 (0.716)	0.401 (0.689)	−0.011 (0.991)

Table 9 shows the learning and growth prospects/governance for the adoption of CE principles. Table 9 states that all parameter intercepts are significantly associated with all CE-R principles, while the non-male executive on board is highly associated with R1, R2, R3, R5, and TCE-6Rs principles. On the other hand, R-DBOD is closely associated with all CE-R principles. However, companies' governance sustainability indicators related to board diversity and racial diversity are nonetheless essential to be taken into consideration because of some approaches accomplished by companies' memorandum.

Table 10 shows that R-DBOD is highly significantly associated with R1, R2, R3, R4, R5, and total CE-6Rs principles. Secondly, the non male executives on barad are significantly engaged with R1, R2, R4, R5, and total CE-6Rs.

The study proposed a CE-BSC to manage vital issues related to environmental, social, economic, and governance perspectives. The study was conducted on collecting the CE principle at annual reports to reveal the companies' action by using the glossaries, and the study also collects the social, environmental, and economic indicators by the Knight, Key performance indicators—KPIs rely on the strategic goals of each corporation. CE-BSC framework proposes to overcome and integrate systematic steps to define the most suitable set of indicators for the calculation of a sustainability index.

The findings indicated that the attention and adoption of the CE-BSC for sustainability are low because this is a primary study and the study includes a limited set of KPIs. The authors state that the delivery side has inspired the diffusion approach of tools and practices, such as the sustainable-oriented balanced scorecard. Thus, the novelty of this paper lies in the proposition of a framework to assess the social, environmental, economic, and governance aspects of the company and propose a combined framework, capable of masking all supply chains: corporation; community; consumers; suppliers; human rights; and human resources. Another novelty is associated with the evaluation of strategic, tactical, and operational indicators, considerably like the concept of a

Table 9 Learning and growth perspectives

	R1	R2	R3	R4	R5	R6	TCE-6Rs
Parameter	t Sig	t Sig	t Sig	t Sig	t Sig	t Sig	t Sig
Intercept	14.517*** (0.000)	14.169*** (0.000)	7.786*** (0.000)	11.000*** (0.000)	6.351*** (0.000)	5.233*** (0.000)	13.477*** (0.000)
N-MEX	−1.757* (0.082)	−1.765* (0.081)	−2.223** (0.029)	0.022 (0.983)	−2.684*** (0.009)	0.193 (0.847)	−2.114** (0.037)
N-MOB	0.488 (0.627)	0.021 (0.983)	1.533 (0.129)	−1.064 (0.290)	−1.672** (0.098)	1.936** (0.056)	0.496 (0.621)
R-DEX	0.430 (0.668)	−0.032 (0.975)	1.327 (0.188)	0.371 (0.711)	−1.499 (0.137)	−0.845 (0.400)	−0.268 (0.789)
R-DBOD	2.745*** (0.007)	2.714*** (0.008)	2.746*** (0.007)	1.691** (0.094)	2.668*** (0.009)	2.394*** (0.019)	3.867*** (0.000)
CEO-P	−0.043 (0.966)	−0.457 (0.649)	−1.655* (0.101)	−0.432 (0.667)	−1.238 (0.219)	0.219 (0.827)	−1.006 (0.317
R^2	0.741	0.719	0.642	0.557	0.709	0.719	0.693
Adj R^2	0.577	0.540	0.415	0.277	0.525	0.541	0.599
N	148						
Year	Included						
Industry	Included						
Country	Included						

Table 10 Robustness analysis of learning and growth perspectives/governance

	R1	R2	R3	R4	R5	R6	TCE-6Rs
Parameter	T	T	T	T	t	t	T
	Sig	Sig	Sig	Sig	Sig	Sig	Sig
Intercept	12.393***	11.574***	6.319***	10.798***	5.326***	5.135***	12.426***
	(0.000)	(0.000)	(0.000)	(0.000)	(0.000)	(0.000)	(0.000)
N-MEX	−1.503*	−1.508*	−1.526*	0.019	−1.957**	0.161	−1.724**
	(0.136)	(0.135)	(0.131)	(0.985)	(0.053)	(0.872)	(0.088)
N-MOB	0.360	0.014	1.102	−0.739	−1.229	1.651*	0.437
	(0.719)	(0.989)	(0.273)	(0.462)	(0.222)	(0.102)	(0.663)
R-DEX	0.462	−0.030	0.974	0.488	−1.112	−0.627	−0.223
	(0.645)	(0.976)	(0.332)	(0.627)	(0.269)	(0.532)	(0.824)
R-DBOD	1.939**	1.920**	2.076**	1.448*	1.656*	1.451	3.053***
	(0.056)	(0.058)	(0.041)	(0.151)	(0.101)	(0.150)	(0.003)
CEO-P	−0.029	−0.300	−1.151	−0.318	−0.935	0.186	−0.668
	(0.977)	(0.765)	(0.253)	(0.751)	(0.352)	(0.853)	(0.506)

balanced scorecard, which was allowed via applying the circular procedure (Hansen et al., 2016). This practice starts with the general values of the decision context (Barnabè & Nazir, 2021).

The CE-BSC measurement allows four pillars of sustainability, social environment and economic and governance that also offer how companies disclose this information in their annual reports. These facts should be helpful to display some unique mechanisms that can be helpful to identify and amend industrial techniques, considering extraordinary situations like COVID-19. This study proposes a framework covering a huge range of sustainability indicators to evaluate sustainability. This framework can be developed with the proposition of a brand-new theory lens to investigate the results. The aggregation of a method can make contributions to the linkage of operations, management and decision analysis areas, sustainability and related ethical elements of the organization. Concerning social, environmental, economic, and governance implications, this paper brings light to exploited subjects in academia and practitioners that have obtained increasing interest and visibility in a practical context.

The implementation of circular economy practices in services and manufacturing industries is an important initiative due to environmental concerns, resource utilization, and waste reduction. There is a significant potential in the way of additional studies in this area (Lihong, 2011). Supply chain managers face complexity in dealing with the performance measurement by transit circular economy adoption because of the circular loop in supply chain management. BSC is an effective framework for overall performance measurement, especially from an organization sustainability perspective. CE-BSC covers the main key indicators in corporations' circular direction. It is not feasible to examine complex practices in industries with generalized methods, so there have to be one-of-a-kind indicators for several structures in organizations to check the overall performance outcomes.

5 Conclusion and Contributions

The basic purpose of this paper was to endorse a framework for the assessment of social, environmental, economic, and governance impact evaluation by indicators, which became possible through the CE-BSC approach. The research investigates the validation of the framework by using services and the manufacturing industry. It became possible to summarize the indicators for the framework at the strategic, tactical, and operational tiers. However, in this research, key performance indicators used at the strategic and tactical phases were evaluated.

Then, it became possible to classify the studied organization in aspects of dedication to social, environmental, governance, and economic sustainability. The study focuses on analyzing the corporation's actions against sustainability impact. The alignment between the top-level management of the corporation and the sectors concerned in enforcing CE initiatives in terms of social dilemmas is crucial because it permits a holistic variation of behaviors. Evaluating the social impact, conjointly with the economic and environmental ones, in a single organization or a supply chain can give inputs to decision-makers to put in force changes in the direction of a circular economy framework transition.

CE practices have gained the interest of companies/corporations to make the supply chain especially sustainable. The study's goal was to provide a framework inside the overall performance dimension of CE more rapidly for sustainability and waste management. From the available literature, KPIs were recognized in CE overall performance size in the direction of sustainability. These KPIs indicators further identified sustainability perspectives in the context of circular economy performance and supply chain management implementation. Research mainly highlights the social, economic, environmental, and governance also combined with the fundamental BSC approach as crucial performance measures closer to sustainability. CE principles' focus is on environmental protection and resource protection with waste reduction. This can be accomplished by checking the circular activities in terms of environmental issues, waste generation, and the effective use of resources and materials.

According to Kaplan and Norton, there must be certain indicators that can be framed by industries based totally on their design strategy for a particular objective. In this research, different prospects are identified in the literature for measuring companies' performance toward sustainability. The modified BSC has an additional approach aside from other directions of holistic BSC. These perspectives in modified BSC are environmental, social, economic, and governance. The proposed (modified BSC) framework will help industrialists and managers explore the performance outcomes in CE-BSC implementation in manufacturing and services industries toward sustainability.

6 Limitations

Despite their limitation, every study has certain limitations that will open a new avenue for future research. The study used the top 100 sustainable companies' KPIs which represent the Knight. The researchers can use the Bloomberg/data stream for the collection of other variable scores and check the different industries participating in the sustainable development agenda.

7 Future Research

First, the chapter contributes to developing a concept for improving the overall performance dimension and new concepts like CE-BSC, but a theoretical framework is required for more in-depth research and qualitative case studies. Secondly, the author used the COVID-19 period companies' dataset and developed a CE-BSC framework. This framework can be used to evaluate the before and after COVID-19 effects.

8 Practical Implications

The practical implications are as follows:

- It will help managers explore the overall performance of specific elements in the aspects of social, environmental, governance, and economic.
- It will be useful for supply chain managers to examine circular principles at each step of the supply chain for essential key indicators' performance measurement.
- The proposed framework will guide the supply chain members in industries where managers have to operate goals and the measures/indicators to be checked for better consequences of their objectives.
- Study explores environmental issues to get better operation for environment safety in nowadays competitive environment.
- The framework provides the indicators as enhancement in social cognizance, sustainability development, organization value creation, eco-friendly material price, decreased environment concerns, and waste reduction.
- The study also allows practitioners and researchers to lead the way for further research on this topic with various other factors and techniques.

Nowadays, government and NGOs are highly concerned with making products and parts that have less harm to the environment and economic costs. This framework is useful to check the environmental effects and social effects and reduce product costs which is a critical element for the management and implementation of CE principles as these elements are lacking inside the holistic BSC approach. The study offers a holistic technique to managers about particular elements for checking their consequences in terms of sustainability perspectives given inside the proposed model. The proposed framework will help the industrialists work for more secure environmental and social aspects with the intention of extra-economic and social benefits in this competitive environment.

Appendix 1: CE Code Book

CE-6Rs	Items	Sources
Reduce (R1)	Reduce energy consumption	WBCSD Glossary, EMF, 2019, Kirchherr et al., 2017, Jawahir and Bradley, 2016, Reike et al. 2018, Fonseca et al., 2018
	Reduce water consumption	WBCSD Glossary, EMF, 2019, Kirchherr et al., 2017, Jawahir and Bradley, 2016, Reike et al. 2018, Fonseca et al., 2018
	Reduce plastic waste	US chamber glossary, WBCSD Glossary, EMF, 2019, Kirchherr et al., 2017, Fonseca et al., 2018
	Reduce material consumption	US chamber glossary, WBCSD Glossary, EMF, 2019, Kirchherr et al., 2017, Jawahir and Bradley, 2016, Reike et al. 2018, Fonseca et al., 2018
	Reduce carbon emission	US chamber glossary, WBCSD Glossary, EMF, 2019, Kirchherr et al., 2017, Jawahir and Bradley, 2016, Reike et al. 2018, Fonseca et al., 2018
Reuse (R2)	Renewable energy	US chamber glossary, WBCSD Glossary, EMF, 2019, Kirchherr et al., 2017, Jawahir and Bradley, 2016, Reike et al. 2018, Fonseca et al., 2018
	Reuse products, parts, material	US chamber glossary, WBCSD Glossary, EMF, 2019, Kirchherr et al., 2017, I.S. Jawahir and Bradley, 2016, Reike et al. 2018, Fonseca et al., 2018
	Product by product	US chamber glossary, WBCSD Glossary, EMF, 2019, Kirchherr et al., 2017, I.S. Jawahir and Bradley, 2016, Reike et al. 2018, Fonseca et al., 2018
	Reuse water	US chamber glossary, WBCSD Glossary, EMF, 2019, Kirchherr et al., 2017, Jawahir and Ryan Bradley, 2016, Reike et al. 2018, Fonseca et al., 2018
	Reuse plastic, packaging	US chamber glossary, WBCSD Glossary, EMF, 2019, Kirchherr et al., 2017, I.S. Jawahir and Bradley, 2016, Reike et al. 2018, Fonseca et al., 2018
Recycle (R3)	Waste to energy productivity	US chamber glossary, WBCSD Glossary, EMF, 2019, Kirchherr et al., 2017, Jawahir and Bradley, 2016, Reike et al. 2018, Fonseca et al., 2018

(continued)

(continued)

CE-6Rs	Items	Sources
	Zero waste	US chamber glossary, WBCSD Glossary, EMF, 2019, Kirchherr et al., 2017, Jawahir and Bradley, 2016, Reike et al. 2018, Fonseca et al., 2018
	Waste material recycling	US chamber glossary, WBCSD Glossary, EMF, 2019, Kirchherr et al., 2017, Jawahir and Bradley, 2016, Reike et al. 2018, Fonseca et al., 2018
	Hazardous materials recycling	US chamber glossary, WBCSD Glossary, EMF, 2019, Kirchherr et al., 2017, Jawahir and Bradley, 2016, Reike et al. 2018, Fonseca et al., 2018
	Packaging, plastic, recycling	US chamber glossary, WBCSD Glossary, EMF, 2019, Kirchherr et al., 2017, Jawahir and Bradley, 2016, Reike et al. 2018, Fonseca et al., 2018
Remanufacture (R4)	Remanufacture	US chamber glossary, WBCSD Glossary, EMF, 2019, Kirchherr et al., 2017, Jawahir and Bradley, 2016, Reike et al. 2018, Fonseca et al., 2018
	Reproduce by original parts or material	US chamber glossary, WBCSD Glossary, EMF, 2019, Kirchherr et al., 2017, Jawahir and Bradley, 2016, Reike et al. 2018, Fonseca et al., 2018
	Repair products and parts	US chamber glossary, WBCSD Glossary, EMF, 2019, Kirchherr et al., 2017, Jawahir and Bradley, 2016, Reike et al. 2018, Fonseca et al., 2018
	Resource digitalization	US chamber glossary, WBCSD Glossary, EMF, 2019, Kirchherr et al., 2017, Jawahir and Bradley, 2016, Reike et al. 2018, Fonseca et al., 2018
	Producer. supplier responsibility	US chamber glossary, WBCSD Glossary, EMF, 2019, Kirchherr et al., 2017, Jawahir and Bradley, 2016, Reike et al. 2018, Fonseca et al., 2018
Redesign (R5)	Redesign old products and parts	US chamber glossary, WBCSD Glossary, EMF, 2019, Kirchherr et al., 2017, Jawahir and Bradley, 2016, Reike et al. 2018, Fonseca et al., 2018
	Repurpose products and parts	US chamber glossary, WBCSD Glossary, EMF, 2019, Kirchherr et al., 2017, Jawahir and Bradley, 2016, Reike et al. 2018, Fonseca et al., 2018

(continued)

(continued)

CE-6Rs	Items	Sources
	Extend the product life cycle	US chamber glossary, WBCSD Glossary, EMF, 2019, Kirchherr et al., 2017, Jawahir and Bradley, 2016, Reike et al. 2018, Fonseca et al., 2018
	Eco-design	US chamber glossary, WBCSD Glossary, EMF, 2019, Kirchherr et al., 2017, Jawahir and Bradley, 2016, Reike et al. 2018, Fonseca et al., 2018
	Regenerative design	US chamber glossary, WBCSD Glossary, EMF, 2019, Kirchherr et al., 2017, Jawahir and Bradley, 2016, Reike et al. 2018, Fonseca et al., 2018
Recover (R6)	Waste recovery	US chamber glossary, WBCSD Glossary, EMF, 2019, Kirchherr et al., 2017, Jawahir and Bradley, 2016, Reike et al. 2018, Fonseca et al., 2018
	Waste hierarchy	US chamber glossary, WBCSD Glossary, EMF, 2019, Kirchherr et al., 2017, Jawahir and Bradley, 2016, Reike et al. 2018, Fonseca et al., 2018
	Recover product, parts	US chamber glossary, WBCSD Glossary, EMF, 2019, Kirchherr et al., 2017, Jawahir and Bradley, 2016, Reike et al. 2018, Fonseca et al., 2018
	Waste to the energy recovery rate	US chamber glossary, WBCSD Glossary, EMF, 2019, Kirchherr et al., 2017, Jawahir and Bradley, 2016, Reike et al. 2018, Fonseca et al., 2018
	Recover natural resources from waste	US chamber glossary, WBCSD Glossary, EMF, 2019, Kirchherr et al., 2017, I.S. Jawahir and Bradley, 2016, Reike et al. 2018, Fonseca et al., 2018

Appendix 2: Dataset of Topmost Sustainable Companies

No.	Companies	Country	N	Industry	N
1	Adidas AG	Australia	6	Appliances and lighting fixtures manufacturing	2
2	Agnico Eagle Mines Ltd	Austria	2	Asset management	2
3	Allianz SE	Brazil	4	Banks	16
4	Alphabet Inc	Canada	22	Cars and trucks manufacturing, including parts	4
5	Alstom SA	China	4	Commercial building construction	4
6	American Water Works Company Inc	Denmark	8	Computers and peripherals manufacturing	8
7	Analog Devices Inc	Finland	8	Food and beverage manufacturing	6
8	Arcelik AS	France	12	Furniture and general manufacturing N.E.C	2
9	AstraZeneca PLC	Germany	10	Grocery stores	2
10	Atlantica Sustainable Infrastructure PLC	Hong Kong	2	HVAC equipment manufacturing	2
11	Autodesk Inc	Ireland	2	Industrial Conglomerates	2
12	Banco do Brasil SA	Italy	2	Insurance companies	6
13	Bank of Montreal	Japan	6	IT services except telecom and hosting	10
14	BNP Paribas SA	Netherlands	4	Machinery manufacturing	4
15	Brambles Ltd	Norway	2	Metal and coal mining	4
16	BT Group PLC	Singapore	6	Non-road transport equipment manufacturing	2

(continued)

(continued)

No.	Companies	Country	N	Industry	N
17	Byd Co Ltd	South Korea	2	Packaging	2
18	Canadian Tire Corporation Ltd	Spain	4	Personal and business services	6
19	CapitaLand Investment Ltd	Sweden	2	Personal products (retail chemical)	6
20	Cascades Inc	Taiwan	2	Pharmaceutical & Biotech	8
21	Chr Hansen Holding A/S	Turkey	2	Plastic and rubber product manufacturing	2
22	Cisco Systems Inc	United Kingdom	10	Power generation	6
23	City Developments Ltd	United States of America	26	Power transmission and distribution	2
24	Cogeco Communications Inc			Real estate and leasing	4
25	Commerzbank AG			Refining, petrochemicals and basic organic chemicals	2
26	Dassault Systems SE			Residential construction	2
27	Eisai Co Ltd			Retail, except grocery and auto	6
28	Henkel AG & Co KgaA			Semiconductor and electronic components manufacturing	8
29	Hewlett Packard Enterprise Co			Smelters and steel-making	2
30	HP Inc			Telecom providers	8
31	Iberdrola SA			Telephones and telecom equipment manufacturing	4

(continued)

(continued)

No.	Companies	Country	N	Industry	N
32	IGM Financial Inc			Textiles and clothing manufacturing	2
33	Industria de Diseno Textil SA			Water and sewage treatment	2
34	ING Groep NV				
35	Intel Corp				
36	Intesa Sanpaolo SpA				
37	Johnson Controls International PLC				
38	Kering SA				
39	Kesko Oyj				
40	Konica Minolta Inc				
41	Koninklijke KPN NV				
42	Lenovo Group Ltd				
43	McCormick & Company Inc				
44	Metso Outotec Corp				
45	National Australia Bank Ltd				
46	Natura & Co Holding SA				
47	Neste Oyj				
48	Nordea Bank Abp				
49	Novozymes A/S				
50	Orsted A/S				
51	Pearson PLC				
52	Prologis Inc				
53	Samsung SDI Co Ltd				
54	Sanofi SA				
55	SAP SE				
56	Schneider Electric SE				
57	Sekisui Chemical Co Ltd				
58	Sims Ltd				
59	Stantec Inc				
60	StarHub Ltd				

(continued)

(continued)

No.	Companies	Country	N	Industry	N
61	Storebrand ASA				
62	Sun Life Financial Inc				
63	Teck Resources Ltd				
64	Telefonaktiebolaget LM Ericsson				
65	Telus Corp				
66	Tesla Inc				
67	Transcontinental Inc				
68	TSMC				
69	Unilever PLC				
70	Verbund AG				
71	Vestas Wind Systems A/S				
72	Vitasoy International Holdings Ltd				
73	Workday Inc				
74	Xerox Holdings Corp				
Total	148				

Appendix 3: Independent Variables

Indicators	KPIs		Description
Financial/ Economic	Sustainable Revenue	REV	Percentage of total revenue derived from products and services that are categorized as "sustainable" according to the Corporate Knights open-source Sustainable Economy Taxonomy, which is informed by a synthesis of, among others, the below sources and best practices: Climate Bonds Taxonomy (Climate Bonds Initiative) - EU Taxonomy for Sustainable Activities - Sustainability Accounting Standards Board (SASB) reporting standards - Environmental Goods and Services Sector (Eurostat) - China Green Bond Endorsed Project Catalogue - Green Bond Principles - TCFD recommended climate opportunity metrics - Other private sector rating agencies with green or sustainability taxonomy - Industry expert consultation covering all relevant CKPG subsectors with solicited feedback on industry definition of sustainable from leading industry experts and government agencies
	Sustainable Investment	INV	Percentage of a company's total investment (R&D, capital expenditures, acquisitions, and others) directed toward projects/ research/companies categorized as "sustainable" according to the Corporate Knights open-source sustainable taxonomy
	Percentage Tax Paid	PTP	Cash tax amount paid/EBITDA – five-year trailing (2017–2021)
	Sanction Deductions	F-Ded	Total fines, penalties and settlements/revenue
Customer Perspective/ Environment	Supplier Sustainability Score	SSS	The supplier with the highest CK Sustainability Score
	Sustainability Pay Link	SPL	Mechanisms that link senior executive pay to sustainability targets

(continued)

(continued)

Indicators	KPIs		Description
	Energy Productivity	ENG-P	Revenue (converted to USD using PPP exchange rate)/(Energy use – renewable energy generated by the company or certified RECs)
	Water Productivity	WAT-P	Revenue (converted to USD using PPP exchange rate)/Water withdrawn
	Waste Productivity	WAST-p	Revenue (converted to USD using PPP exchange rate)/Total non-recycled waste generated
	VOC Productivity	VOC-P	Revenue (converted to USD using PPP exchange rate)/VOC emissions
	NOx Productivity	NOX-P	Revenue (converted to USD using PPP exchange rate)/NOx emissions
	SOx Productivity	SOX-P	Revenue (converted to USD using PPP exchange rate)/SOx emissions
	Particulate Matter Productivity	PM-P	Revenue (converted to USD using PPP exchange rate)/Particulate matter emissions
	GHG Productivity	GHG-P	Revenue (converted to USD using PPP exchange rate)/GHG emissions: scope 1 & 2
Internal Process/Social	Injuries	ING	Lost time incidents rate per 200,000 hours for both employees and contractors
	Fatalities	FAT	Fatalities/total number of full-time equivalent employees
	Employee Turnover	EMP	Number of departures (voluntary and involuntary)/total average employees
	Paid Sick Leave	PSL	Paid sick leave (10+ days, 50%+ of pay) offered to employees in the country where the company is headquartered
	Pension Fund Quality	PFQ	75% × (total DB and DC employer contributions/FTE employees percent-ranked* against peers) + 25% × ((fair value of DB plan assets/FTE employees percent-ranked* against peers) – (1 – (fair value of DB plan assets/liability percent-ranked* against peers))

(continued)

(continued)

Indicators	KPIs		Description
Learning and growth perspective/ Governance	Non-males in Executive Management	N-MEX	Non-male representation on the executive management team (percent-ranked* against all companies in the universe)
	Non-males on Boards	N-MOB	Non-male representation on board of directors (percent-ranked* against all companies in the universe)
	Racial Diversity Among Executives	R-DEX	Number of top-tier executives who are members of a visible minority compared to the population of their executive peers in headquarters country (percent-ranked* against all companies in the universe)
	Racial Diversity on Board of Directors	R-DBOD	Number of board directors who are members of a visible minority compared to the population of their director peers in headquarters country (percent-ranked* against all companies in the universe)
	CEO-Average Employee Pay	CEO-P	CEO compensation or highest-paid Exec/average employee compensation

References

Alin, A. (2010). Multicollinearity. Wiley interdisciplinary reviews: computational statistics, 2(3), 370–374.

Barnabè, F., & Nazir, S. (2021). Investigating the interplays between integrated reporting practices and circular economy disclosure. *International Journal of Productivity and Performance Management, 70*(8), 2001–2031.

Barnabè, F., & Nazir, S. (2022). Conceptualizing and enabling circular economy through integrated thinking. *Corporate Social Responsibility and Environmental Management, 29*(2), 448–468.

Begum, R. A., Siwar, C., Pereira, J. J., & Jaafar, A. H. (2009). Attitude and behavioral factors in waste management in the construction industry of Malaysia. *Resources, Conservation and Recycling, 53*(6), 321–328.

Berelson, B. (1952). Content analysis in communication research.

Burnard, P. (1995). Nurse educators' perceptions of reflection and reflective practice: A report of a descriptive study. *Journal of Advanced Nursing, 21*(6), 1167–1174.

Calzolari, T., Genovese, A., & Brint, A. (2022). Circular economy indicators for supply chains: A systematic literature review. *Environmental and Sustainability Indicators, 13*, 100160.

Crespo-Rosas, N., & Franco-García, L. (2023). Improving gender equality with social entrepreneurship and circular economy: A Mexican case. *The social dimensions of the circular economy* (pp. 241–263). Springer International.

de Oliveira, C. T., & Oliveira, G. G. A. (2023). What circular economy indicators really measure? An overview of circular economy principles and sustainable development goals. *Resources, Conservation and Recycling, 190*, 106850.

Downe-Wamboldt, B. (1992). Content analysis: Method, applications, and issues. *Health Care for Women International, 13*(3), 313–321.

Duman, G. M., Taskaynatan, M., Kongar, E., & Rosentrater, K. A. (2018). Integrating environmental and social sustainability into performance evaluation: A balanced scorecard-based grey-DANP approach for the food industry. *Frontiers in Nutrition, 5*, 65.

Elkington, J., & Rowlands, I. H. (1999). Cannibals with forks: The triple bottom line of 21st century business. *Alternatives Journal, 25*(4), 42.

Esmaeilian, B., Wang, B., Lewis, K., Duarte, F., Ratti, C., & Behdad, S. (2018). The future of waste management in smart and sustainable cities: A review and concept paper. *Waste Management, 81*, 177–195.

Gacser, N. G., & Szoka, K. (2021). Sustainability accounting-historical development and future perspectives of the discipline. *PressAcademia Procedia, 14*(1), 1–4.

Guthrie, J., & Abeysekera, I. (2006). Content analysis of social, environmental reporting: What is new? *Journal of Human Resource Costing & Accounting, 10*(2), 114–126.

Hansen, E. G., & Schaltegger, S. (2016). The sustainability balanced scorecard: A systematic review of architectures. *Journal of Business Ethics, 133*, 193–221.

Hernández-Arzaba, J. C., Nazir, S., Leyva-Hernández, S. N., & Muhyaddin, S. (2022). Stakeholder pressure engaged with circular economy principles and economic and environmental performance. *Sustainability, 14*(23), 16302.

Hockerts, K. (2001, January). Corporate sustainability management, towards controlling corporate ecological and social sustainability. In *Proceedings of greening of industry network conference* (pp. 21–24).

Hopwood, B., Mellor, M., & O'Brien, G. (2005). Sustainable development: Mapping different approaches. *Sustainable Development, 13*(1), 38–52.

Janubová, B., & Grešš, M. (2016). Urbanization of poverty and the sustainable development of urban areas in Chile. *Theoretical and Empirical Researches in Urban Management, 11*(4), 17–29.

Kaplan, R. S. (2009). Conceptual foundations of the balanced scorecard. *Handbooks of Management Accounting Research, 3*, 1253–1269.

Kaplan, R. S., & Norton, D. P. (1996). *The balanced scorecard: translating strategy into action.* Harvard Business Press.

Kaplan, R. S., & Norton, D. P. (2000). Having trouble with your strategy? Then map it. *Focusing Your Organization on Strategy—With the Balanced Scorecard, 49*(5), 167–176.

Kirchherr, J., & Piscicelli, L. (2019). Towards an education for the circular economy (ECE): Five teaching principles and a case study. *Resources, Conservation and Recycling, 150*, 104406.

Krippendorff, K. (2004). Reliability in content analysis: Some common misconceptions and recommendations. *Human Communication Research, 30*(3), 411–433.

Lamba, H. K., Kumar, N. S., & Dhir, S. (2023). Circular economy and sustainable development: A review and research agenda. *International Journal of Productivity and Performance Management* (ahead-of-print).

Lihong, W. (2011). Development of circular economy and optimization of industrial structure for Shandong province. *Energy Procedia, 5*, 1603–1610.
Long, T., & Johnson, M. (2000). Rigour, reliability and validity in qualitative research. *Clinical Effectiveness in Nursing, 4*(1), 30–37.
Maroun, W., & Prinsloo, A. (2020). Drivers of combined assurance in a sustainable development context: Evidence from integrated reports. *Business Strategy and the Environment, 29*(8), 3702–3719.
Milne, M. J., & Adler, R. W. (1999). Exploring the reliability of social and environmental disclosures content analysis. *Accounting, Auditing & Accountability Journal, 12*(2), 237–256.
Neuendorf, K. A. (2010). Reliability for content analysis. In *Media messages and public health* (pp. 85–105). Routledge.
Pask, F., Lake, P., Yang, A., Tokos, H., & Sadhukhan, J. (2017). Sustainability indicators for industrial ovens and assessment using Fuzzy set theory and Monte Carlo simulation. *Journal of Cleaner Production, 140*, 1217–1225.
Reh, L. (2013). Process engineering in circular economy. *Particuology, 11*(2), 119–133.
Sassanelli, C., Rosa, P., Rocca, R., & Terzi, S. (2019). Circular economy performance assessment methods: A systematic literature review. *Journal of Cleaner Production, 229*, 440–453.
Scheel, C. (2016). Beyond sustainability. Transforming industrial zero-valued residues into increasing economic returns. *Journal of Cleaner Production, 131*, 376–386.
Steen-Olsen, K., Owen, A., Barrett, J., Guan, D., Hertwich, E. G., Lenzen, M., & Wiedmann, T. (2016). Accounting for value added embodied in trade and consumption: An intercomparison of global multiregional input–output databases. *Economic Systems Research, 28*(1), 78–94.
Torgautov, B., Zhanabayev, A., Tleuken, A., Turkyilmaz, A., Borucki, C., & Karaca, F. (2022). Performance assessment of construction companies for the circular economy: A balanced scorecard approach. *Sustainable Production and Consumption, 33*, 991–1004.
Tsai, F. M., Bui, T. D., Tseng, M. L., Lim, M. K., & Hu, J. (2020). Municipal solid waste management in a circular economy: A data-driven bibliometric analysis. *Journal of Cleaner Production, 275*, 124132.
WCED, S. W. S. (1987). World commission on environment and development. *Our Common Future, 17*(1), 1–91.
Weber, R. P. (1990). *Basic content analysis* (Vol. 49). Sage.
Wilson, S. M. (2013). Professional development for science teachers. *Science, 340*(6130), 310–313.

Wine, J. (1971). Test anxiety and direction of attention. *Psychological Bulletin, 76*(2), 92.

Witjes, S., & Lozano, R. (2016). Towards a more circular economy: Proposing a framework linking sustainable public procurement and sustainable business models. *Resources, Conservation and Recycling, 112*, 37–44.

Wixom, B. H., Yen, B., & Relich, M. (2013). Maximizing value from business analytics. *MIS Quarterly Executive, 12*(2), Article 6.

Zarbakhshnia, N., Govindan, K., Kannan, D., & Goh, M. (2023). Outsourcing logistics operations in circular economy towards sustainable development goals. *Business Strategy and the Environment, 32*(1), 134–162.

7
Conclusion

1 Conclusion

The main aim of this book is to explore the corporate reporting practices' role in the implementation of CE activities by firms, which is informative for the internal and external stakeholders in the decision-making process (Linder & Williander, 2017). These stakeholders want to know whether practices reflect all three aspects of SD, i.e., economic, social, and environmental.

At present, the level of information on social, economic, and environmental aspects given by firms is a subject of great interest in the literature on sustainability. Book chapters have been focused on investigating the consideration of sustainable development information in yearly records by utilizing social, economic, and environmental procedures (Mathews, 2008), disclosure practices and accounting in green business (Burritt & Schaltegger, 2010; Gray & Laughlin, 2012; Llena et al., 2007), and cleaner manufacture processes (Aranda-Usón et al., 2020). The book not only covers financial and non-financial reporting information for sustainability but also highlights the quality as a matter raised by CE researchers and practitioners (Stewart & Niero, 2018). Year after year, an expanding number of big organizations have been publishing corporate

S. Nazir and A. Capocchi, *Sustainability Reporting Practices and the Circular Economy*,
https://doi.org/10.1007/978-3-031-51845-4_7

social responsibility and sustainability reports that provide information to their internal and external stakeholders for rational decision-making and the promotion of sustainable development practices (A4S, 2022; KPMG, 2008, 2010), but companies fail disclosed CE activities into their reporting practices.

The literature review chapter set out how and to what extent similarities, differences, and relationships exist between the CE and SD in the context of the business economy. The literature found that many modern organizations have yet to recognize the potential opportunities available from CE. The evidence from this systematic review paper suggests that reporting may help them not only to think and rethink the relationships among resources across the various sectors of the organization but also to deliver new accounting information for better strategic decision-making, investment decisions, and sustainable performance. It shows the various compatibilities between CE practices and SD goals. CE aligns with a range of R imperatives, e.g., 3Rs, 4Rs, 5Rs, 6Rs, 7Rs, 8Rs, 9Rs, and 10Rs (Reike et al., 2018), but most practitioners, academic researchers, and organizations are using 3R's (reduce, reuse, recycle). This study attempts to fill the research gap between CE and IR.

Chapter 3 explored the primary nexus of integrated reporting with CE issues and activities. In detail, through content analysis, the study provided data useful to investigate how and to what extent integrated reports disclose circular economy-related information. Subsequently, the paper inspected a sample of integrated reports looking for CE-related visual representations and found that CE and IR have a typical relationship.

Chapter 4 investigates how and to what extent CE activities are developing within companies and being disclosed in reporting practices, and how it impacts environmental performance. Most multinational companies annually or biannually publish sustainability reports, annual reports that present their strategies concerning internal and external practices. Competent sustainability reveals the long-term outcomes of a company in a single report, containing every single important point of view. Generally, annual reports demonstrate business activities that are identified with the information utilized by the organization's management

(IIRC, 2013). The paper represents R principles that integrate with environment key performance indicators and inputs, material manufactured, product use, and waste in the corporate sector. CE can be considered as a framework for the effective management of resources, whereby inputs and outputs are utilized circularly, and the outputs of each industrial procedure turn on the inputs by a different process (Korhonen et al., 2018). The CE approach can also enhance the product lifecycle (Tukker, 2015) by implementing the R principal approach into the production process (Reike et al., 2018).

Chapter 5 explored how and to what extent CE-6Rs principles into integrated reporting practices, and additionally, how and to what extent, do institutional pressures (coercive, normative, and mimetic) impact integrated reporting in the context of circular economy activities? This paper provides a disclosure of the existing IR practices and CE activities in different regions. Industries and year-wise evidence, as well as institutional pressure, revealed that coercive, normative, and mimetic isomorphism has a certain impact on CE-6Rs and IRs practices. This may represent the ideal fit not only to contribute to organizations in representing and disclosing financial and non-financial information but also to stimulate the full integration of such issues of value creation processes with a holistic approach (i.e., considering simultaneous economic, social, and environmental issues).

Chapter 6 investigated the companies' overall performance and endorsed a framework for the assessment of social, environmental, economic, and governance impact evaluation by indicators, which became possible through the circular economy and balanced scorecard approach. The chapter investigates the validation of the framework by using services and the manufacturing industry. Research mainly highlights the social, economic, environmental, and governance also combined with the fundamental BSC approach as crucial performance measures closer to sustainability. CE principles' focus is on environmental protection and resource protection with waste reduction. This can be accomplished by checking the circular activities in terms of environmental issues, waste generation, and the effective use of resources and materials. The study goal was to provide a framework inside the overall performance dimension of CE more rapidly for sustainability and waste management. This framework also helps policymakers and trendsetters to prompt and deploy social, environmental, governance, and economic sustainability perspectives. The book explores the mechanism between management accounting practices and circular economy and considers the role of CE in sustainable development. Furthermore, the next section states the limitations and practical implications of this research.

2 Limitations Transit Future Research Agenda

The finding of this research applies certain limitations for future research into the CE role and reporting practices. The systematic literature review paper sample size of the articles covers 2021. But the reader can add and could enhance the scope of the literature review and find out more research gaps. Furthermore, the literature review covered the business and economic area, if material science, energy fuels, computer, etc., areas could be considered in the future for the comparative studies that could be beneficial for finding more patterns as well as provide a broad view of CE and SD.

Chapter 3 presents some limitations that should be highlighted in future research agendas. The research explored the primary relationship between the CE and the SD. The amount of disclosure of CE-relative terms in integrated reports is quite limited which will refer to further explore the CE-related terms by circular economic principles. Furthermore, content analysis has traditionally an excessive focus on the quantity rather than the quality of disclosure (Guthrie & Abeysekera, 2006). Stated differently, the quantity of disclosure does not necessarily mean that an organization is disclosing information of high quality, or relevance for its stakeholders. Another limitation of this study is that it draws upon a rather limited sample or integrated reports. The sample of data collection research only disclosed the before COVID-19 effects, but it could be helpful for future research during COVID-19 analysis and could do comparative analysis. Anyhow, these limitations also open up avenues for further research, specifically toward the development of a qualitative exploratory case study (Yin, 1994; Ryan, 2002). Additionally, statistical analyses could be performed to correlate data emerging from the content analysis with a range of other factors considered to be relevant for CE.

Chapter 4 circular economy ties with environmental performance, this research indicates several limitations and future directions for researchers and practitioners developing strategies and participating in enhancing SD. Firstly, the study adopted a mixed methodology approach, a qualitative content analysis, and a quantitative analysis in-depth approach, if in future utilizing the structure and semi-structured interviews of responsible persons and policymakers of companies, an analysis of which would enhance this current research and produce new prospective ideas to test. Secondly, a study could be undertaken to test the framework by applying it with time to see the COVID-19 effects and then comparing the results with this research. Thirdly, further studies could be conducted to compare this research to develop new accounting GRI standards that identify how and to what extent these companies implement and promote CE-related reporting practices, and what policies and barriers to change such regions may endure.

Chapter 5 contains certain limitations with this study, and the most significant limitations of the research, which open doors for further research, are as follows. Every organization is driven by an ever-expanding emphasis on sustainability issues and discloses these practices to the general public, stakeholders, and policymakers, while reconsidering the way organizations frame their framework that can deliver the financial and non-financial information to the general public and stakeholders, step by step, i.e., inputs, business activities, outputs, and outcomes. First, the basic quantitative limitation of the research is related to the IIRC database; information may not demonstrate the full critical effect of the CE-related strategy and enactment in the IR. Furthermore, IR will collect from the other database to explore how and to what extent CE terms into integrated reports. In any case, the connection between industry standards (e.g., G4, GRI, UN 2030, EU directives) for sustainable development (accepted as best practices) and the CE-related IR practices should be additionally investigated whether any other patterns of CE can be identified. The paper used the World

Business Council for Sustainable Development [WBCSD] (https://www.ceguide.org/Glossary) and the US Chamber of Commerce Foundation (https://www.uschamberfoundation.org/circular-economy-toolbox/about-circularity/glossary) glossaries on CE even though another glossary provides the other CE-related terms that could be effective. Hence, a comprehensive investigation is required through expert surveys, interviews, and case studies.

Chapter 6 has also highlighted certain limitations that will open a new avenue for future research. First, the study used the top 100 sustainable companies' KPIs which represent the Knight. The researchers can use the Bloomberg/data stream for the collection of other variable scores and check the different industries participating in the sustainable development agenda. Secondly, the author used the COVID-19 period companies' dataset and developed a CE-BSC framework. This framework can be used to evaluate the before and after COVID-19 effects.

3 Practical Implications

The proposed frameworks will help industrialists and managers explore the performance outcomes in CE implementation in manufacturing and services industries toward sustainability. The industrial implications are as follows:

- It will help managers to explore the overall performance of specific elements in the aspects of social, environmental, governance, and economic.
- It will be useful for supply chain managers to examine circular principles at each step of the supply chain for essential key indicators performance measurement.
- The proposed framework will guide the supply chain members in industries where managers must operate goals and the measures/indicators to be checked for better consequences of their objectives.
- The study explores environmental issues to get better operation for environmental safety in nowadays competitive environment.

- These frameworks provide indicators such as enhancement in social cognizance, sustainability development, organization value creation, eco-friendly material price, decreased environment concerns, and waste reduction.
- Lastly, the study also allows practitioners and researchers to lead the way for further research on this topic with various other factors and techniques.

Book Summary

The papers summarize the literature review, theoretical framework, research design, contribution, limitation, and implications of the research underpinning this book, although every chapter has a portion of the circular economy and corporate reporting literature for contributing to the sustainable development debate. However, this study suggests that CE and corporate are strongly linked with sustainability reporting practices as well as interlinked with each other. Furthermore, the study unfolds the CE practices into corporate reports that could be beneficial to all stakeholders to see the organization picture in broad view while to policymakers to adopt or deploy CE activities into their organizations.

References

A4S. (2022). *Accounting for sustainability*. https://www.accountingforsustainability.org/content/a4s/corporate/en/activities/reporting/response-ifrs-sustainability-disclosure-standards.html

Aranda-Usón, A., Portillo-Tarragona, P., Scarpellini, S., & Llena-Macarulla, F. (2020). The progressive adoption of a circular economy by businesses for cleaner production: An approach from a regional study in Spain. *Journal of Cleaner Production, 247*, 119648.

Burritt, R. L., & Schaltegger, S. (2010). Sustainability accounting and reporting: Fad or trend? *Accounting, Auditing & Accountability Journal., 23*(7), 829–846.

Gray, R., & Laughlin, R. (2012). It was 20 years ago today Sgt Pepper. *Accounting, Auditing & Accountability Journal, Green Accounting and the Blue Meanies, 25*(2), 228–255.

IIRC. (2013). *Business model. Background paper for IR*. International Integrated Reporting Council. https://integratedreporting.org/wp-content/uploads/2013/03/Business_Model.pdf

Korhonen, J., Honkasalo, A., & Seppala, J. (2018). Circular economy: The concept and its limitations. *Ecological Economics, 143*, 37–46.

KPMG. (2008). *Climate change your business*. https://inis.iaea.org/search/search.aspx?orig_q=RN:40052557.

KPMG. (2010). *KPMG promotes integration of company reports*. http://www.kpmg.com/RO/en/IssuesAndInsights/ArticlesPublications/Press-releases/Pages/Integrated-Reporting.aspx

Linder, M., & Williander, M. (2017). Circular business model innovation: Inherent uncertainties. *Business Strategy and the Environment, 26*(2), 182–196.

Llena, F., Moneva, J. M., & Hernandez, B. (2007). Environmental disclosures and compulsory accounting standards: The case of Spanish annual reports. *Business Strategy and the Environment., 16*, 50–63.

Mathews, M. R. (2008). Further thoughts on maga-accounting and the need for standards. *Issues in Social and Environmental Accounting, 2*(2), 158–175.

Reike, D., Vermeulen, W. J. V., & Witjes, S. (2018). The circular economy; New or refurbished as CE 3.0? Exploring controversies in the conceptualization of the circular economy through a focus on history and resource value retention options. *Journal of Cleaner Production, 135*, 246–264.

Ryan, B. (2002). *Research methods and methodology in finance and accounting*. Cengage Learning EMEA.

Stewart, R., & Niero, M. (2018). Circular economy incorporates sustainability strategies: A review of corporate sustainability reports in the fast-moving consumer goods sector. *Business Strategy and the Environment, 27*(7), 1005–1022.

Tukker, A. (2015). Product services for a resource-efficient and circular economy—A review. *Journal of Cleaner Production, 97*, 76–91.

Yin, R. K. (1994). *Case study research: Design and methods* (2nd ed.). Sage.

References

A4S. (2022). *Accounting for sustainability*. https://www.accountingforsustainability.org/content/a4s/corporate/en/activities/reporting/response-ifrs-sustainability-disclosure-standards.html

A4S. (2010). *Accounting for sustainability*. http://www.accountingforsustainability.org/output/page186.asp

Abbasi, K. R., Hussain, K., Haddad, A. M., Salman, A., & Ozturk, I. (2022). The role of financial development and technological innovation towards sustainable development in Pakistan: Fresh insights from consumption and territory-based emissions. *Technological Forecasting and Social Change, 176*, 121444.

Abbasi, S., & Choukolaei, H. A. (2023). A systematic review of green supply chain network design literature focusing on carbon policy. *Decision Analytics Journal*, 100189.

Abbasi, S., Zahmatkesh, S., Bokhari, A., & Hajiaghaei-Keshteli, M. (2023). Designing a vaccine supply chain network considering environmental aspects. *Journal of Cleaner Production, 417*, 137935.

Abrutyn, S., & Turner, J. H. (2011). The old institutionalism meets the new institutionalism. *Sociological Perspectives, 54*(3), 283–306.

Adams, C. A. (2015). The international integrated reporting council: A call to action. *Critical Perspectives on Accounting, 27*, 23–28.

S. Nazir and A. Capocchi, *Sustainability Reporting Practices and the Circular Economy*, https://doi.org/10.1007/978-3-031-51845-4

Adams, C. A., & Abhayawansa, S., (2022). Connecting the COVID-19 pandemic, environmental, social and governance (ESG) investing and calls for harmonisation of sustainability reporting. *Critical Perspectives on Accounting, 82*, 102309.

Adams, R. B., Licht, A. N., & Sagiv, L. (2011). Shareholders and stakeholders: How do directors decide? *Strategic Management Journal, 32*(12), 1331–1355.

Adams, S., & Simnett, R. (2011). Integrated reporting: An opportunity for Australia's not-for-profit sector. *Australian Accounting Review, 21*(3), 292–301.

Aguilar-Hernandez, G. A., Rodrigues, J. F. D., & Tukker, A. (2021). Macroeconomic, social and environmental impacts of a circular economy up to 2050: A meta-analysis of prospective studies. *Journal of Cleaner Production, 278*, 123421.

Aguilar-Rivera, N. (2022). Bioindicators for the sustainability of sugar agroindustry. *Sugar Tech*, 1–11.

Alin, A. (2010). Multicollinearity. Wiley interdisciplinary reviews: computational statistics, 2(3), 370–374.

Andrews, D. (2015). The circular economy, design thinking and education for sustainability. *Local Economy, 30*(3), 305–315.

Aranda-Usón, A., Portillo-Tarragona, P., Marín-Vinuesa, L. M., & Scarpellini, S. (2019). Financial resources for the circular economy: A perspective from businesses. *Sustainability, 11*(3), 888.

Aranda-Uson, A., Portillo-Tarragona, P., Scarpellini, S., & Llena-Macarulla. F. (2020). The progressive adoption of a circular economy by businesses for cleaner production: An approach from a regional study in Spain. *Journal of Cleaner Production, 247*, 119648.

Arif, M., Hasan, M., Alawi, S. M., & Naeem, M. A. (2021). COVID-19 and time-frequency connectedness between green and conventional financial markets. *Global Finance Journal, 49*, 100650.

Atkins, J. F., Solomon, A., Norton, S., & Joseph, N. L. (2015a). The emergence of integrated private reporting. *Meditari Accountancy Research, 23*(1), 28–61.

Atkins, J., Atkins, B. C., Thomson, I., & Maroun, W. (2015b). "Good" news from nowhere: Imagining utopian sustainable accounting. *Accounting, Auditing & Accountability Journal, 28*(5), 651–670.

Barnabè, F., & Nazir, S. (2021). Investigating the interplays between integrated reporting practices and circular economy disclosure. *International Journal of Productivity and Performance Management, 70*(8), 2001–2031.

Barnabè, F., & Nazir, S. (2022). Conceptualizing and enabling circular economy through integrated thinking. *Corporate Social Responsibility and Environmental Management, 29*(2), 448–468.

Beattie, V., & Smith, S. J. (2013). Value creation and business models: Refocusing the intellectual capital debate. *The British Accounting Review, 45*(4), 243–254.

Begum, R. A., Siwar, C., Pereira, J. J., & Jaafar, A. H. (2009). Attitude and behavioral factors in waste management in the construction industry of Malaysia. *Resources, Conservation and Recycling, 53*(6), 321–328.

Bell, E., & Davison, J. (2013). Visual management studies: Empirical and theoretical approaches. *International Journal of Management Reviews, 15*(2), 167–184.

Bellis, D. N. (2009). *Bibliometrics and citation analysis.* Scarecrow Press.

Berelson, B. (1952). Content analysis in communication research.

Blomsma, F., & Brennan, G. (2017). The emergence of circular economy: A new framing around prolonging resource productivity. *Journal of Industrial Ecology, 21*(3), 603–614.

Bocken, N. M., De Pauw, I., Bakker, C., & Van Der Grinten, B. (2016). Product design and business model strategies for a circular economy. *Journal of Industrial and Production Engineering, 33*(5), 308–320.

Boiral, O., & Gendron, Y. (2011). Sustainable development and certification practices: Lessons learned and prospects. *Business Strategy and the Environment, 20*(5), 331–347.

Burke, J. J., & Clark, C. E. (2016). The business case for integrated reporting: Insights from leading practitioners, regulators, and academics. *Business Horizons, 59*(3), 273–283.

Burnard, P. (1995). Nurse educators' perceptions of reflection and reflective practice: A report of a descriptive study. *Journal of Advanced Nursing, 21*(6), 1167–1174.

Burritt, R. L., & Schaltegger, S. (2010). Sustainability accounting and reporting: Fad or trend? *Accounting, Auditing & Accountability Journal., 23*(7), 829–846.

Busco, C., Frigo, M. L., Riccaboni, A., & Quattrone, P. (2013). *Integrated reporting. Concepts and cases that redefine corporate accountability.* Switzerland.

Busco, C., Malafronte, I., Pereira, J., & Starita, M. G. (2018). The determinants of companies' levels of integration: Does one size fit all? *The British Accounting Review, 51*(3), 277–298.

Calzolari, T., Genovese, A., & Brint, A. (2022). Circular economy indicators for supply chains: A systematic literature review. *Environmental and Sustainability Indicators, 13*, 100160.

Cameron, E. J. (1997). A formal AIN service creation, feature interactions analysis and management environment: An industrial application. In Proceedings of Fourth Workshop on Feature Interactions in Telecommunications Systems, July 1997.

Campbell, J. L. (2007). Why would corporations behave in socially responsible ways? An institutional theory of corporate social responsibility. *Academy of Management Review, 32*(3), 946–967.

Casiano Flores, C., Bressers, H., Gutierrez, C., & de Boer, C. (2018). Towards Circular economy—A wastewater treatment perspective, the Presa Guadalupe case. *Management Research Review, 41*(5), 554–571.

Cohen, J. L., Holder-Webb, L., Nath, L., & Wood, D. (2012). Corporate reporting on nonfinancial leading indicators of economic performance and sustainability. *Accounting Horizons, 26*(1), 65-90.

Corvellec, H., Böhm, S., Stowell, A., & Valenzuela, F. (2020). Introduction to the special issue on the contested realities of the circular economy. *Culture and Organization, 26*(2), 97–102.

Crespo-Rosas, N., & Franco-García, L. (2023). Improving gender equality with social entrepreneurship and circular economy: A Mexican case. In *The social dimensions of the circular economy* (pp. 241–263). Springer International Publishing.

Cristina, D. M., Popescu, M. F., Jean, A., & Mieila, M. (2018). Developments of the circular economy in Romania under the new sustainability paradigm. *Economic Computation and Economic Cybernetics Studies and Research, 52*(2), 125–183.

D'ALFONSO, A. (2020). Sustainable Europe Investment Plan.

Davison, J. (2014). Visual rhetoric and the case of intellectual capital. *Accounting, Organizations and Society, 39*(1), 20–37.

Davison, J. (2015). Visualising accounting: An interdisciplinary review and synthesis. *Accounting and Business Research, 45*(2), 121–165.

de Oliveira, C. T., & Oliveira, G. G. A. (2023). What circular economy indicators really measure? An overview of circular economy principles and sustainable development goals. *Resources, Conservation and Recycling, 190*, 106850.

De Vaus, D. (1982). The impact of geographical mobility on adolescent religious orientation: an Australian study. *Review of Religious Research*, 391–403.

de Villiers, C., & Sharma, U. (2017). A critical reflection on the future of financial, intellectual capital, sustainability and integrated reporting. *Critical Perspectives on Accounting*, corrected proof (in press). 70, 101999. https://www.sciencedirect.com/science/article/pii/S1045235417300606

De Villiers, C., & Sharma, U. (2020). A critical reflection on the future of financial, intellectual capital, sustainability and integrated reporting. *Critical Perspectives on Accounting, 70*, 101999.

De Villiers, C., Rinaldi, L., & Unerman, J. (2014). Integrated Reporting: Insights, gaps and an agenda for future research. *Accounting, Auditing & Accountability Journal., 27*(7), 1042–1067.

DeLorenzo, A., Parizeau, K., & Von Massow, M. (2019). Regulating Ontario's circular economy through food waste legislation. *Society and Business Review, 14*(2), 200–216.

DiMaggio, P. J., & Powell, W. W. (1983a). The iron revisited; Institutional isomorphism and collective rationality in organizational fields. *American Sociological Review, 48*(2), 147–160.

DiMaggio, P. J., & Powell, W. W. (1983b). *The new institution in organizational analysis*. University of Chicago Press.

Downe-Wamboldt, B. (1992). Content analysis: Method, applications, and issues. *Health Care for Women International, 13*(3), 313–321.

Duman, G. M., Taskaynatan, M., Kongar, E., & Rosentrater, K. A. (2018). Integrating environmental and social sustainability into performance evaluation: A balanced scorecard-based grey-DANP approach for the food industry. *Frontiers in Nutrition, 5*, 65.

Dumay, J. (2016). A critical reflection on the future of intellectual capital: From reporting to disclosure. *Journal of Intellectual Capital, 17*(1), 168–184.

Eaton, K. A., Newman, H. N., & Widström, E. (2003). A survey of dental hygienist numbers in Canada, the European Economic area, Japan and the United States of America in 1998. *British Dental Journal, 195*(10), 595–598.

Eccles, R. G., & Krzus, M. P. (2010). *One report: Integrated reporting for a sustainable strategy*. Wiley.

EC—European Commission. (2014). *Critical raw materials—CRM list 2014*. https://rmis.jrc.ec.europa.eu/?page=crm-list-2014-34bfe8

EC—European Commission. (2015). *First circular economy action plan*. https://ec.europa.eu/environment/topics/circular-economy/first-circular-economy-action-plan_en

EC—European Commission. (2017). *Critical raw materials*. https://ec.europa.eu/growth/sectors/raw-materials/areas-specific-interest/critical-raw-materials_en

EC—European Commission. (2020). *Circular economy action plan*. https://ec.europa.eu/environment/strategy/circular-economy-action-plan_en

EC—European Commission. (2021). *Proposal for a Corporate Sustainability Reporting Directive (CSRD)*. https://ec.europa.eu/info/business-economy-euro/company-reporting-and-auditing/company-reporting/corporate-sustainability-reporting_en

EC—European Commission. (2018). *Regulation (EU) 2018/1999 on the Governance of the Energy Union and Climate Action*. https://www.iea.org/policies/11773-regulation-eu-20181999-on-the-governance-of-the-energy-union-and-climate-action

EEA—European Environment Agency. (2015). *Climate change impacts and adaptation*. https://www.eea.europa.eu/soer/2015/europe/climate-change-impacts-and-adaptation

El-Kassar, A. N., Dagher, G. K., Lythreatis, S., & Azakir, M. (2022). Antecedents and consequences of knowledge hiding: The roles of HR practices, organizational support for creativity, creativity, innovative work behavior, and task performance. *Journal of Business Research, 140*(c), 1–10.

Elkington, J., & Rowlands, I. H. (1999). Cannibals with forks: The triple bottom line of 21st-century business. *Alternatives Journal, 25*(4), 42.

Ellen MacArthur Foundation. (2012). *Economic and business rationale for an accelerated transition. Towards a circular economy* (Vol. 2). Ellen MacArthur Foundation: Cowes. https://www.ellenmacarthurfoundation.org/publications

Ellen MacArthur Foundation. (2013). *Opportunities for the consumer goods sector. Towards a circular economy*. https://www.ellenmacarthurfoundation.org/publications

Ellen MacArthur Foundation. (2014). *Accelerating the scale-up across global supply chains. Towards the circular economy*. https://www.ellenmacarthurfoundation.org/publications

Ellen MacArthur Foundation. (2015a). *Delivering the circular economy—A toolkit for policymakers*. https://www.ellenmacarthurfoundation.org/publications

Ellen MacArthur Foundation. (2015b). *Potential for Denmark as a circular economy*. https://www.ellenmacarthurfoundation.org/publications

Ellen MacArthur Foundation. (2015c). *Towards a circular economy: Business rationale for an accelerated transition.* https://www.ellenmacarthurfoundation.org/publications

Ellen MacArthur Foundation. (2017a). *The new plastic economy: Rethinking the future of plastics & catalysing action.* https://www.ellenmacarthurfoundation.org/publications

Ellen MacArthur Foundation. (2017b). *A new textile economy, redesigning fashion's future.* Ellen MacArthur Foundation: Cowes. https://www.ellenmacarthurfoundation.org/publications

El-Kassar, A. N., & Singh, S. K. (2019). Green innovation and organizational performance: The influence of big data and the moderating role of management commitment and HR practices. *Technological forecasting and social change, 144*, 483–498.

EMF—Ellen-Macarthur Foundation. (2020). *Global-Commitment-2020-Progress-Report.* https://emf.thirdlight.com/link/il0mcm1dqjtn-knjubr/@/preview/1?o

EMF—Ellen-Macarthur Foundation. (2022). *Circular economy introduction.* https://ellenmacarthurfoundation.org/topics/circular-economy-introduction/glossary

Esmaeilian, B., Wang, B., Lewis, K., Duarte, F., Ratti, C., & Behdad, S. (2018). The future of waste management in smart and sustainable cities: A review and concept paper. *Waste Management, 81*, 177–195.

EU, (1994). *Directive 94/62/EC on packaging and packaging waste.* http://eur-lex.europa.eu/LexUriServ/LexUriServ.do?uri=CELEX:31994L0062:EN:HTML

EU—European Union. (2014a). *Scoping study to identify potential circular economy actions, priority sectors, material flows and value chains.* Publications Office of the European Union. https://op.europa.eu/en/publication-detail/-/publication/0619e465-581c-41dc-9807-2bb394f6bd07

EU—European Union. (2014b). *Non-financial reporting.* Publications Office of the European Union. https://ec.europa.eu/info/business-economy-euro/company-reporting-and-auditing/company-reporting/non-financial-reporting_en

EU—European Union. (2019). *The European Green Deal.* https://ec.europa.eu/commission/presscorner/detail/en/ip_19_6691

European Commission. (2000a). *EU financial reporting strategy: The way forward.* https://eur-lex.europa.eu/legal-content/en/ALL/?uri=CELEX:52000DCO359

European Commission. (2000b). *Company reporting*. https://ec.europa.eu/info/business-economy-euro/company-reporting-and-auditing/company-reporting_en

European Commission. (2008). *Directive 2008/98/EC of the European Parliament and the Council*. https://eur-lex.europa.eu/legal-content/EN/TXT/?uri=CELEX:32008L0098

European Commission. (2014). *Towards a circular economy: A zero waste programme for Europe*. European Commission.

European Commission. (2015a). *EU resource efficiency scoreboard*. https://ec.europa.eu/environment/resource_efficiency/targets_indicators/scoreboard/index_en.htm

European Commission. (2015b). *Closing the loops—An EU action plan for the circular economy. COM/2015/0614 final*. https://eur-lex.europa.eu/legal-content/EN/TXT/?uri=CELEX:52015DC0614

European Commission. (2015c). Communication from the commission to the European Parliament, the council, the European Economic and Social Committee and the committee of the regions. COM (2015) 614/2.

European Commission. (2017). *The role of waste-to-energy in the circular economy*. https://ec.europa.eu/environment/waste/waste-to-energy.pdf

European Commission. (2018a). *A European strategy for plastics in a circular economy*. https://ec.europa.eu/environment/circular-economy/pdf/plastics-strategy.pdf

European Commission. (2018b). *EU raw material week 2018—Closing the loop on critical raw materials*. https://ec.europa.eu/easme/en/news/eu-raw-materials-week-2018-closing-loop-critical-raw-materials

European Commission. (2012). *Manifesto for a resource-efficient Europe, MEMO 12/989/*. http://europa.eu/rapid/press-release_MEMO-12-989_en.htm.

European Commission. (2014a). *Scoping study to identify potential circular economy actions, priority sectors, material flows, and value chains*. https://op.europa.eu/en/publication-detail/-/publication/0619e465-581c-41dc-9807-2bb394f6bd07

European Commission. (2014b). *Towards a circular economy: A Zero Waste Programme for Europe, COM (2014)398*. https://www.eumonitor.eu/9353000/1/j9vvik7m1c3gyxp/vjl4tamjogxb

European Commission. (2015a). Communication from the Commission to the European Parliament, the Council, the European Economic and Social Committee and the Committee of the regions closing the loop—An EU action plan for the Circular Economy. COM (2015) 614. https://ec.europa.eu/transparency/documents-register/detail?ref=COM(2015)614&lang=en

European Commission. (2015b). *Resource efficiency scoreboard.* https://ec.europa.eu/environment/resource_efficiency/targets_indicators/scoreboard/index_e

European Union. (2014). Directive 2014/24/EU of the European Parliament and of the Council of 26 February 2014 on public procurement and repealing Directive 2004/18/EC. Office Journal of European Union, 65–242. https://eur-lex.europa.eu/legal-content/EN/TXT/PDF/?uri=CELEX:32014L0024

European Union. (2017). *Guidelines on non-financial reporting*. https://ec.europa.eu/anti-trafficking/sites/antitrafficking/files/guidelines_on_non-financial_reporting.pdf

European Union. (2020). *Global alliance on circular economy and resource efficiency*. https://ec.europa.eu/environment/international_issues/gacere.html

European Union. (2022). *Communication from the commission to the European parliament, the council, the European Economic and Social Committee and the committee of the regions on making sustainable products the norm, com/2022/140 final*. https://eur-lex.europa.eu/legal-content/EN/TXT/?uri=CELEX%3A52022DC0140&qid=1649112555090

Eurostat. (2016). https://ec.europa.eu/eurostat/data/database

Fetscherin, M., & Heinrich, D. (2015). Consumer brand relationships research: A bibliometric citation meta-analysis. *Journal of Business Research, 68*(2), 380–390.

Fonseca, L. M., Domingues, J. P., Pereira, M. T., Martins, F. F., & Zimon, D. (2018). Assessment of circular economy within Portuguese organizations. *Sustainability, 10*(7), 2521.

Fonseca, L. M., Portela, A. R., Duarte, B., Queiros, J., & Paiva, L. (2018). Mapping higher education for sustainable development in Portugal. *Management & Marketing: Challenges for the Knowledge Society, 13*(3), 1064–1075.

Gacser, N. G., & Szoka, K. (2021). Sustainability accounting-historical development and future perspectives of the discipline. *PressAcademia Procedia, 14*(1), 1–4.

Garvare, R., & Johansson, P. (2010). Management for sustainability—A stakeholder theory. *Total Quality Management and Excellence Journal, 21*(7), 737–744.

Gaur, V.K., Regar, R.K., Dhiman, N., Gautam, K., Srivastava, J.K., Patnaik, S., Kamthan, M., & Manickam, N. (2019). Biosynthesis and characterization of sophorolipid biosurfactant by Candida spp.: Application as food emulsifier and antibacterial agent. *Bioresource Technology, 285*, 121314.

Geissdoerfer, M. S., Moriorka, S. N., de Carvalho, M. M., & Evans, S. (2018). Business models and supply chains for the circular economy. *Journal of Cleaner Production, 190*, 712–721.

Geissdoerfer, M., Sayaget, P., Bocken, N. M. P., & Hultin, E. J. (2017). The circular economy—A new sustainability paradigm? *Journal of Cleaner Production, 143*, 757–768.

Geng, Y., & Doberstein, B. (2008). Development of the circular economy in China: Challenges and opportunities for achieving 'leapfrog' development. *International Journal of Sustainable Development, 3*, 231–239.

Ghisellini, P., Cialani, C., & Ulgiati, S. (2016). A review on circular economy: The expected transition to a balance interplay of environmental and economic systems. *Journal of Cleaner Production, 114*, 11–32.

Giorgino, M. C., Barnabe, F., & Paoicelli, N. (2016). Searching for the missing link between business model and strategy. The integrated reporting perspective. In A. Jablonski (Ed.), *Business models: Strategies, impact and challenges.* Nova Science Publisher.

Global Reporting Initiative. (2011). *Global reporting initiative mission-history.* https://www.globalreporting.org/about-gri/mission-history/

Gray, C., & Charter, M. (2007). *Remanufacturing and product design designing of the 7th generation.* The Centre for Sustainable Design, University College for the Creative Arts and SEEDA: Farnham.

Gray, R. (2002a). Of messiness, systems, and sustainability: Towards more social and environmental finance and accounting. *The British Accounting Review, 34*, 357–386.

Gray, R. (2002b). The social accounting project and Accounting Organizations and Society Privileging engagement, imaginings, new accountings and pragmatism over critique? *Accounting, Organizations and Society, 27*(7), 687–708.

Gray, R., Adams, C. A., & Owen, D. (2014). Accounting, social responsibility and sustainability: Accounting for the society and the environment. *Social and Environmental Accountability Journal, 34*(3), 193–194.

Gray, R., & Laughlin, R. (2012). It was 20 years ago today Sgt Pepper. *Accounting, Auditing & Accountability Journal, Green Accounting and the Blue Meanies, 25*(2), 228–255.

Gregson, N., Crang, M., Fuller, S., & Holmes, H. (2015). Interrogating the circular economy: The moral economy of resource recovery in the EU. *Economy and Society, 44*(2), 218–243.

GRI. (2010). *Global conference executive brief: Rethink, rebuilt, report*. http://www.amsterdamgriconference.org/2010_GRI_Global_Conference_Executive_Briefing.pdf

GRI. (2017). *GRI 300: Environmental disclosures*. https://reports.clariant.com/2017/gri-report/additional-information/gri-300-environmental-disclosures.html

GRI. (2022). *Global reporting initiatives*. https://www.globalreporting.org/

Gurbo, M. (2017). *Why are sustainable development goals important: Supporting the implementation of UN sustainable development goals in Georgia project*. Institute for Development of Freedom of Information.

Guthrie, J., & Abeysekera, I. (2006). Content analysis of social, environmental reporting: What is new? *Journal of Human Resource Costing and Accounting, 10*(2), 114–126.

Guthrie, J., Petty, R., Yongvanich, K., & Ricceri, F. (2004a). Using content analysis as a research method to inquire into intellectual capital reporting. *Journal of Intellectual Capital, 5*(2), 282–293.

Guthrie, J. R., Dennerstein, L., Taffe, J. R., Lehert, P., & Burger, H. G. (2004b). The menopausal transition: A 9-year prospective population-based study. *The Melbourne Women's Midlife Health Project. Climacteric, 7*(4), 375–389.

Hansen, E. G., & Schaltegger, S. (2016). The sustainability balanced scorecard: A systematic review of architectures. *Journal of Business Ethics, 133*, 193–221.

Hao, L. N., Umar, M., Khan, Z., & Ali, W. (2021). Green growth and low carbon emission in G7 countries: How critical the network of environmental taxes, renewable energy and human capital is? *Science of the Total Environment, 752*, 141853.

Hermann, R. R., Jensen, A., & Gianiodis, P. (2021). Opportunity domains for new entrants in the circular economy: A keyword-in-context analysis of Norwegian RD tax incentive projects. In *Research handbook of innovation for a circular economy* (pp. 316–325). Edward Elgar Publishing.

Hernández-Arzaba, J. C., Nazir, S., Leyva-Hernández, S. N., & Muhyaddin, S. (2022). Stakeholder pressure engaged with circular economy principles and economic and environmental performance. *Sustainability, 14*(23), 16302.

Hockerts, K. (2001, January). Corporate sustainability management, towards controlling corporate ecological and social sustainability. In *Proceedings of greening of industry network conference* (pp. 21–24).

Hopwood, B., Mellor, M., & O'Brien, G. (2005). Sustainable development: Mapping different approaches. *Sustainable Development, 13*(1), 38–52.

IIRC. (2011). *Discussion paper. Towards integrated reporting. Communicating value in the 21st century.* International Integrated Reporting Council. https://integratedreporting.org/wp-content/uploads/2011/09/IR-Discussion-Paper-2011_spreads.pdf

IIRC. (2013a). *The international IR framework.* International Integrated Reporting Council. https://integratedreporting.org/resource/international-ir-framework/

IIRC. (2013b). *Business model. Background paper for IR.* International Integrated Reporting Council. https://integratedreporting.org/wp-content/uploads/2013/03/Business_Model.pdf

IIRC. (2013c). *Capitals. Background paper for IR.* International Integrated Reporting Council. https://integratedreporting.org/wp-content/uploads/2013/03/IR-Background-Paper-Capitals.pdf

IIRC. (2013d). *Value creation. Background paper.* International Integrated Reporting Council. https://integratedreporting.org/wp-content/uploads/2013/08/Background-Paper-Value-Creation.pdf

IIRC. (2016). *Creating value: The cyclical power of integrated thinking and reporting*. International Integrated Reporting Council. https://integratedreporting.org/wp-content/uploads/2016/11/CreatingValue_IntegratedThinking_.pdf

Inigo, E. A., & Blok, V. (2019). Strengthening the socio-ethical foundations of the circular economy: Lessons from responsible research and innovation. *Journal of Cleaner Production, 233*, 280–291.

Jacobs, L. F. (1996). The economy of winter: Phenotypic plasticity in behavior and brain structure. *The Biological Bulletin, 191*(1), 92–100.

Jadaun, J. S., Bansal, S., Sonthalia, A., Rai, A. K., & Singh, S. P. (2022). Biodegradation of plastics for sustainable environment. *Bioresource Technology*, 126697.

Jain, S., Jain, N. K., & Metri, B. (2018). Strategic framework towards measuring a circular supply chain management. *Benchmarking: An International Journal, 25*(8), 3238–3252.

Janubová, B., & Grešš, M. (2016). Urbanization of poverty and the sustainable development of urban areas in Chile. *Theoretical and Empirical Researches in Urban Management, 11*(4), 17–29.

Jawahir, I. S., & Bradley, R. (2016). Technological elements of circular economy and the principles of 6R-based closed-loop material flow in sustainable manufacturing. *Procedia CIRP, 40*, 103–108.

Jayal, A. D., Badurdeen, F., Dillon Jr., O. W., & Jawahir, I. S. (2010). Sustainable manufacturing, modeling and optimization challenges at the product, process and system levels. CIRP *Journal of Manufacturing Science and Technology*, 3, 144–152.

Johansen, M. R., Christensen, T. B., Ramos, T. M., & Syberg, K. (2022). A review of the plastic value chain from a circular economy perspective. *Journal of Environmental Management, 302*, 113975.

Kamp-Roelands, N. (2013). A commentary on 'Integrated reporting: A review of developments and their implications for the accounting curriculum.' *Accounting Education, 22*(4), 357–359.

Kaplan, R. S. (2009). Conceptual foundations of the balanced scorecard. *Handbooks of Management Accounting Research, 3*, 1253–1269.

Kaplan, R. S., & Norton, D. P. (1996). *The balanced scorecard: Translating strategy into action.* Harvard Business Press.

Kaplan, R. S., & Norton, D. P. (2000). Having trouble with your strategy? Then map it. *Focusing Your Organization on Strategy—With the Balanced Scorecard*, *49*(5), 167–176.

Kaplan, R. S., & Norton, D. (1992). The balanced scorecard: Measures that drive performance. *Harvard Business Review, 70*(1), 71–79.

Katz-Gerro, T., & Lopez Sintas, J. (2019). Mapping circular economy activities in the European Union: Patterns of implementation and their correlates in small and medium-sized enterprises. *Business Strategy and the Environment, 28*(4), 485–496.

Kirchherr, J., & Piscicelli, L. (2019). Towards an education for the circular economy (ECE): Five teaching principles and a case study. *Resources, Conservation and Recycling*, *150*, 104406.

Kirchherr, J., & Urban, F. (2018). Technology transfer and cooperation for low carbon energy technology: Analysing 30 years of scholarship and proposing a research agenda. *Energy Policy, 119*, 600–609.

Kirchherr, J., Piscicelli, L., Bour, R., Kostense-Smit, E., Muller, J., Huibrechtse-Truijens, A., & Hekkert, M. (2018). Barriers to the circular economy: Evidence from the European Union (EU). *Ecological Economics, 150*, 264–272.

Kirchherr, J., Reike, D., & Hekkert, M. (2017). Conceptualizing the circular economy: An analysis of 114 definitions. *Resources, Conservation and Recycling, 127*, 221–232.

Knight. (2022). *Global 100 sustainable corporations.* https://www.corporateknights.com/rankings/global-100-rankings/2022-global-100-rankings/

Korhonen, J., Honkasalo, A., & Seppala, J. (2018). Circular economy: The concept and its limitations. *Ecological Economics, 143*, 37–46.

Kovacic, Z., Strand, R., & Völker, T. (2020). *The circular economy in Europe: Critical perspectives on policies and imaginaries* (p. 208). Taylor & Francis.

KPMG. (2008). *Climate change your business.* https://inis.iaea.org/search/search.aspx?orig_q=RN:40052557.

KPMG. (2010). *KPMG promotes integration of company reports.* http://www.kpmg.com/RO/en/IssuesAndInsights/ArticlesPublications/Press-releases/Pages/Integrated-Reporting.aspx

Kraaijenhagen, C., Van Oppen, C., & Bocken, N. (2016). Circular business: Collaborate and circulate. Circular collaboration.

Krippendorff, K. (2004a). *Content analysis: An introduction to its methodology.* SAGE.

Krippendorff, K. (2004b). Reliability in content analysis: Some common misconceptions and recommendations. *Human Communication Research, 30*(3), 411–433.

Krippendorff. K. (1989). Content analysis. In E. Barnouw, G. Gerbner, W. Schramm, T. L. Worth, & L. Gross (Eds.), *International encyclopaedia of communication* (Vol. 1, pp. 403–407). Oxford University Press.

Krippendorff, K. (2018). *Content analysis: An introduction to its methodology.* Sage.

Kristensen, H., & Remmen, A. (2019). A framework for sustainable value propositions in product-service-system. *Journal of Cleaner Production, 223*, 25–35.

Krylov, S. I. (2014). Theoretical aspects of economic balanced scorecard analysis. *Asian Journal of Finance & Accounting, 6*(1), 90.

Kühl, C., Bourlakis, M., Aktas, E., & Skipworth, H. (2022). Product-service systems and circular supply chain practices in UK SMEs: The moderating effect of internal environmental orientation. *Journal of Business Research, 146*, 155–165.

Lacy, P., & Rutqvist, J. (2015). *Waste to wealth: The circular economy advantage.* Macmillan.

Lacy, P., Long, J., Spindler, W., Lacy, P., Long, J., & Spindler, W. (2020). Introduction: The path to transformation is circular. *The Circular Economy Handbook: Realizing the Circular Advantage*, 1–14.

Lamba, H. K., Kumar, N. S., & Dhir, S. (2023). Circular economy and sustainable development: a review and research agenda. *International Journal of Productivity and Performance Management* (ahead-of-print).

Lang, M., & Marsden, T. (2018). Rethinking growth: Towards the well-being economy. *Local Economy, 33*(5), 496–514.

Lazarevic, D., & Valve, H. (2017). Narrating expectations for the circular economy: Towards a common and contested European transition. *Energy Research & Social Science, 31*, 60–69.

Levi Jaksic, M., Rakicevic, J., & Jovanovic, M. (2018). Sustainable technology and business innovation framework comprehensive approach. *Amfiteatru Economic, 20*(48), 418–436.

Lewandowski, M. (2016). Designing the business models for circular economy—Towards the conceptual framework. *Sustainability, 8*(1), 43.

Li, F., & Ding, Z. D. (2013). The effect of institutional isomorphic pressure on the internationalization of the firm in an emerging economy: Evidence from China. *Asia Pacific Business Review, 19*(4), 506–525.

Lieder, M., & Rashid, A. (2016). Towards circular economy implementation: A comprehensive review in the context of manufacturing industry. *Journal of Cleaner Production, 115*, 36–51.

Lihong, W. (2011). Development of circular economy and optimization of industrial structure for Shandong Province. *Energy Procedia, 5*, 1603–1610.

Linder, M., & Williander, M. (2017). Circular business model innovation: Inherent uncertainties. *Business Strategy and the Environment, 26*(2), 182–196.

Liu, J., & Peifer, J. L. (2022). A moral foundations framing approach: Retail investors' investment intention in ethical mutual funds. *Business & Society, 61*(7).

Liu, Z., Adams, M., Cote, R. P., Geng, Y., Chen, Q., Liu, W., Sun, L., & Yu, X. (2017). Comprehensive development of industrial symbiosis for the response of greenhouse gas emission mitigation: Challenges and opportunities in China. *Energy Policy, 102*(C), 88–95.

Llena, F., Moneva, J. M., & Hernandez, B. (2007). Environmental disclosures and compulsory accounting standards: The case of Spanish annual reports. *Business Strategy and the Environment, 16*, 50–63.

Long, T., & Johnson, M. (2000). Rigour, reliability and validity in qualitative research. *Clinical Effectiveness in Nursing, 4*(1), 30–37.

Low, J. S. C., & Ng, Y. T. (2018). Improving the economic performance of remanufacturing systems through flexible design strategies: A case study based on remanufacturing laptop computers for the Cambodian market. *Business Strategy and the Environment, 27*, 503–527.

Maroun, W., & Prinsloo, A. (2020). Drivers of combined assurance in a sustainable development context: Evidence from integrated reports. *Business Strategy and the Environment, 29*(8), 3702–3719.

Martins, N. O. (2016). Ecosystems, strong sustainability, and the classical circular economy. *Ecological Economics, 129*, 32–39.

Mathews, J. A., & Tan, H. (2011). Progress toward a circular economy in China: The drivers (and inhibitors) of eco-industrial initiative. *Journal of Industrial Ecology, 15*(3), 435–457.

Mathews, J. A., Tang, Y., & Tan, H. (2011). China's move to a circular economy as a development strategy. *Asian Business & Management, 10*(4), 463–484.

Mathews, M. R. (2008). Further thoughts on maga-accounting and the need for standards. *Issues in Social and Environmental Accounting, 2*(2), 158–175.

Mattera, M., & Ruiz-Morales, C. A. (2020). UNGC principles and SDGs: Perception and business implementation. *Marketing Intelligence & Planning*.

Mavropoulos, A., & Nilsen, A. W. (2020). *Industry 4.0 and circular economy: Towards a wasteless future or a wasteful planet?* Wiley.

McDonough, W., & M. Braungart. 2002. Cradle to Cradle. Remaking the Way We Make Things. New York: North Point Press.

McNaught, C., & Lam, P. (2010). Using wordle as a supplementary research tool. *The Qualitative Reports, 15*(3), 630–643.

Merli, R., Preziosi, M., & Acampora. A. (2018). How do scholars approach the circular economy? A systematic literature review, *Journal of Cleaner Production, 178*, 703–722.

Milne, M. J., & Adler, R. W. (1999). Exploring the reliability of social and environmental disclosures content analysis. *Accounting, Auditing & Accountability Journal, 12*(2), 237–256.

Milne, M. J., & Gray, R. (2013). W (h) ither ecology? The triple bottom line, the global reporting initiative, and corporate sustainability reporting. *Journal of Business Ethics, 118*, 13–29.

Moroney, R., & Trotman, K. T. (2016). Differences in auditors' materiality assessment when auditing financial statements and sustainability reports. *Contemporary Accounting Research, 33*(2), 551–575.

Mourad, M. (2016). Recycling, recovering and preventing "food waste": Competing solutions for food systems sustainability in the United States and France. *Journal of Cleaner Production, 126*, 461–477.

Murray, A., Skene, K., & Haynes, K. (2017). The circular economy: An interdisciplinary exploration of the concept and application in a global context. *Journal of Business Ethics, 140*(3), 369–380.

Naeem, M. A., Adekoya, O. B., & Oliyide, J. A. (2021a). Asymmetric spillovers between green bonds and commodities. *Journal of Cleaner Production, 314*, 128100.

Naeem, M. A., Farid, S., Ferrer, R., & Shahzad, S. J. H. (2021b). Comparative efficiency of green and conventional bonds pre-and during COVID-19: An asymmetric multifractal detrended fluctuation analysis. *Energy Policy, 153*, 112285.

Naeem, M. A., & Karim, S. (2021). Tail dependence between bitcoin and green financial assets. *Economics Letters, 208*, 110068.

Naeem, M. A., Karim, S., Nor, S. M., & Ismail, R. (2022). Sustainable corporate governance and gender diversity on corporate boards: evidence from COVID-19. *Economic Research-Ekonomska Istraživanja*, 1–19.

Nasr, M., & Thurston, M. (2006). Remanufacturing: A key enable to sustainable product systems. 13th CIRP International Conference of Life Cycle Engineering, 15–18.

Nathaniel, S., Anyanwu, O., & Shah, M. (2020). Renewable energy, urbanization, and ecological footprint in the Middle East and North Africa region. *Environmental Science and Pollution Research, 27*, 14601–14613.

Nathaniel, S. P. (2021). Environmental degradation in ASEAN: Assessing the criticality of natural resources abundance, economic growth and human capital. *Environmental Science and Pollution Research, 28*(17), 21766–21778.

Neuendorf, K. (2002). The content analysis guidebook. In *Library of congress*. Sage Publications, Inc.

Neuendorf, K. A. (2010). Reliability for content analysis. In *Media messages and public health* (pp. 85–105). Routledge.

Nguyen, K. H., & Kakinaka, M. (2019). Renewable energy consumption, carbon emissions, and development stages: Some evidence from panel cointegration analysis. *Renewable Energy, 132*, 1049–1057.

Nikseresht, A., Hajipour, B., Pishva, N., & Mohammadi, H. A. (2022). Using artificial intelligence to make sustainable development decisions considering VUCA: A systematic literature review and bibliometric analysis. *Environmental Science and Pollution Research*, 1–30.

Nishitani, K., Kokubu, K., Wu, Q., Kitada, H., Guenther, E., & Guenther, T. (2022). Material flow cost accounting (MFCA) for the circular economy: An empirical study of the triadic relationship between MFCA, environmental performance, and the economic performance of Japanese companies. *Journal of Environmental Management, 303*, 114219.

Niskanen, J., Anshelm, J., & McLaren, D. (2020). Local conflicts and national consensus: The strange case of circular economy in Sweden. *Journal of Cleaner Production, 261*, 121117.

Nunnally, J. C. (1978). *Psychometric theory* (2nd ed.). McGraw.

OECD. (2015a). *Enable the productive revolution.* OECD Publishing. https://www.oecd.org/sti/OECD-Innovation-Strategy-2015

OECD. (2015b). *OECD compendium of productivity indicators.* OECD Publishing. https://www.oecd.org/sti/OECD-Innovation-Strategy-2015

OECD. (2015c). *Compendium of productivity indicators.* https://www.oecd-ilibrary.org/industry-and-services/oecd-compendium-of-productivity-indicators_22252126

Pan, L., Cui, Z., Cai, J., & Li, L. (2022). Bio-inspired computing: Theories and applications: 16th international conference, BIC-TA 2021, Taiyuan, China, December 17–19, 2021, Revised Selected Papers, Part I. Springer Nature.

Pask, F., Lake, P., Yang, A., Tokos, H., & Sadhukhan, J. (2017). Sustainability indicators for industrial ovens and assessment using Fuzzy set theory and Monte Carlo simulation. *Journal of Cleaner Production, 140*, 1217–1225.

Pata, U. K. (2021). Renewable and non-renewable energy consumption, economic complexity, CO_2 emissions, and ecological footprint in the USA: Testing the EKC hypothesis with a structural break. *Environmental Science and Pollution Research, 28*, 846–861.

Pata, U. K., & Samour, A. (2022). Do renewable and nuclear energy enhance environmental quality in France? A new EKC approach with the load capacity factor. *Progress in Nuclear Energy, 149*, 104249.

Pieroni, M. P., McAloone, T. C., & Pigosso, D. C. (2019). Business model innovation for circular economy and sustainability: A review of approaches. *Journal of Cleaner Production, 215*, 198–216.

Quattrone, P. (2017). Embracing ambiguity in management controls and decision-making processes: On how to design data visualisations to prompt wise judgment. *Accounting and Business Research, 47*(5), 588–612.

Rahman, M. M., Alam, K., & Velayutham, E. (2022). Reduction of CO_2 emissions: The role of renewable energy, technological innovation and export quality. *Energy Reports, 8*, 2793–2805.

Ranta, V., Stenroos, A. L., & Makinen, J. S. (2018). Creating value in the circular economy: A structured multiple-case analysis of business models. *Journal of Cleaner Production, 201*, 998–1000.

Reh, L. (2013). Process engineering in circular economy. *Particuology, 11*(2), 119–133.

Reike, D., Vermeulen, W. J. V., & Witjes, S. (2018). The circular economy; New or refurbished as CE 3.0? Exploring controversies in the conceptualization of the circular economy through a focus on history and resource value retention options. *Journal of Cleaner Production, 135*, 246–264.

Riding, J. M., Herbert, B. M. J., Ricketts, L., Dodd, I., Ostle, N., & Semple, T. K. (2014). Harmonising conflicts between science, regulation, perception and environmental impact: The case of soil conditioners from bioenergy. *Environmental International, 74*, 52–67.

Ryan, B. (2002). *Research methods and methodology in finance and accounting*. Cengage Learning EMEA.

Sarkar, B., Bolan, N. S., Mukhopadhyay, R., Bolan, S. S., Kirkham, M. B., & Rinklebe, J., (2020). Management of particulate plastic waste input to terrestrial and aquatic environments. In *Particulate plastics in terrestrial and aquatic environments* (pp. 397–411). CRC Press.

Sassanelli, C., Rosa, P., Rocca, R., & Terzi, S. (2019). Circular economy performance assessment methods: A systematic literature review. *Journal of Cleaner Production, 229*, 440–453.

Schandl, H., Hatfield-Dodds, S., Wiedmann, T., Geschke, A., Cai, Y., West, J., Newth, D., Baynes, T., Lenzen, M., & Owen, A. (2016). Decoupling global environmental pressure and economic growth: scenarios for energy use, materials use and carbon emissions. *Journal of Cleaner Production, 132*, 45–56.

Schanes, K., Dobernig, K., & Gözet, B. (2018). Food waste matters—A systematic review of household food waste practices and their policy implications. *Journal of Cleaner Production, 182*, 978–991.

Scheel, C. (2016). Beyond sustainability. Transforming industrial zero-valued residues into increasing economic returns. *Journal of Cleaner Production, 131*, 376–386.

Schilling, J. (2006). On the pragmatics of qualitative assessment. *European Journal of Psychological Assessment, 22*(1), 28–37.

Schroeder, P., Anggraeni., K, & Weber, U. (2018). The relevance of circular economy practices to the sustainable development. *Journal of Industrial Ecology*.

Scott, W. R. (2005). *Social movement and organization movement*. Cambridge University Press.

Shammi, M., Behal, A., & Tareq, S. M. (2021). The escalating biomedical waste management to control the environmental transmission of COVID-19 pandemic: A perspective from two South Asian countries. *Environmental Science & Technology, 55*(7), 4087–4093.

Sihvonen, S., & Partanen, J. (2017). Eco-design practices with a focus on quantitative environmental targets: An exploratory content analysis within ICT sector. *Journal of Cleaner Production, 143*, 769–783.

Speich, I. (2019a). *Wir werden firmen aussortieren.* Handelsblatt. https://www.handelsblatt.com/finanzen/banken-versicherungen/ingo-speich-im-interview-chefstratege-der-deka-bank-wir-werden-firmen-aussortieren/24582180.html?ticket=ST-41870794-BXWhTrs1Q69EsvtkedTv-ap5

Speich, I. (2019b). *ESG-investing: MiFID II als game-changer*. https://e-fundresearch.com/funds/artikel/36237-esg-investing-mifid-ii-als-game-changer?region=de

Stahel, W. (1982). *Product-life factor*. http://product-life.org/en/major-publications/the-product-life-factor.

Stahel, W. R. (2014a). *Reuse is the key to the circular economy*. European Commission. http://ec.europa.eu/environment/ecoap/about-eco-innovation/expertsinterviews/reuse-is-the-key-to-the-circular-economy.

Stahel, W. R. (2014b). *The business angle of a circular economy—Higher competitiveness, higher resource security and material efficiency*. The Product-Life Institute: Geneva. www.product-life.org

Stahel, W. R. (2016). The circular economy. *Nature, 531*(7595), 435–438.

Stahel, W. R., & MacArthur, E. (2019). *The circular economy: A user's guide.* Routledge.

Starovoytova, D. (2018). Solid Waste Management (SWM) at a University Campus (Part 1/10): Comprehensive review on legal framework and background to waste management, at a global Context. *Journal of Environment and Earth Science, 8*(4), 2225–948.

Steen-Olsen, K., Owen, A., Barrett, J., Guan, D., Hertwich, E. G., Lenzen, M., & Wiedmann, T. (2016). Accounting for value added embodied in trade and consumption: An intercomparison of global multiregional input–output databases. *Economic Systems Research, 28*(1), 78–94.

Sterman, J. D. (2000). *Business dynamics*. McGraw-Hill.

Stewart R., Niero M., Murdock K., & Olsen, S. I. (2018). Exploring the implementation of a circular economy strategy. Procedia CIRP 25th Life Cycle Engineering Conference, 30 April–2 May, Copenhagen, Denmark.

Stewart, R., & Niero, M. (2018). Circular economy incorporates sustainability strategies: A review of corporate sustainability reports in the fast-moving consumer goods sector. *Business Strategy and the Environment, 27*(7), 1005–1022.

Taghizadeh-Hesary, F., Rasoulinezhad, E., & Yoshino, N. (2019). Energy and food security: Linkages through price volatility. *Energy Policy, 128*, 796–806.

Temesgen, A., Storsletten, V., & Jakobsen, O. (2021). Circular economy–reducing symptoms or radical change? *Philosophy of Management, 20*(1), 37–56.

Tettamanzi, P., Venturini, G., & Murgolo, M. (2022). Sustainability and financial accounting: A critical review on the ESG dynamics. *Environmental Science and Pollution Research*, 1–4.

Torgautov, B., Zhanabayev, A., Tleuken, A., Turkyilmaz, A., Borucki, C., & Karaca, F. (2022). Performance assessment of construction companies for the circular economy: A balanced scorecard approach. *Sustainable Production and Consumption, 33*, 991–1004.

Tsai, F. M., Bui, T. D., Tseng, M. L., Lim, M. K., & Hu, J. (2020). Municipal solid waste management in a circular economy: A data-driven bibliometric analysis. *Journal of Cleaner Production, 275*, 124132.

Tukker, A. (2015). Product services for a resource-efficient and circular economy—A review. *Journal of Cleaner Production, 97*, 76–91.

U.S. Chamber of Commerce Foundation. (2022). *U.S. Chamber of Commerce Foundation, CE glossary*. https://www.uschamberfoundation.org/circular-economy-toolbox/about-circularity/glossary

Umar, M., Su, C. W., Rizvi, S. K. A., & Lobonţ, O. R. (2021a). Driven by fundamentals or exploded by emotions: Detecting bubbles in oil prices. *Energy, 231*, 120873.

Umar, M., Su, C. W., Rizvi, S. K. A., & Shao, X. F. (2021b). Bitcoin: A safe haven asset and a winner amid political and economic uncertainties in the US. *Technological Forecasting and Social Change, 167*, 120680.

UN—United Nations. (2015). *Transforming our world: The 2030 agenda for sustainable development.* https://sustainabledevelopment.un.org/

Valenzuela, F., & Böhm, S. (2017). Against wasted politics: A critique of the circular economy. *Ephemera: Theory & Politics in Organization, 17*(1), 23–60.

Velis, C. (2018). No circular economy if current systemic failures are not addressed. *Waste Management & Research, 36*(9), 757–759.

Völker, T., Kovacic, Z., & Strand, R. (2020). Indicator development as a site of collective imagination? The case of European Commission policies on the circular economy. *Culture and Organization, 26*(2), 103–120.

Wang, Y., Yang, F., Hua, C., Hu, J., Wang, J., Zhou, J., Feng, Z., Zhang, C., Ye, J., Zhang, J., & Leng, X. (2021). Comparing the efficiencies of individual-scoring and complementarity-based algorithms in prioritizing existing protected areas. *Ecological Indicators*, 125, 107539.

Warren, S., & Davison, J. (2017). Visual methodologies for accounting and accountability. In *The Routledge companion to qualitative accounting research methods* (pp. 136–152). Routledge.

WBCSD. (2018). *World business council for sustainable development*. https://www.ceguide.org/Glossary

WCED SWS. (1987). World commission on environment and development. *Our Common Future, 17*(1), 1–91.

Weber, M., Eisenführ, F., & Von Winterfeldt, D. (1988). The effects of splitting attributes on weights in multiattribute utility measurement. *Management Science, 34*(4), 431–445.

Weber, R. P. (1990). *Basic content analysis* (Vol. 49). Sage.

Webster, K. (2021). A circular economy is about the economy. *Circular Economy and Sustainability, 1*(1), 115–126.

Winans, K., Kendall, A., & Deng, H. (2017). The history and current applications of the circular economy concept. *Renewable and Sustainable Energy Reviews, 68*, 825–833.

White., A., & Schmidt Katia. (2005). Systematic literature reviews. *Complementary Therapies in Medicine, 13*, 54–60.

WHO. (2022). *WHO Coronavirus (COVID-19) dashboard*. https://covid19.who.int/

Wilson, C. (2013a). *Brainstorming and beyond: A user-centered design method*. Newnes.

Wilson, S. M. (2013b). Professional development for science teachers. *Science, 340*(6130), 310–313.

Wine, J. (1971). Test anxiety and direction of attention. *Psychological Bulletin, 76*(2), 92.

Winer, B. J (1971). *Statistical principles in experimental design* (2nd ed.) McGraw-Hill and Kogakusha Ltd.

Witjes, S., & Lozano, R. (2016). Towards a more circular economy: Proposing a framework linking sustainable public procurement and sustainable business models. *Resources, Conservation and Recycling, 112*, 37–44.

Wixom, B. H., Yen, B., & Relich, M. (2013). Maximizing value from business analytics. *MIS Quarterly Executive, 12*(2).

World Economic Forum (WEF) (2020). Nature Risk Rising: Why the Crisis Engulfing Nature Matters for Business and the Economy. New Nature

Economy Series. Retrieved From, https://www.weforum.org/publications/nature-riskrising-why-the-crisis-engulfing-nature-matters-for-business-and-the-economy/

Yang, X. J., Hu, H., Tan, T., & Li, J. (2016). China's renewable energy goals by 2050. *Environmental Development, 20*, 83–90.

Yin, R. K. (1994). *Case study research: Design and methods* (2nd ed.). Sage.

Zarbakhshnia, N., Govindan, K., Kannan, D., & Goh, M. (2023). Outsourcing logistics operations in circular economy towards to sustainable development goals. *Business Strategy and the Environment, 32*(1), 134–162.

Zhu, J., Fan, C., Shi, H., & Shi, L. (2019). Efforts for a circular economy in China: A comprehensive review of policies. *Journal of industrial ecology, 23*(1), 110–118.

Zhuo, N., Ji, C., & Yin, N. (2021). Supply chain integration and resilience in China's pig sector: Case study evidence from emerging institutional arrangements. *Environmental Science and Pollution Research, 28*(7), 8310–8322.

Index

S. Nazir and A. Capocchi, *Sustainability Reporting Practices and the Circular Economy*, https://doi.org/10.1007/978-3-031-51845-4

The manufacturer's authorised representative in the EU is Springer
Nature Customer Service Centre GmbH, Europaplatz 3, 69115 Heidelberg,
Germany. If you have any concerns regarding our products, please
contact ProductSafety@springernature.com

Printed and bound by CPI Group (UK) Ltd, Croydon, CR0 4YY
01/10/2026
02225894-0013